THE BISHOPS AND THE BOMB

THE BISHOPS AND THE
BOMB

Waging Peace in a Nuclear Age

Jim Castelli

Image Books
A Division of
DOUBLEDAY & COMPANY, INC., GARDEN CITY, NEW YORK,
1983

Library of Congress Cataloging in Publication Data

Castelli, Jim.
The bishops and the bomb.

1. Atomic warfare—Religious aspects—Catholic Church. 2. Catholic Church—United States—Pastoral letters and charges. I. Title.

BX1795.A85C37   1984   261.8'73
ISBN 0-385-18760-2 (pbk.)
Library of Congress Catalog Card Number: 82-48706
Copyright © 1983 by Jim Castelli
All Rights Reserved
Printed in the United States of America
First Edition

37,440

CONTENTS

ACKNOWLEDGMENTS

When the American bishops launched the unusually open process leading up to the passage of their pastoral letter, "The Challenge of Peace: God's Promise and Our Response," they took a number of risks. Perhaps the least known was the decision to allow a journalist unprecedented access to committee files while the process was underway to help him in writing a book about the historic document.

In arranging access, I spoke with Archbishop John Roach, president of the bishops' conference, and all five members of the committee drafting the pastoral. All approved, with the only ground rule being that the research was to be used for the book and that I could quote directly from correspondence to the committee—from bishops or outside experts—only if I received permission from the person involved.

But this is in no way an "authorized" version, and the bishops involved should be given credit for giving me access without any guarantee about how my project—or theirs—would turn out.

I would like to thank those already mentioned, the many others interviewed for the project, and the bishops' public affairs staff—Russ Shaw, Bill Ryan and Bob Wonderly—for their help.

A special word of thanks is in order to Ed Doherty of the U.S. Catholic Conference and Yale University Professor Bruce Martin Russett for their invaluable help in telling this story.

I'd also like to thank everyone who offered encouragement, tips and clippings for the effort.

And, of course, there's no way to thank my wife, Jayne, and my sons, Matt and Dan, for putting up with my absence—and, what was often worse, my presence—during the hectic period in which I put this together.

THE BISHOPS AND THE BOMB

FOREWORD

In October of 1981, I was walking back to my office after a campus teach-in on nuclear disarmament when I felt something close to a religious experience.

I thought of my long involvement with human and civil rights—with immigration and refugees, hunger, the developing nations, higher education, race relations. It suddenly occurred to me that all this would be moot if there were no people left on earth. So I decided to put all else on the back burner.

Nuclear force is one of the few things on earth that's evil per se. It's not a weapon, it's a means of mutual suicide.

The scope of the problem is expressed well in a statement that was presented in Pope John Paul II by an international group of scientists, a quarter of them from the Soviet bloc, in September 1982, and later endorsed by a prestigious group of religious leaders representing the world's major faiths.

In that statement, scientists speak from their own expertise and religious leaders speak after being tutored by the men who created nuclear weapons:

> For the first time, it is possible to cause damage on such a catastrophic scale as to wipe out a large part of civilization and to endanger its very survival. The large-scale use of such weapons could trigger major and irreversible ecological and genetic changes, whose limits cannot be predicted. . . . All disputes that we are concerned with today, including political, economic, ideological and religious ones, are small compared to the hazards of nuclear war.

In issuing "The Challenge of Peace: God's Promise and Our Response," the finest document ever to emerge from the U.S. Catholic hierarchy, the bishops have taken a courageous step. Never before has humanity or the church faced a moral problem like that posed by nuclear weapons—the possibility and probability of reversing creation, both God's and humanity's.

There were no precedents to invoke, no history to depend upon for a wise lesson, no real body of theology except for that which dates back to pacifism or a just-war doctrine that was first applied in a day of spears, swords, and bows and arrows, not ICBMs.

On the other hand, if the bishops did not speak out on this primordial problem of total human life or death, they could hardly address with credibility any of the lesser problems that confront us today.

No one will agree with everything they have written, nor do they expect that. But they have given us a framework of reason and faith, some certain and some not so certain moral judgments.

I was impressed by the modesty with which they did it, by their call for a discussion of what they said, by Catholics and non-Catholics, who share in the formation of public opinion in this country. I was particularly impressed by their call for charity and civility in the discussion that will inevitably follow.

The bishops offer a vision of humanity transcending its differences to avoid nuclear holocaust. I would suggest that no one hasten to criticize their work without reading the entire pastoral letter, reflecting over it prayerfully and asking, "What is the alternative vision?" Certainly not being vaporized, burned, blasted or radiated.

As the discussion of the bishops' work proceeds, *The Bishops and the Bomb: Waging Peace in a Nuclear Age* offers valuable insight into the forces, movements, ideas, issues, beliefs and personalities that shaped this extraordinary document which altered the terms of the public debate in America even before it was completed.

This book also clearly shows that the bishops are neither pawns of church bureaucracies nor Johnny-come-latelies looking for headlines. It reveals them as flesh-and-blood human beings with unique responsibilities who accepted a unique opportunity to help their nation and their world try to avoid a nuclear finale that too often seems inevitable.

REV. THEODORE M. HESBURGH, C.S.C.

I. VARIA

Every August the general secretary of the National Conference of Catholic Bishops sends each member a letter asking if he has anything to bring up during time reserved for "varia"—a sort of "new business" session—at the bishops' November meeting. In recent years, varia items led to major policy statements on human rights in Eastern Europe and Marxist communism and to the creation of a special committee on the parish.

The August 1980 letter from Bishop Thomas Kelly came at a time when Auxiliary Bishop P. Francis (Frank) Murphy of Baltimore was deeply involved in a continuing personal study of the church's role as a peacemaker. The forty-seven-year-old Murphy, who had the résumé of a typical church bureaucrat when he was ordained a bishop in 1976, had begun that study only a few years before.

As vice-chancellor of the diocese and secretary to Cardinal Lawrence Shehan (from 1965 to 1974), Murphy had never been mistaken for an activist, even though Shehan was one of the first bishops to oppose the Vietnam War. The closest he came to the Catholic peace movement of the sixties was when he helped Shehan get an ailing Philip Berrigan—a Josephite priest who, with his brother Daniel, a Jesuit, was a major symbol of that activism—an early release from federal prison, where he was serving time for a draft-board raid.

Shortly after becoming a bishop himself, Murphy joined a handful of bishops who were members of Pax Christi U.S.A., the American branch of an international Catholic peace organization. In June 1979, he addressed a panel on "The Moral Imperative of Halting the Arms Race" at the United Nations Special Session on Disarmament, a major focus of interfaith activity.

Murphy begins an explanation of his "conversion" this way: "On August 6, 1945, I was twelve years old. While I remember some feelings of sadness for the victims of the atomic bomb, I remember my predominant feelings of celebration that the war was ended and we were the victors."

For that attitude, and a later indifference to the arms race, Murphy now frequently does penance. His growing concern about peace and the danger of nuclear war was fueled by contact with the thoughts of others, including some who had had to deal with the issues on a personal basis.

He was moved, for example, by the story of Franz Jaegerstatter, an Austrian peasant beheaded for his refusal to fight for the Nazis; by Pope Paul VI's plea for "No more war! War never again" at the United Nations; by a 1977 sermon on peace by Cardinal John Dearden of Detroit, the first president of the U.S. bishops' conference after Vatican II; and by people, particularly young people, from the Baltimore area, who told him of their fears for the future.

But the major influence on Murphy may have been Father George Zabelka, a Catholic priest who, as an Air Force chaplain, had blessed the men who dropped the atomic bombs on Hiroshima and Nagasaki, just as he had previously blessed the men who were inflicting massive bombing damage on civilians in Tokyo.

Murphy quotes from an interview with Zabelka in the evangelical Christian magazine, *Sojourners:*

> I knew that civilians were being destroyed, and knew it in a way perhaps that others didn't. Yet I never preached a single sermon against killing civilians to the men who were doing it.
>
> . . . I was "brainwashed." It never entered my mind to publicly protest the consequences of these massive air raids. I was told it was necessary; told openly by the military and told implicitly by my church's leadership. To the best of my knowledge, no American cardinals or bishops were opposing these mass air raids in 1945. Silence in such matters, particularly by a public body like the American bishops, is a stamp of approval.

Responding to Kelly's request, Murphy said he'd like to offer a varium calling for a concise summary of the church's teaching on war and peace and a strong educational effort on those issues within the church. Kelly said the proposal was acceptable.

In between the time Kelly accepted Murphy's varium and the meeting itself, something happened which gave the peace discussion more urgency—the election of Ronald Reagan as President of the United States. Reagan had campaigned strongly against the SALT II arms limitation treaty negotiated by President Jimmy Carter—and endorsed by the bishops—while talking about getting tough with the Russians and calling for a massive arms buildup.

The nuclear issue was a major concern of the bishops during Carter's presidency; many of the policies that became a public issue for the bishops during the Reagan administration were born under the Carter and Ford administrations. But Reagan's election—with the rhetoric and policies he brought to office—was the single greatest factor influencing the bishops' discussion in November 1980 and all that followed.

As the 1980 meeting approached, Murphy caucused with several other bishops, including Auxiliary Bishop Thomas Gumbleton of Detroit, president of Pax Christi, and other Pax Christi members, including Walter Sullivan of Richmond and James Lyke, a black auxiliary from Cleveland. They agreed that Murphy's varium offered an opportunity to air the peace issue before the whole conference.

"I talked to a couple of fellows," Murphy says now, "but what happened went way beyond any orchestration."

On Wednesday afternoon as the bishops' meeting neared its close, Murphy opened his varium by praising church teaching but voicing concerns about "its familiarity and effectiveness." "Increased tensions in the world have contributed to a sense of anxiety, genuine fear and deep insecurity among many of our people," he said. "Do we need," he asked, "to speak more specifically about the nature and numbers of nuclear armaments, about the morality of their development and use, and especially about the morality of diverting massive human and material resources to their creation?"

Murphy's varium was followed by two others on the same general subject, but coming from different perspectives—and from men sometimes regarded as mavericks within the conference. One was Bishop Edward O'Rourke of Peoria. O'Rourke attracted national attention in the late seventies when he was on a plane that was hijacked; he gave the last rites to his fellow passengers, an action that comforted some and frightened others.

In 1978, O'Rourke disagreed with a conference statement opposing the deployment of the neutron bomb when it was under consideration by the Carter administration; he argued that the neutron bomb was a moral advance because it could be restricted to military targets.

His varium used the same approach. He began by mentioning

Carter's Presidential Directive 59, which shifted American nuclear targeting away from Soviet cities, giving priority to military targets.* O'Rourke said Carter's directive might create a "second deterrent"— nuclear attack on military targets—standing between conventional war and all-out nuclear war. He acknowledged the concern of some that this approach "might start a series of events that would lead to that dreaded ultimate holocaust." But he then suggested that "a re-examination of the neutron bomb might be considered."

Ironically, the U.S. bishops' first condemnation of the neutron bomb came in 1968, when the weapon was still science fiction. In the pastoral letter "Human Life in Our Day," they said "one philosopher declares that the manner in which it would leave entire cities intact, but totally without life, makes it, perhaps, the symbol of our civilization. It would be perverse indeed if the Christian conscience were to be unconcerned or mute in the face of the multiple moral aspects of these awesome prospects."

In echoing Murphy's call for a new study, O'Rourke said many of the bishops' statements aren't taken seriously because "some think that we are saying that we should stand before the communist aggressor naked and without any real hope of defense. This is not a proposal easily accepted." He said he hoped any committee formed to study the subject would include an expert in "the technology of weapons."

The third varium on war and peace came from Archbishop John Whealon of Hartford, one of the most conservative bishops—both theologically and politically—in the country. Whealon had in the past opposed conference positions opposing the death penalty and supporting the Humphrey-Hawkins full-employment bill.

He asked the bishops to review their position, taken in 1968, in support of selective conscientious objection—the claim by those who follow the just-war theory that they can serve in a just war but conscientiously object to one they believe is unjust. "My point is not to challenge this teaching," Whealon said, "but only to say that it seems now, after twelve years, so vague and presumptive as to make us restudy it and in the meantime be cautious about applying this doctrine to any current developments in the nation."

When the bishops' conference president, Archbishop John Quinn of San Francisco, turned to the floor for discussion of the varia, the first

* Interestingly enough, Murphy says the directive wasn't a factor in his decision to introduce a varium, because he didn't fully understand its implications at the time.

to speak was Bishop Victor Balke of Crookston, Minnesota. In the kind of barb that was once unheard of but is now rather common in floor debates, Balke quoted recent popes who had called for education for peace, and said, "If I can editorialize a bit, I think education for peace would leave every young man and woman a selective conscientious objector—at least that, if not an objector to all war, at least that."

The next speaker was Cardinal Terence Cooke of New York, head of the Military Vicariate, in effect the diocese for Catholics in the armed services. A low-key, personable man, the fifty-nine-year-old Cooke, a bishop since 1965, had suffered from the assumption that as the hawkish Cardinal Francis Spellman's hand-picked successor, he must share his views. Cooke was particularly pained by the criticism that came his way during the Vietnam War, and it's clear that he felt torn between his anguish at the human cost of the war and his duty to minister to those in the military. After the war ended, Cooke became more visible in conference affairs, heading the bishops' Ad Hoc Committee on Pro-Life Activities, formed to counter the Supreme Court's 1973 decisions legalizing most abortions.

At a crucial point during the bishops' debate on support for the Panama Canal treaties when it seemed sentiment against the treaties might pick up steam after a critical comment from Cardinal John Krol of Philadelphia, a former conference president, Cooke backed the treaties, turning the corner and leading to the bishops' support. Typically, neither Cooke's comments nor presentation were particularly forceful; but they were strategic. His comments on the peace varia bordered on the innocuous, but he had already given his endorsement to a controversial undertaking.

He noted that military vicars from twenty-five countries had recently discussed their responsibility to work for peace. He said they had received a report summarizing church teaching on war and peace and offered it to the rest of the bishops, adding, "It's just a beginning. Much, much more work has to be done in all these areas, as we can see from the varia that have been proposed."

Then Quinn called on Gumbleton. The short, slim bishop with wire-rimmed glasses and stylishly barbered silvery hair thanked Murphy, O'Rourke and Whealon for their varia. He said there was an urgent need for a new study of the morality of nuclear war. "If we need any convincing of it," he said, "a very quick review of what has happened in our country in the past thirty-five years since we entered the atomic era will help us realize that there is an urgency today that means, in fact, that time is very short before the nuclear holocaust could indeed happen.

"We went for a long time after August 6, 1945, with the unspoken presumption that even though that terrible thing did happen—and many of us would have said it had to happen, it was a terrible thing but it had to happen—it would never happen again.

". . . More recently, as we entered the decade of the seventies especially, we became ever more explicit about our public policy of Mutual Assured Destruction, and we began to speak as if it could, perhaps would, indeed happen again in retaliation.

"And in 1975 our Secretary of Defense at the time explicitly stated that we, the United States, would be the first to use nuclear weapons if we determined we had to. So we had a first-use policy that was explicitly defined by our officials.

"As we move on out of the seventies and into the eighties, we find ourselves now with a further evolution of our public policy that says we are moving toward a counterforce strategy with first-strike capability. We are also finding out that our leaders are telling us that a nuclear war, a limited nuclear war, is possible, something which none of us would ever have believed before—and rightly would not have believed before.

". . . We've just elected a President who has stated his conviction that we can have superiority in nuclear weapons, an utter impossibility. We have a Vice-President who has clearly stated that one side could win a nuclear war and that we must be prepared to fight one and to win it. When we have that kind of thinking going on, it seems to me we are getting ever more close to the day when we will wage that nuclear war and it will be the war that will end the world as we know it. We are at a point of urgent crisis. We have to face this question and face it very clearly."

Then Gumbleton cited Pope John Paul II's 1980 World Day of Peace statement calling for a turn to nonviolence and urged study of "nonviolent civil defense" and "nonviolent alternatives to war." As Gumbleton concluded, the applause began at the same level of politeness most speakers received, but then it built in intensity, continuing for twenty seconds, making it clear he had struck a responsive chord.

"This is a very serious issue and one in which we are all intensely interested and about which we are profoundly concerned," Quinn said, ending the discussion before a coffee break. Just before calling the session back to order, he told Kelly, "They're really interested; they could take the rest of the meeting on this."

Quinn asked the burly Bishop Edward Head of Buffalo, outgoing chairman of the bishops' Committee on Social Development and World Peace, to respond to the varia; Head joked that this might be the time to announce the winner of the election for his successor. He recommended that the bishops accept the formal responsibility to deal with the issue and to consider whether to assign it to his committee or an ad hoc committee. Quinn accepted Head's recommendation.

The following January, Quinn's successor as conference president, Archbishop John Roach of St. Paul-Minneapolis, announced the creation of an ad hoc committee on war and peace with the task of drafting a statement for debate at the bishops' November 1982 meeting. Roach picked perhaps the most respected member of the American hierarchy, Archbishop Joseph Bernardin of Cincinnati, a former conference president known for his ability to build a consensus, to run the committee. Bernardin named Gumbleton and Auxiliary Bishop John O'Connor of the Military Ordinariate—author of the background paper mentioned by Cooke—to the committee, along with Bishop Daniel Reilly of Norwich, Connecticut and Auxiliary Bishop George Fulcher of Columbus, Ohio.

While the pastoral letter eventually became a watershed, the bishops' involvement in contemporary social issues was not brand new. Father J. Bryan Hehir, U.S. Catholic Conference associate secretary for international justice and peace, places it in a long tradition.

Historically, Christianity has been no stranger to social concern. Hehir notes that the bishops have been active for quite a while. "It's the response that's changed." He notes, for example, that Cardinal Dearden testified at the first House hearings on human rights in foreign policy in 1973. And the attention focused on the bishops on the nuclear question stands in stark contrast to the lack of attention on their support for the Panama Canal treaties—support Jimmy Carter, Cyrus Vance and Hamilton Jordan all called indispensable in winning Senate ratification.

Hehir says the general reason for the bishops' increased visibility on social justice issues is "a series of themes building very slowly, but very significantly, in recent years." He points out that the church's teaching has always been social in nature, emphasizing relationships and community, particularly after the Industrial Revolution, beginning with Pope Leo XIII. The Second Vatican Council, particularly the Pastoral Constitution on the Church in the Modern World *(Gaudium et Spes)* "took the whole social idea in ministry and brought it very close to the center of what the church is all about."

The council influenced bishops and theologians who began seeking ways to bring the social dimension to the church's daily life. "That's the basis for everything the church does—on nuclear weapons, budget cuts, human rights in foreign policy," Hehir says. "Each issue has its own line of argumentation, but protecting human dignity is a thoroughly evangelical task, a thoroughly gospel task, that the church must be involved in. Because of the social dimension, it can't be done outside of the political arena. That's why the church does it, it's not trying to impress people with being *au courant.*"

Another factor in the increased visibility for social justice issues has been the emphasis on collegiality, the sharing of power within the hierarchy, emphasized by Vatican II. When Archbishop Pio Laghi, who served on the staff at the Apostolic Delegation in the 1950s, returned to the United States to head the delegation in 1981, one of the major changes he noted was the growth of collegiality. "An auxiliary bishop has the same voice as a cardinal, the archbishop of New York the same vote as the bishop of Gallup."

The bishops' social concern is also partly a pastoral response, according to Msgr. Francis Lally, USCC secretary for social development and world peace. "People are asking them about the impact of unemployment and inflation on families," Lally says. "The same with war and peace, which is now a present peril."

Msgr. John Tracy Ellis, the foremost historian of the U.S. Catholic Church, adds historical and sociological explanations for the bishops' growing activity in the political arena. He argues that as an immigrant church, "a despised and scorned minority," American Catholics traditionally avoided criticism of the government. But, he says, in the past few decades, American Catholics have "arrived." The election of a Catholic President was one factor, he notes. Catholic political power has become entrenched. After the November 1982 elections, Catholics increased their representation in Congress to 142, the largest group ever from any denomination.

Congressional influence in the House of Representatives is particularly striking—including Speaker Tip O'Neill, Majority Whip and Agriculture Committee Chairman Thomas Foley, Budget Committee Chairman Jim Jones, Judiciary Committee Chairman Peter Rodino, Ways and Means Committee Chairman Daniel Rostenkowski, and Intelligence Committee Chairman Edward Boland.

Increasing economic as well as political power was a factor in increasing Catholic visibility, according to Ellis. He notes a sharp increase in per capita income among Catholics in the past few decades and points out that Father Andrew Greeley has compiled statistics showing Catholics rank ahead of all Protestant denominations and only slightly behind Jews in per capita income.

Noting that Catholics now make up one fourth of the U.S. population—they've been the largest U.S. denomination since 1850, he adds —Ellis says "numbers and money bespeak power. Catholics are in a much more secure position to speak out than they were in the past."

Two political developments since Vatican II also greatly influenced the bishops. The first was the Vietnam War. The 1971 bishops' resolution concluding that it was no longer a "just war" was a particularly wrenching experience, the first time the U.S. bishops had opposed their government on a major foreign policy issue.

The second event was the Supreme Court's legalization of most abortions, a move that further alienated the bishops from the government. As the bishops geared up their antiabortion efforts in the legislative area, they became more and more used to political involvement. At the same time, their emphasis on the broad meaning of "pro-life" led many to seek consistency on other issues—a factor, for example, in the bishops' opposition to the restoration of capital punishment in the United States.

As Bernardin noted in an interim report a year later, his committee did not "start from scratch"—statements from popes, the Second Vatican Council, and the U.S. bishops themselves offered a solid base.

The Pastoral Constitution on the Church in the Modern World adopted at the Second Vatican Council said: "Any act of war aimed indiscriminately at the destruction of entire cities or of entire areas along with their population is a crime against God and man himself. It merits unequivocal and unhesitating condemnation."

The council supported the right to legitimate self-defense and stopped short of condemning all war or all use of nuclear weapons; it said nuclear deterrence provides "peace of a sort."

The first major statement by the U.S. bishops after the council came in the pastoral letter of November 15, 1968, "Human Life in Our Day." "We join wholeheartedly," the bishops said, "in the Council's condemnation of wars fought without limitation. We recognize the right of legitimate self-defense and, in a world society still unorganized, the necessity for recourse to armed defense and to collective security action in the absence of a competent authority on the international level and once peaceful means have been exhausted. But we seek to limit warfare and to humanize it, where it remains a last resort, in the maximum degree possible. Most of all, we urge the enlisting of the energies of all men of good will in forging the instruments of peace, to the end that war may at last be outlawed."

The American bishops returned to the issue of nuclear warfare in "To Live in Christ Jesus," a pastoral letter issued on November 11, 1976:

With respect to nuclear weapons, at least those with massive destructive capability, the first imperative is to prevent their use. As possessors of a vast nuclear arsenal, we must also be aware that not only is it wrong to attack civilian populations, but it is also wrong to threaten to attack them as part of a strategy of deterrence. We urge the continued development and implementation of policies which seek to bring these weapons more securely under control, progressively reduce their presence in the world and ultimately remove them entirely.

The declaration that it is wrong to threaten to use nuclear weapons against civilians was the most dramatic change in church teaching on nuclear war since the council; ironically, in stark contrast to the deliberate approach used by the Bernardin committee, it was adopted without any substantive discussion. Even Archbishop Philip Hannan of New Orleans, a major hawk in the conference, failed to question this change in church teaching, even though he recommended minor changes in the same paragraph. Everyone knew that while the 1976 pastoral touched on other issues, it was primarily about sexual morality; that may have left many bishops less attentive to the rest of the document.

The notion that it is wrong to threaten to use nuclear weapons came originally from the pen of Russell Shaw, the U.S. Catholic Conference secretary for public affairs. Shaw, who looks a little like Wally Cox, is a trusted aide who has helped write scores of speeches and statements for church officials. Like any ghostwriter, Shaw tries to keep a low profile; he points out that while he did a great deal of writing and rewriting, the pastoral was written by a committee.

But he says he takes "a certain pride of authorship" in the section attacking the threat to use nuclear weapons, "a position I deeply hold myself."

"I felt honestly at the time it was a new step for the bishops," Shaw says. "It was logically consistent with things individual bishops and the conference itself had said. It was another step forward in a logical progression.

"Did they know? Who knows? I've wondered sometimes myself. There was nothing tricky about it; it was flat, bold, unequivocal. There was nothing deceptive about it—it was there in black and white. Sometimes I wondered how long it would take people to catch on to what the bishops did."

One person who caught on right away was Edward Doherty, a retired Foreign Service officer working in the USCC Office of International Justice and Peace. Doherty argued inside the conference— without much reaction—that the statement meant Catholics could not serve in the nuclear branch of the military.

Doherty and his boss, Father Hehir, came to grips with that question almost three years later as they prepared conference testimony supporting President Carter's SALT II treaty. The decision to back the treaty was made only after a highly unusual session of the bishops' Administrative Committee, an elected body which acts in the name of the entire conference in between general meetings.

The committee invited Gumbleton and Bishop Carroll Dozier of Memphis to debate the issue; as members of Pax Christi, they had opposed SALT II, arguing it would only perpetuate the arms race. The debate within the bishops' conference was the opposite of the secular political debate, in which the Carter administration was beseiged by conservatives charging the treaty weakened America.

The SALT testimony was ultimately delivered by Krol, an acknowledged leader of church conservatives. "Krol" is Polish for "king," and the tall, white-haired cardinal carries himself with a regal bearing; if he has ever had self-doubts, he's never let on in public.

The choice of Krol—a friend of Richard Nixon's—to deliver the testimony was an effort to defuse conservative criticism of the treaty, as was the case when Krol testified earlier in support of the Panama

Canal treaties. But Krol, who delivered a major address on the arms race at the 1971 Synod of Bishops—a triannual meeting of bishops representing the world episcopal conferences—has always been out front on the issue; he tells questioners, "I first spoke on disarmament before the VFW in Philadelphia in 1969." Some people think Krol takes a particular pride in being so "liberal" on peace.

Krol's testimony neatly summarized the church's subtle position; it's been quoted many times since. "The moral judgment of this statement," he said in explaining the 1976 pastoral, "is that not only the use of strategic nuclear weapons, but also the declared intent to use them involved in our deterrence policy, are both wrong. This explains the Catholic dissatisfaction with nuclear deterrence and the urgency of the Catholic demand that the nuclear arms race be reversed. It is of the utmost importance that negotiations proceed to meaningful and continuing reductions in nuclear stockpiles, and eventually to the phasing out altogether of nuclear deterrence and the threat of Mutual Assured Destruction.

"As long as there is hope of this occurring, Catholic moral teaching is willing, while negotiations proceed, to tolerate the possession of nuclear weapons for deterrence as the lesser of two evils. If that hope were to disappear, the moral attitude of the Catholic Church would almost certainly shift to one of uncompromising condemnation of both use and possession of such weapons."

◇ ◇ ◇

A week after his testimony, Krol delivered another speech that received less attention but was in many ways far more radical. He told a "Religious Consultation on SALT" that during the hearings, several senators had argued that no one could doubt the President's resolve to use air- and sea-based nuclear weapons in retaliation if the Soviet Union attacked U.S. land-based missiles. "I ask you," he said, "if the Christian conscience, after analysis of the facts and reflection on the consequences, could even be tempted to engage in such a senseless act of retaliation?"

As a Pole with deep ties to his communist-dominated homeland, Krol spoke with the credibility of one not likely to be thought soft on communism. "The history of certain countries occupied during World War II shows that there are other means of resistance which are in keeping with the nature of human beings," he said. "The history of certain countries under communist rule today shows that not only are human means of resistance available and effective, but also that human life does not lose all meaning with the replacement of one political system by another.

"History goes on and political systems are subject to change. As long as life exists, there is hope, hope that God's grace will enable suffering and oppressed peoples to endure. A nuclear holocaust would wipe out that hope. Therefore, we must resist tyranny and aggression by every human means, but not act in an irrational and suicidal way, and thus forfeit the grace which God will otherwise give us to enable us to persevere."

II. CRESCENDO

On February 25, 1981, Pope John Paul II went to Hiroshima. In a talk at the Peace Memorial Park, he repeated his theme four times—"To remember the past is to commit oneself to the future."

"In the past," he said, "it was possible to destroy a village, a town, a region, even a country. Now it is the whole planet that has come under threat. This fact should compel everyone to confront a basic moral consideration: From now on, it is only through a conscious choice and through a deliberate policy that humanity can survive. The moral and political choice that faces us is putting all the resources of mind, science and culture at the service of peace and building up of a new society."

Less than three weeks later, seventeen bishop members of Pax Christi sent Archbishop Bernardin a letter asking his committee to consider questions like these:

—"Can the nuclear arms race between the superpowers be continued without greatly increasing the risks of war?"

—"If the indiscriminate use of weapons of mass destruction is morally wrong (as Catholic teaching clearly holds), how can the threat to use them (which is essential to our strategy of deterrence), be morally justifiable?"

—"Is it right, then, for our country to possess nuclear weapons?"

—"Is it realistic to expect that nuclear war can be fought on a limited basis?"

—"Is it morally responsible for policy makers to suggest that nuclear wars can be won?"

The bishops in Pax Christi were a notable mix of men considered to be in the hierarchy's peace wing and those considered part of the establishment: in addition to Gumbleton, Murphy, Walter Sullivan, Lyke and Balke, there were Archbishop John May of St. Louis, Archbishop Daniel Sheehan of Omaha and Bishop James Rausch of

Phoenix, Bernardin's successor as general secretary of the bishops' conference, who died a few months after the letter was sent.

The Pax Christi bishops said the challenge of the present arms race is "whether, given the character of modern weapons, it is possible for states to wage a morally justifiable war." The letter also said, "We must explore carefully the possibility of advocating unilateral initiatives as a way of breaking the current deadlock."

The first dramatic gesture within the American hierarchy came on June 12, when Archbishop Raymond Hunthausen of Seattle—known as "Dutch" to his friends—spoke in Tacoma to the Pacific Northwest Synod of the Lutheran Church in America. Hunthausen had previously emerged as a major critic of the Trident submarine, which was being built in neighboring Puget Sound. But he took several giant steps in the Tacoma talk when he called for unilateral nuclear disarmament and said he was considering withholding half of his federal income tax as a protest against U.S. nuclear policy.

"I can recall vividly hearing the news of the atomic bombing of Hiroshima in 1945," said the fifty-nine-year-old archbishop, a member of the hierarchy since 1962. "I was deeply shocked. I could not then put into words the shock I felt from the news that a city of hundreds of thousands of people had been devastated by a single bomb.

"Hiroshima challenged my faith as a Christian in a way I am only now beginning to understand. That awful event and its successor at Nagasaki sank into my soul, as they have in fact sunk into the souls of all of us, whether we recognize it or not.

"I am sorry to say that I did not speak out against the evil of nuclear weapons until many years later," Hunthausen said. One catalyst to that decision to speak out was an article entitled "It's a Sin to Build a Nuclear Weapon" by Jesuit Father Richard McSorley, a pacifist, in a 1976 issue of *U.S. Catholic.* Hunthausen quoted McSorley:

> The taproot of violence in our society today is our intention to use nuclear weapons. Once we have agreed to that, all other evil is minor in comparison. Until we squarely face the question of our consent to use nuclear weapons, any hope of large-scale improvement of public morality is doomed to failure.

"I agree," Hunthausen said. He said he was also challenged to speak out by the construction of the Trident—with "the first-strike nuclear doctrine" it represents—in his archdiocese. The Trident, he said, can destroy as many as 408 separate areas, each with a bomb five times more powerful than the one dropped on Hiroshima. The Trident and the MX missile have such accuracy and power they can only be understood as first-strike missiles, he said. "First-strike nuclear weapons are immoral and criminal. They benefit only arms corporations and the insane dreams of those who wish to 'win' a nuclear holocaust.

"I was moved to speak out against Trident," he said, "because it is being based here. We must take special responsibility for what is in our own back yard. And when crimes are being prepared in our own name, we must speak plainly. I say with deep consciousness of these words that Trident is the Auschwitz of Puget Sound."

Hunthausen said unilateral disarmament is one way of taking up "the cross." "I am told by some that unilateral disarmament in the face of atheistic communism is insane," he said. "I find myself observing that nuclear armament by anyone is itself atheistic and anything but sane."

Hunthausen readily acknowledged that others might reject his "tactics," but said one thing remained certain: "We must demand over and over again that our political leaders make peace and disarmament, and not war and increased armaments, their first priority. . . . We must challenge every politician who talks endlessly about building up our arms and never about efforts for peace."

Just about two months later, on August 21, a little-known bishop from a diocese with a small Catholic population—Leroy Matthiessen of Amarillo, Texas—caused a furor locally and nationally when he denounced the Reagan administration's decision to deploy the neutron bomb. If Hunthausen had the Trident in his backyard, Matthiessen had the Pantex plant—final assembly point for U.S. nuclear weapons, including the neutron bomb—in his, fifteen miles from Amarillo.

The sixty-year-old Matthiessen, who was ordained a bishop in March 1980, is a former newspaper editor; his statement, compressing explosive ideas into ten short paragraphs, was far better suited for an editorial than a pastoral statement. Calling the neutron bomb decision "the latest in a series of tragic anti-life decisions taken by our government," he said: "Let us stop this madness. . . . We beg our administration to stop accelerating the arms race. We beg our military to use common sense and moderation in our defense posture. We urge individuals involved in the production and stockpiling of nuclear bombs to consider what they are doing, to resign from such activities and to seek employment in peaceful pursuits."

It was that last point that caused an explosion of its own in Amarillo, heavily dependent on Pantex for jobs and spending.

As local criticism of Matthiessen mounted, the twelve other Catholic bishops in Texas issued a statement supporting him on September 10. "The bishops wanted to support Bishop Matthiessen in order to dispel any impression that his stand did not reflect the opinion of the other bishops in Texas or the teachings of the church on nuclear weapons," Bishop Joseph Fiorenza of San Angelo, secretary of the Texas conference, explained to reporters.

Matthiessen had earlier questioned plans to base the MX missile in the Texas Panhandle. "There is no way we can do the enemy in without them doing us in," he said.

Matthiessen's grandfather came to the United States from Germany in 1870 because he was sick of that country's endless wars. Matthiessen's father was a pacifist of sorts, although he relented and gave the young Leroy a Stevens .22 single-shot rifle for Christmas when he was twelve.

"Once, in a pickup," Matthiessen says, "a rifle in my hands went off accidentally. The bullet sped within inches of a friend's head. I said simply, 'I didn't know the gun was loaded.'

"I really paid little attention to the dropping of the atomic bombs on Hiroshima and Nagasaki in 1945, grateful only that the war was over soon thereafter and that my brother could come home. I did not realize then what it was with which the guns of Hiroshima and Nagasaki were loaded."

Matthiessen too speaks of Father Zabelka. "What of me?" he asks. "For thirty-three years I lived . . . at the very portals of Pantex, and for those thirty-three years I said nothing, either as a priest or a bishop, until a Catholic employee and his wife came to me with troubled consciences. They had begun to think that what he was doing was wrong.

"Other events had preceded them. . . . I finally was moved to speak. I had come to the realization, with Martin Luther King, Jr., that the choice really is between nonviolence and nonexistence. I finally could no longer say, 'I didn't know the gun was loaded.' "

One dynamic in the bishops' growing involvement in the nuclear issue—and the public's awareness of that involvement—is that many important developments were not widely publicized at the time, probably because they didn't fit the prevailing conception of "news." But as other dramatic incidents—like Hunthausen's and Matthiessen's statements—became news, those missed stories became part of a broader pattern.

One such missed event was the publication of a study paper by Bishop Anthony Pilla of Cleveland on August 6, 1981, the twenty-sixth anniversary of the bombing of Hiroshima. Pilla phrased his statement in a series of questions focused around the church's just-war tradition, going back to St. Augustine, which holds that to be just, a war must meet these conditions:

1. The decision for war must be made by a legitimate authority.
2. The war must be fought for a just cause.
3. War must be taken only as a last resort.
4. There must be a reasonable chance of "success."
5. The good to be achieved by the war must outweigh the evil that will result from it (proportionality).
6. The war must be waged with just means (in accordance with international and natural law).

"If even one of these conditions were not met in a particular conflict," Pilla said, "the conflict would be perceived by the church as contrary to the Fifth Commandment, morally reprehensible and a crime against God. The criteria are so constructed that though they allow some wars to be perceived as just, most fall into the latter category and are condemned."

Pilla said: "Nuclear weapons made possible the total destruction of entire innocent civilian populations in a very short amount of time. Not only was such annihilation against rules 5 and 6 of the just war doctrine, it far overstepped Rule 4 by giving the aggressor overwhelming odds for success. Also, the simplicity and power of one atomic warhead made Rule 1 . . . and Rule 2 . . . easily bypassable by anyone in control of a bomb.

"Finally, the presence of nuclear technology led to the 'first-strike' philosophy and the arms race, thus negating Rule 3. So nuclear weapons break all St. Augustine's standards for justice. Even more, they create the potential for mass destruction even if they are used in accordance with the just war doctrine."

Pilla urged the church to oppose modern war "as strongly as we oppose abortion, racism and poverty." He called on church institutions to promote education for peace and the formation of conscience, including establishing a justice and peace commission in every parish council. Stopping short of the more judgmental language Matthiessen used, Pilla urged Catholics "involved in the production of weapons of mass destruction to reconsider the moral implications of their jobs; those who are asked to give or obey orders to use nuclear weapons ought to meditate on the morality of such actions."

And Pilla urged "supporting and participating in the nuclear freeze campaign," then a little-noticed, fledgling effort to have Congress urge the President to propose a bilateral, verifiable freeze on the building, testing and deployment of nuclear weapons to the Soviet Union.

The study paper had been in preparation for several months. Pilla, forty-nine, had been an auxiliary bishop since 1979; he became ordinary of the diocese on January 6, 1981, several months after Bishop James Hickey of Cleveland had been named Archbishop of Washington, D.C. The Italian-American bishop wondered on what issues he could exercise his role as a teacher in his diocese.

"After a lot of thought, I came up with two ideas—the whole question of peace and the whole question of the poor. I thought I'd first address the issue of peace because a lot of people had been coming with concern about this, looking for direction. I was concerned about the lack of consistency with which they were being presented the tradition of the church."

Pilla decided to issue a pastoral on peace, to be followed by one on poverty and then a linkage of the two—in Advent 1982, he emphasized the papal theme "If you want peace, work for justice."

He asked the diocesan Catholic Commission for Community Action to research the peace pastoral and gave it guidelines. "We were not trying to tell people what to think . . . the approach was a teaching document—what has been the tradition of the church, not what I think. . . . Now, you can accept it or you can reject it, but you should know it."

The diocesan Justice and Peace Commission is itself a new structure in the post-Vatican II period. The Cleveland commission used broad consultation with church and community leaders. "How can we be patriotic if we take these positions?" Pilla said. "Those who govern us do so by our consent. Patriotism neither presupposes nor requires acquiescence to their every decision. Our nation's democratic traditions support, indeed are hinged upon, the right and responsibility of the governed to question and scrutinize the decisions of public officials. Our country has witnessed much social progress in the last two decades, notably in civil rights, because of the courage of relatively few people who were willing to challenge the policies and practices of the many."

"The overwhelming response was positive," Pilla says. Every school in the diocese developed a peace education plan.

Pilla's personal endorsement of the nuclear freeze resulted from a separate process. "I'm convinced that as a starting point, we have to change the psychology of our whole defense policy . . . we have to stop and begin thinking along new patterns, because if you don't freeze and start thinking about it, where does it happen? When does it happen? Someone has to be strong enough to be able to start that process, and I think we are."

Noting that his master's degree in history and political science at John Carroll University in Cleveland was in European history and the development of communism, Pilla says, "I have found historically that the strongest defense against communism—the particular area of my study—has not been armaments, it's been just and nonoppressive societies."

Less than a week after Pilla issued his statement, on August 12, Archbishop Roach, speaking as president of the bishops' conference, issued a statement criticizing the Reagan administration's decision to build and stockpile neutron bombs. He said the conference position had not changed since 1978, and he quoted the statement Quinn had made then:

It can be argued that this weapon is less objectionable than existing tactical nuclear weapons. . . . In terms of traditional moral theology, this characteristic would be judged as a favorable recommendation for this type of weapon.

In making an ethical judgment on the neutron warhead, however, I believe it is necessary to calculate its moral implications in a broadly defined framework. A principal consideration is the impact of this decision on the arms race. I am concerned, in the spirit so often expressed by Pope Paul VI, that we forestall any major decisions which will intensify the nuclear arms spiral.

A second argument against development of the neutron warhead is that the introduction of this new and more "manageable" weapon tends to narrow the gap politically and psychologically between conventional war and nuclear war. In other words, it could render more probable the escalation of any war in Europe to the level of nuclear warfare.

"The very danger against which Archbishop Quinn warned in 1978," Roach said, "appears closer to realization today. . . . One must seriously ask whether the decision to develop the neutron warhead serves to blur the distinction between conventional war and the qualitative moral-political leap one makes in moving to nuclear war in any form.

"The questions and concerns of this statement are based on the conviction that the political and moral barriers to nuclear war should be made clearer and stronger today. I question whether the neutron warhead serves that objective."

At about the time that Roach, Pilla and Matthiessen were issuing their statements, Quinn was looking ahead to October 4, the eight hundredth anniversary of the birth of St. Francis of Assisi, patron saint of his city, and planning what to say in a homily on that day. "I wanted to show that a saint like St. Francis has an enduring relevance . . . to the problems of our times," Quinn says. "I thought that one of the most notable problems would be the issue of nuclear war."

Quinn, fifty-two, is a short, slender man with slicked-back salt-and-pepper hair. He often creates the impression of being cold and aloof, perhaps because of an innate shyness. When he was elected president of the bishops' conference in 1977, ten years after first being named an auxiliary bishop in San Diego, he had the reputation of being a conservative; but on social issues, his record as archbishop of Oklahoma City before he went to San Francisco and his later record contained all the statements—such as a condemnation of the Christmas bombing of North Vietnam and a statement on prison reform—that earned others, like Bernardin, a reputation as liberals.

Quinn had led the American delegation to the 1980 Synod of Bishops on the family, where he made a dramatic appeal for recognition of the fact that millions of American Catholics remain loyal to the church despite their rejection of its ban on artificial means of birth control.

Quinn's language in his twenty-five-hundred-word St. Francis homily was strong, arguing that "nuclear weapons and the arms race must be condemned as immoral." He said the neutron bomb, "even though it is being promoted as a 'clean' bomb for use only as a 'theater' or 'tactical' weapon, is a deadly instrument of mass destruction, and its use could easily ignite a global nuclear conflagration. It contributes to the dangerous illusion that a 'limited' nuclear war can be fought and won."

Quinn said: "The billions of dollars presently being spent on arms each year throughout the world is surely an appalling form of theft in a world where so many persons die each day of starvation and privation. The obsessive drive for security through nuclear weaponry has not brought security, either for the six nations which now have strategic nuclear capacity or for the forty other nations which will possess that capacity by 1985."

Like Pilla, Quinn laid out the requirements of the just-war doctrine. "If we apply each of these traditional principles to the current international arms race," he said, "we must conclude that a 'just' nuclear war is a contradiction in terms.

"Strategic nuclear weapons are designed precisely and exclusively to destroy entire cities and their populations," he said. "It is hard to imagine a more lethal instrument of indiscriminate mass destruction of civilian noncombatant populations. Furthermore, physicians, physicists and even military planners have described all too graphically the biological, environmental and genetic damage that will result for generations from the explosive and radioactive power of a single thermonuclear weapon.

"What good could possibly be proportional to such uncontrollable destruction and suffering? Is it likely that survivors of such a holocaust could describe themselves in any sense as victors?"

Quinn called for educational programs on peace (he now has two people working full-time on this) and a day of fasting each month for penance and political action, and he endorsed the nuclear freeze campaign.

Quinn closed his homily by reciting the prayer of St. Francis: "Lord, make me an instrument of your peace . . ." He was stunned when the cathedral full of people burst into applause and gave him a standing ovation.

"I never expected it at all," he says. "In fact, I really expected a very grim and hostile reaction. It was during Mass—I went and began to say the Credo, the Creed, because I certainly appreciated the goodness of the people to express themselves in that way, but it was in the middle of the Mass."

A month after the St. Francis celebration, Quinn spoke about nuclear weapons again at the Doheny Campus of Mount St. Mary's College in Los Angeles. He emphasized his concern that the "political and psychological firebreak (between conventional and nuclear war) is in danger of being eroded, increasing the possibility of actual nuclear conflict."

He credited an article by Father Hehir of the USCC with helping him to focus on that concern. Quinn also addressed the morality of nuclear deterrence, arguing that "while in principle the possession of nuclear weapons targeted at cities cannot be justified morally, there is some reliable body of moral opinion that would tolerate the possession of nuclear weapons, but only as an interim instrument of policy."

But, he said, "There are signs, now, that the arms race has gone beyond this reluctantly tolerated policy of deterrence. . . . The traditional policy . . . has now shifted to a first-strike or 'counterforce' strategy. It is now becoming clearer that the Trident II submarine missile system is a first-strike weapon, as indeed is the M-X missile system. . . . This escalation of forces to a first-strike posture underscores the compelling logic of the Council's prophetic observation that nuclear weapons even as a deterrent is not a safe way to preserve a steady peace."

Quinn says the nuclear issue began to take hold of him about a year before his St. Francis homily. He told the San Francisco Commonwealth Club the following summer that "when I became a priest almost thirty years ago, I used to preach on Sundays about the Creed, about the sacraments, about the life of Our Lord and other strictly religious truths. I taught religion each day in the parish school, trained altar boys and visited the sick at the local hospitals.

"I helped people deal with marriage and family problems, and I was chaplain to the scout troop and to the parish teen club. I listened to the often unannounced callers who came to talk about their problems. In other words, my work was almost entirely what could be called 'religious.'"

How did he move from that stage of his priesthood to the present?

"The major influence was the Second Vatican Council, particularly the Constitution on the Church in the Modern World, which says it all, it situates the church in the world," Quinn says. "It was really the mind and spirit of the council that I've tried to assimilate and absorb and internalize that led me to this."

Statements by Quinn and the others, along with the Reagan administration's neutron bomb decision, continued rhetoric about limited and winnable nuclear wars, and the growing peace movement in Europe, opened a floodgate of comments from other bishops.

Concern was heightened on October 16 when Reagan, answering a question at a press conference about the possibility of fighting a limited nuclear war in Europe, said: "I don't honestly know. I could see where you could have an exchange of tactical weapons against troops in the field without it bringing either one of the superpowers into pushing the button."

The bishops' statements came in bunches, creating a crescendo leading up to the November conference meeting.

In a local religion program aired over WNBC-TV in New York on October 18, Bishop Frank Rodimer of Paterson, New Jersey, called building the neutron warhead "a sin against humanity." Writing in his column in the diocesan newspaper, Rodimer said that on a practical level, Soviet tanks—the would-be targets of the neutron bomb—would be widely spread out, causing the use of a number of neutron bombs and damage not really much less than that caused by normal nuclear weapons.

The best way to appreciate the flood of bishops' peace statements and comments may be by looking at stories run by National Catholic News Service, the news wire serving U.S. diocesan papers.

"Recent months have seen a notable increase in concern over the arms race by U.S. Catholic bishops," was the understated lead on a two-thousand-word round-up sent out October 19 over the by-line of Jerry Filteau, an NC reporter and former Rome bureau chief. In addition to the statements by Roach, Quinn, Pilla, Matthiessen and Hunthausen, Filteau pulled together both brand-new statements and some that had not received national publicity earlier to create a stunning picture of a hierarchy up in arms over the arms race:

Bishops Elden F. Curtiss of Helena and Thomas J. Murphy of Great Falls-Billings, both in Montana, took the same basic position (as Matthiessen) against the M-X, declaring that "continued stockpiling of arms, in a world already capable of destroying itself, is a false and precarious means of assuring lasting peace."

In a weekly column for *The Florida Catholic* of Oct. 23, Bishop Thomas Grady of Orlando, Fla., asked, "Is it moral even to possess nuclear weapons?"

"Nuclear war should be opposed as an unjust war," he wrote. "Nuclear weapons should be banned."

"It is immoral to possess nuclear weapons," wrote Bishop Raymond Lucker of New Ulm, Minn., in his monthly diocesan paper in September. "Nuclear weapons may not be used for attack or for first strike," he said. "They may not be used in defense. They may not be threatened to be used. Therefore it seems to me that even to possess them is wrong."

The month before [Pilla's statement] Bishop Michael Kenny of Juneau, Alaska, had declared himself "categorically opposed not only to the use but to the possession of nuclear weapons," and said he was personally becoming a pacifist because of his meditation on Christian teaching.

In a series of essays on peace and disarmament in his archdiocesan newspaper, *The Leaven,* Archbishop Ignatius Strecker of Kansas City, Kan., asked where the moral issue of the arms race is in American discussions of weapons systems and strategy, and declared that "pacificism greatly needs a clear voice and a strong witness in the church, in our nation, in the world."

Bishop Walter Sullivan of Richmond, Va., a board member of Pax Christi USA . . . told a largely military audience in Virginia Beach, Va., in September that it is "immoral to be associated with the production or use" of nuclear weapons.

Archbishop John L. May of St. Louis wrote Oct. 16 in his archdiocesan newspaper, the *St. Louis Review,* "The neutron bomb is being pushed as a clean, tactical nuclear weapon. The idea of a limited, winnable nuclear war is now being sold as a further refinement beyond increasingly horrendous conventional weapons."

Eight months earlier he had written in a similar vein, decrying "a lot of tough talk in Washington, talk about perfecting the neutron bomb, winning the nuclear arms race and even winning a nuclear war. . . . We know deep down that there is no way to win a nuclear war."

Bishop Phillip F. Straling of San Bernardino, Calif., who had written to Reagan in July urging him "to consider less spending on military and implements of war and more for people in need," also issued a public statement backing Archbishop Roach and questioning the neutron warhead decision.

"As our nation puts greater emphasis on mightier and more destructive weapons of war, especially the neutron warhead . . . it is a contradiction to the message and spirit of the word of God," he said.

Bishop Edward O'Rourke of Peoria, Ill., . . . wrote an editorial in his diocesan paper, *The Catholic Post,* warning against Pax Christi's orientation toward unilateral disarmament, saying that this was dangerous, unrealistic and not in accord with papal teachings on the right of nations to self-defense.

But in the editorial Bishop O'Rourke also said that after carefully studying the issue, "I have reached the conclusion that present diplomatic policies and negotiating procedures are inadequate to meet the seriousness and urgency of this crisis. . . . We must boldly suggest a radically different manner in which disarmament and peace can be discussed and pursued. Failure to do so may occasion a nuclear war which would destroy civilization as we now know it."

Other NC stories in the following days focused on European peace demonstrations, a Vatican Radio attack on the arms race, and the decision of a parish in Indianapolis to withhold part of the federal tax on its phone bill to protest military spending. And more bishops spoke out:

—Nov. 9: An interfaith group of Oregon church leaders, including Archbishop Cornelius Power and Auxiliary Bishop Paul Waldschmidt of Portland, called on Reagan and Congress to begin negotiations with other countries to ban nuclear weapons by the year 2000.

—Nov. 10: Bishop James Niedergeses of Nashville issued a pastoral as a four-page insert in his diocesan paper, *The Tennessee Register,* calling nuclear war "folly of unbelievable proportions" and citing Krol's SALT testimony.

—Nov. 12: Another Filteau round-up:

At least three more U.S. bishops have publicly entered the nuclear arms debate, bringing the number of American prelates who have recently commented on the issue to more than 30.

"The U.S. has a moral right to have a deterrent power sufficient to protect our freedom and the freedom of the west," said Archbishop Philip M. Hannan in a column questioning the opposition to American nuclear weaponry.

In Ohio, meanwhile, Bishop Albert H. Ottenweller of Steubenville declared that "there is no way we can apply the just war norms to machines with such destructive power [as nuclear bombs]. We must say that their very use is madness and immoral."

Bishop Francis Quinn of Sacramento, Calif., condemned even the possession of nuclear weapons and urged the United States to take unilateral initial steps toward disarmament. "A bilateral reduction of arms will not begin until something unilateral happens," he said.

—Nov. 13: A story on Quinn's Los Angeles speech.

—Nov. 17: Bishop Bernard Flanagan of Worcester, Mass., condemned a new "nuclear doctrine" he said had been advanced by members of both the Carter and Reagan administrations "that a nuclear war can be controlled and is winnable."

As the crescendo mounted, Filteau asked himself a question reporters often ask themselves: "Am I reporting the news or creating it?" He concluded that his collecting of quotes on nuclear weapons from a variety of pastoral letters and newspaper columns was indeed legitimately reporting the news. But Filteau also notes that the press did help move the story along: "Reporters ask the local bishop, 'And what do you think?' and another statement is made."

As the bishops' meeting approached, an air of anticipation grew, even though no action on the peace pastoral was planned. When reporters came to the meeting at the Capitol Hilton Hotel in Washington, they found in their press kits a list of more than forty bishops who had spoken out on the peace issue in recent months. But a close look revealed that the list was incomplete—statements were coming out literally too fast to follow.

III. INTERIM REPORT

The 1981 bishops' meeting opened November 16, like all others, with an address by the conference president.

Roach opened his talk by challenging a relevant cliché: "As a rule of thumb for keeping friends, 'never discuss religion or politics' has a long history in our culture. It has received the status of a secular commandment. At times it is even taken as a corollary of the constitutional principle of church and state.

"On the one hand," he said, "Catholic theology can and should support and defend the separation of church and state, the principle that religious organizations should expect neither favoritism nor discrimination because they are religious. On the other hand," he said, "we should not accept or allow the separation of church and state to be used to separate the church from society."

Accepting this, he said, would reduce the church to "a purely private role" and prevent it from fulfilling "an essential dimension of its ministry."

He then applied this approach to the question of the Moral Majority, the name of a particular organization, but also the generic name for newly active right-wing Christian groups. In the first major comment on the movement by a prominent Catholic bishop, he defended the right of the "Moral Majority or any religious organization to address the public issues of the day."

But, he said, "religious organizations should be subjected to the same standards of rational, vigorous presentation of their views as any other participant in the public debate. Moreover, religious organizations, which address the moral dimensions of public issues, are to be judged by the standards of competent moral analysis. Particularly relevant," Roach said, "are the issues of 'how one defines a moral issue' and the consistency with which moral principles are defended across a range of moral issues."

When the Catholic Church speaks on public policy issues, he said, "it must be made clear that these actions are rooted in, directed by, in fulfillment of a theologically grounded conception of the church's ministry."

The first theme of church teaching, Roach said, is "the religious conviction about the dignity of the human person" and its protection within the political process; the second, he said, is in the Second Vatican Council's definition of "the protection of human dignity and the promotion of human rights as properly ecclesial tasks, an integral part of the church's ministry.

"A consistent moral vision rooted in Catholic social thought," Roach said, "would link opposition to the arms race with opposition to abortion and support for the rights of the poor." Noting that "strategic arms limitations talks are presently stalemated," he said, "The church needs to say 'no' clearly and decisively to the use of nuclear weapons. This is surely the direction of Vatican II teachings on the arms race and its condemnation of attacks on civilian centers. The 'no' we utter should shape our policy advice and our pastoral guidance of Catholics."

Returning to the theme of his statement on the neutron bomb, Roach said, "It is not useful to blur the line of moral argument about the use of nuclear weapons at a time when the secular debate is openly discussing the use of limited nuclear weapons and winnable nuclear wars."

Shifting to abortion, Roach spoke of the "carnage" and "scandal" created by the Supreme Court's 1973 decisions and urged all "prolife people" to unite behind the Hatch amendment.

The Hatch amendment was a major focus of the meeting. Earlier in the year, Roach and Cooke had backed the amendment, introduced by Republican Senator Orrin Hatch of Utah, that would give the states and the federal government concurrent power to regulate abortion, providing that the strictest law would prevail. This marked the first time the bishops had backed a specific amendment, departing from their reference to a set of principles they said should characterize an amendment.

While the bishops argued that the Hatch amendment met those principles, many hard-line right-to-lifers charged that it was a states' rights approach that was unacceptable because it would allow some states to remain abortion havens. During the bishops' meeting, Cooke's report sparked an unusually frank debate, which featured

Cardinal Humberto Medeiros of Boston attacking Cooke and Roach's actions. After what one bishop described as "caucusing," particularly during the bishops' executive session, the bishops closed ranks behind Cooke and Roach, with only one bishop dissenting.

Concluding his speech, Roach discussed poverty in the context of the Reagan administration's plans for spending $1.5 trillion on arms over the next five years: "In the past it was presumed in the United States that we could spend whatever we decided for defense and still be a compassionate society. That assumption is today denied in fact; what is spent for guns directly reduces what is available for the quality of care and life for the least among us."

Roach also challenged the Administration's argument that the private and voluntary sectors could "fill the gaps" created by budget cutbacks in social programs. "We have neither the resources, nor, I suppose, even the mandate, to do this," he said. "We will do our part, but our own social teaching calls upon the state to do its part."

At almost the same time that Roach was speaking, President Reagan was giving a speech of his own. It contained a bombshell of sorts, as well as evidence that the Administration took the bishops and the growing antinuclear movement seriously. It was Reagan's first major arms control proposal—a "zero option plan" under which the United States would not deploy new intermediate-range ballistic missiles in Europe if the Soviet Union would dismantle all of its similar weapons in the area. The plan seemed an uneven trade to some—but it was the first sign of Administration movement on the issue.

Bernardin gave his interim report on Wednesday afternoon, describing the committee's makeup and process and summarizing church teaching. He said that while the committee's major focus was on nuclear war, "our experience with the moral turmoil provoked by Vietnam highlights the need for an assessment of non-nuclear uses of force. Periodically in the last decade the threat of an oil boycott has produced proposals to fight a conventional war over oil. Some of these proposals seem to take it for granted that the justification to do this for oil or other resources is self-evident."

Returning to nuclear weapons, Bernardin said, "The failure, after so many years, of effective arms limitation, the growing official readiness to contemplate the use of nuclear weapons and the introduction of highly integrated command and control systems, which may heighten the thrust toward automatic use of our weapons if deterrence fails, all make the need to evaluate existing policy more evident."

He said that "much expert opinion seriously doubts" that nuclear war could be kept limited.

"We are fully aware," he went on, "that current tensions are by no means attributable to U.S. policy alone. Clearly, the enormous build-up of nuclear and conventional arms pursued by the Soviet Union in recent years has done more than its share to heighten the peril of the present moment. The duty of responsible moral action falls equally on both superpowers. But if we direct our attention particularly to the United States, it is for the simple reason that we are American citizens and have a right and duty to address our government."

As Bernardin neared the end of his text, he used dramatic language, unusually dramatic language for him. "We need to be convinced," he said, "that some actions can never be taken, even for survival; that there are limits to the argument that, because our adversaries are considering something, we must be prepared to do it also. We need to recall that as Americans and as people of faith we are expected to have our own principles, to be prepared to live by them and, in faith, to accept the consequences of doing so."*

Concluding his interim report, Bernardin argued that "the very created order is threatened by nuclear war. We must learn how to evaluate war with an entirely new attitude."

He received a standing ovation. It was one of two votes of confidence the bishops gave Bernardin at the meeting; the other came when he was elected a delegate to the 1983 Synod of Bishops.

The two signs were important, because they came at a time when Bernardin was dealing with unwanted publicity. During the messy dispute over the activities of Cardinal John Cody in Chicago, a reporter published materials from the papers of Andrew Greeley—a priest, sociologist and author—revealing Greeley's plans to elect a liberal pope by getting Bernardin into the College of Cardinals by moving him to Chicago. Greeley's scheme would have removed Cody by getting a newspaper to do an investigative report on his financial dealings.

Greeley responded that the scenario was transcribed from a fantasy

---

* At a press conference later that day, Bernardin explained that the "action" to which he referred was the use of nuclear weapons which would destroy thousands and millions of civilians.

dictated late at night after too much wine. No one seriously thought Bernardin had any part in Greeley's scheming, but the concern was widespread that the incident might hurt Bernardin's chance to succeed Cody, a move that had been rumored for years. (The Washington *Post* later quoted a church figure as saying, "Bernardin is no more responsible for his role in Andy Greeley's fantasies than Jodie Foster is for hers in John Hinckley's").

When Roach went to the floor for discussion after Bernardin's report, the first to speak was the new convert to pacifism, forty-four-year-old Michael Kenny of Juneau.

"When we as a church ally ourselves too closely with a particular country or age, we tend to weaken our prophetic role," he said. "In several notable instances in our past, such alliances have gotten us into serious trouble. As followers of Christ . . . our kingdom is not of this world."

Next, Bishop O'Rourke, sixty-four, criticized Kenny and others by implication. "I recall," he said, "that several of our fellow bishops have declared publicly that all use or threat to use nuclear weapons is immoral." (O'Rourke apparently didn't remember the 1976 pastoral very well.) "Some have suggested unilateral disarmament by the United States.

"Indeed, some of our brother bishops have expressed the opinion that we are approaching a consensus at least on the first of these views. Lest we be stampeded into that opinion, I rise to state that many bishops have great reservations about both of these declarations."

O'Rourke said that if the bishops backed unilateral disarmament, the Russians would probably refuse to engage in meaningful SALT talks. "If this body declares that all use or threat to use nuclear weapons is immoral," he said, the Russians might launch a nuclear first strike against the United States or a conventional attack upon its enemies.

O'Rourke was followed by Walter Sullivan, who became the first to voice a strategy agreed on earlier by a number of peace bishops—to urge the bishops to continue to speak out at the local level while the Bernardin committee continued its process.

Just as O'Rourke had taken on Kenny, the salty Sullivan took on O'Rourke. "I agree with Bishop O'Rourke," he said. "I'm not sure who in this body is for doing away with every type of defense. I always almost think that that's a straw man that comes to make the position look foolish."

Sullivan suggested those who agree with O'Rourke join in supporting the nuclear freeze campaign. "This is a bilateral freeze, it's not a unilateral freeze."

Auxiliary Bishop Francis Stafford of Baltimore called for independent de-escalatory initiatives that don't threaten defense.

Archbishop Peter Gerety of Newark seconded Sullivan's call for statements at the local level. "It seems to me," he said, "that we have a duty . . . not to lose heart. We do have the possibility in this country of influencing our government. We have already had evidence of that, I think, this morning. The President, in giving in to public opinion, apparently, has expressed his willingness, I understand, to go into negotiations. . . . We've got to form a constituency for peace to speak up."

Matthiessen urged the committee to address "the very real plight of the workers who are currently involved in the development of these nuclear weapons."

Joseph McNicholas of Springfield, Illinois, said, "We cannot operate in an ivory tower. . . . I think the public record shows that there have been few uses of force in the last twenty years that have not directly involved the threat of worldwide communism."

Next to speak was Hannan, who had launched his first salvo against the antinuclear bishops just before the meeting. A paratrooper during World War II, the sixty-eight-year-old archbishop had long defended nuclear deterrence and a strong military. As an auxiliary bishop from Washington, D.C., attending the Second Vatican Council, he helped organize the effort that led the council to stop short of condemning war altogether.

Hannan opened his comments at the bishops' meeting by saying, "For the record, I'd like to say that I abhor war together with the members of the committee and also view with great dismay the use of nuclear weapons. However," he continued, "to me the basic question in this and which has not been addressed at all, and I wish it could be included actually in the wording of the topic, is the question of freedom under God. War is unintelligible without a consideration of freedom under God and the dignity of man and human rights."

Hannan urged the Bernardin committee to have a military expert among its advisers. He also defended low-yield nuclear weapons, noting that "Thomas E. Murray, a very devout Catholic, when he was the head of the Atomic Energy Commission, was the one that forwarded the development of nuclear weapons of comparatively low yield.

"The governments of western Europe, especially Mitterand, a socialist, have recognized that they must have a nuclear deterrent for their own defense," Hannan said. "And let me say that a deterrent has always worked. For instance, in World War I, there was poisonous gas."

In a comment that suggested additional personal basis for Hannan's concern, he said, "Unfortunately, I lost a cousin, killed by poisonous gas. But just as soon as we developed a deterrent, then there was no longer the use of poisonous gas except by the Soviet Union in those countries which do not have a deterrent of poisonous gas, that is, in Vietnam, Laos, Cambodia, and in Afghanistan.

"I'd like also simply to say," Hannan concluded, "that Pius XII said that 'a nation has a duty to defend itself,' at a time that nuclear weapons existed."

After Hannan spoke, Auxiliary Bishop Peter Rosazza of Hartford, a bearded activist who had demonstrated with the Berrigans at the Pentagon, continued the testy tone of the floor debate by noting, "We see the United States as the largest, as far as I know, supplier of arms in the world, to even Latin American dictatorships, which does cut down [undermine] those who are living in situations of injustice and would like to overthrow that yoke."

The comment was particularly relevant; the bishops were to vote the next day on a proposed statement from the bishops' Justice and Peace Committee critical of U.S. policy in Central America—El Salvador, Nicaragua and Guatemala. Only about a half-dozen bishops opposed the statement. One was Hannan; another was O'Connor, who argued that more consultation with the local hierarchies in those countries was needed.

O'Connor's impassioned speeches delivered few, if any, of the other bishops from the New York delegation; Hannan could not even deliver his own vicar general, Bishop Nicholas D'Antonio, who had served as a missionary in Honduras. Less than a year later, D'Antonio also backed the nuclear freeze movement. That kind of split between an ordinary and his auxiliary—as Whealon and Rosazza have similarly disagreed—offers another example of the institutionalization of pluralism within the American hierarchy.

After referring to Latin America, Rosazza called for devoting one day a week to prayer and fasting for peace as the Anglican bishops had already done.

"I just end up by saying," he concluded, "that listening to this debate, I am extremely proud to be a member of this body."

Archbishop Quinn spoke next, reminding the bishops that nuclear proliferation "is spreading like some kind of lethal epidemic over the world" and repeating his concern about the erosion of the psychological firebreak between conventional and nuclear war.

Citing Reagan's speech that morning, Quinn said, "This change in attitude has been brought about through informed public opinion, and I think it's very important to recognize that this public opinion now is not coming from one single segment of society, it is coming from all segments of society. There is something stirring very deeply in the soul of humanity about this issue. . . . I think we have a very grave obligation to encourage and sustain that public opinion at this moment when there has been some indication of movement forward."

Lyke then noted that twenty-five bishops had joined Pax Christi since the previous bishops' meeting and asked others to join as well.

Bishop Norman McFarland of Reno-Las Vegas asked the committee to follow the church's teaching to its ultimate conclusions: "If the conclusion amounts to 'Better Red than Dead,' then the document should say it. Otherwise, it cannot be credible and we cannot be making a real contribution."

Frank Murphy urged that Roach's and Bernardin's talks be sent to priests as a coming attraction.

Niedergeses urged that the pastoral treat injustice as the root cause of all evil. Noting that John Paul II has emphasized ecumenism, he praised recent Presbyterian and Episcopalian statements. Finally, he urged Friday abstinence and prayer for peace.

Bishop Mark Hurley of Santa Rosa, Head's successor as chairman of the Committee on Social Development and World Peace, said there was a consistency between the bishops' position on nuclear war and their opposition to abortion. But, he said: "We do not affirm that life is an absolute. Now this cuts both ways; it can cut one way in saying that because we believe in a resurrection, it really doesn't matter much whether we are annihilated in the long run by atomic bombs or by cancer. . . . The other way it cuts, however, is that there are people who believe and will affirm that freedom is greater even than life itself and that therefore we are willing to fight and die for our country."

Hurley was the final speaker on the subject. The bishops hold a press conference after each morning and afternoon session, with bishops involved in floor action during the session appearing on a panel.

Bernardin took questions on his interim report. He spoke with the occasional hesitations in his voice that mark his impromptu performances. Several questions dealt with Reagan's speech; asked about the relationship between that talk and the bishops' work, Bernardin smiled and said, "Your guess is as good as mine." He said he was "encouraged" by Reagan's initiative, but said, "Even if this initiative progresses well, that doesn't resolve all of the problems we are concerned with."

Discussing the committee's process, he said the group would hear from a variety of technical experts. In discussing his interim report, he gave a clue to the process that guided the actual preparation of the pastoral drafts themselves. He said the committee "had an all-day meeting last Friday. I went over this report with all the members; we made a few stylistic changes and they all agreed and said that they wanted me to present it."

Speaking of his hopes for the finished product, Bernardin said, "We intend to be prophetic, but at the same time, we don't want to operate in an ivory tower." He said he hoped for "if not a total consensus, at least agreement on the part of the vast majority of the bishops." A pastoral letter needs the approval of two thirds of the bishops to pass.

The bishops' meeting ended the next day and Roach held a solo press conference, a tradition for the conference president at the close of a meeting.

A ruddy-faced man with a crew cut, the build of a football player (which he once was) and a Minnesota twang in his speech, Roach, sixty, is as freewheeling as Bernardin is cautious; if he doesn't feel comfortable speaking for a consensus, he steps aside from his role as president and says what he thinks personally.

Roach deftly handled a query from Lester Kinsolving, a veteran gadfly famous for asking two-part, have-you-stopped-beating-your-wife questions. Kinsolving asked whether Roach thought President Roosevelt was right to threaten to use chemical weapons in World War II to deter the Germans from using their poison gas.

Roach said he didn't know enough to address the specifics, but he answered on a broader level, referring to a book he had just read on the history of the American churches and slavery. He said there was a "tragic silence" on the part of the churches on slavery: "I'm satisfied that had the churches spoken more directly to that moral question than they did, that that great national sin would not have been in our midst as long as it was.

"The churches have had a very uneven record on speaking to moral questions," he said, "and, frankly, one of the reasons that some of us are fairly passionate on the question of speaking to moral issues today is that there has been too great a silence in the past."

Asked about Bishop Hurley's comments about life not being an absolute, Roach said, "I remember that. He was a little poetic, I thought, at that point. I think what he was saying . . . was that there is a hope in resurrection and the absolute goal is not, in a sense, the retention of life, but of salvation. That's a defensible kind of position.

"I frankly felt," Roach said, "and if Bishop Hurley were here, I would say it to him—that, as I recall at least, that didn't add a lot to the argument at the time he said it."

Asked how he thought American Catholics felt about the antinuclear movement, Roach said he thought they had about the same sensitivity as the rest of the population: "I see society moving very quickly on that question. I think that it's almost dramatic to see what's happened to people on the question of nuclear war—there's not just a nervousness, there's an excitement, I think, about saying, 'We've got to face this, we've had enough!' "

There were two important postscripts to the November 1981 meeting. On November 30, Roach wrote to Navy Secretary John Lehman urging him to change the name of a nuclear submarine scheduled to be commissioned as the *Corpus Christi.* Roach acknowledged that the Navy's intention was to honor the Texas city of that name, but noted that "this Latin phrase"—meaning the Body of Christ—"also expresses one of the most sacred mysteries in the faith of millions of Americans. For them, the naming of a war vessel in this manner is not merely inappropriate, but very nearly sacrilegious."

The submarine issue had been a major one in Corpus Christi and for many Protestant as well as Catholic figures. The bishops had supported the letter at the request of Bishop Thomas Drury of Corpus Christi. But the issue wasn't discussed publicly at the November meeting because Drury had brought it up during executive session; it became public only when Roach released the text of his letter.

Lehman said he understood the bishops' concern but could not agree with them. He noted that other warships have been named *Corpus Christi* and cited Augustine's and Aquinas' support for legitimate self-defense. "I must, however," he said, "express to you my concern as a Catholic about the theme that seems to underlie this issue: that naval ships and even military service are somehow profane and less worthy of association with the Sacred Name than, for example, the City itself. I cannot accept such an implication.

"I am sure that the religious significance of the name . . . so suggestive of unity and peace among men will be reflected in the professional actions of her commander and crew. They recognize their essential mission is to keep the peace, a noble, ethical and virtuous mission. . . . I believe that a venerable name like Corpus Christi is a valuable asset to those responsible for the management of the fearful weapons of our national defense."

On December 3, Roach sent Reagan a letter congratulating him on his November 18 speech as well as copies of Roach's presidential address and Bernardin's interim report. "We receive your words, Mr. President, as a sign of hope," Roach wrote. "We encourage you to pursue arms reductions and nuclear disarmament with steadfast determination."

"It is our hope, Mr. President," Roach concluded, "that all of us may work together to pursue a conscious policy of reversing the arms race and using the resources presently committed to it to build a world in which the rights of each person and every nation are respected and their human needs fulfilled."

About five weeks later, Roach received a pro forma response and a transcript of Reagan's speech and press conference from an assistant secretary of defense.

IV. THE FREEZE

As 1981 drew to a close, Pope John Paul II once again entered the nuclear arms debate.

At a general audience on November 29, he announced he had sent personal letters to President Reagan and Soviet Premier Brezhnev on the eve of the opening of U.S.-Soviet talks in Geneva on nuclear arms reduction in Europe, urging them to take steps to avoid a nuclear conflict.

Two weeks later, John Paul announced he was sending delegations from the Pontifical Academy of Sciences to Reagan and Brezhnev—as well as the heads of England and France and the president of the United Nations General Assembly—to present a document on "the disastrous effects" of nuclear war.

The paper, based on evidence presented by fourteen experts at an academy hearing on October 7 and 8, echoed the rising opposition to nuclear weapons in the United States from the medical community, particularly through the leadership of Dr. Helen Caldicott and Physicians for Social Responsibility. Psychologist Jerome Frank, a freeze movement leader, credits two "establishments"—the Catholic bishops and the medical community—with giving the new antinuclear movement its credibility.

"Recent talk about winning or even surviving a nuclear war," the academy paper said, "must reflect a failure to appreciate a medical reality: any nuclear war would inevitably cause death, disease and suffering of pandemic proportions and without the possibility of effective medical intervention.

"Even a nuclear attack directed only at military facilities would be devastating to the country as a whole," the paper said, "because military facilities are widespread rather than concentrated at only a few points. Thus, many nuclear weapons would be exploded. Furthermore, the spread of nuclear radiation due to the natural winds and the atmospheric mixing would kill vast numbers of people and contaminate large areas.

"Our knowledge and credentials as scientists and physicians do not, of course, permit us to discuss security issues with expertise," the academy members said. "However, if political and military leaders have based their strategic planning on mistaken assumptions concerning the medical aspects of a nuclear war, we feel that we do have a responsibility. . . . If we remain silent, we risk betraying ourselves and our civilization."

President Reagan thanked the group, repeated his position that negotiations must be built on strength, and quoted from the Book of Revelation (16:16–21) describing the end of the world.

As the Christmas season approached, U.S. bishops' statements on the nuclear issue took on a certain inevitable sameness. But most reflected the individual personalities and situations of the bishops involved. The steady stream of individual statements also pointed out an irony in the focus on the preparation of the national-level pastoral: the degree of authority behind a statement by a national bishops' conference, still a fairly new institution in the church, is not clearly defined; ultimately, the teaching authority of a bishop in his own diocese may well be greater than that of the National Conference of Catholic Bishops speaking to Catholics in the whole country.

Two of the more interesting Christmas pastorals came from bishops —William McManus of Fort Wayne-South Bend, Indiana, a bishop since 1967, and James Malone of Youngstown, Ohio, a bishop since 1968—from a more lonely generation of liberals than those named bishops in the middle and late 1970s.

Malone, bishops' conference vice-president for the second time, said, "We are not required to advocate unilateral disarmament— indeed, to do so might hasten, rather than impede, our introduction to nuclear conflict. However, given the total destructive capacity of nuclear weapons, we cannot indefinitely justify the possession of such arms in the name of peace."

McManus wrote in a conversational, almost folksy tone, complaining that Jesus would be called a "bleeding heart" in today's climate. He said "loose irresponsible talk" about nuclear war "should anger us"; he criticized both U.S. and Soviet policy, but noted, shortly after the declaration of martial law in Poland, that "Poland will be no better off if we refuse to go through with disarmament talks already scheduled with the Soviets."

McManus said reasonable people would disagree on specific issues. "Reasonable Catholics, however," he said, "have no right to indulge in slaphappy oversimplifications, e.g., 'Better to be dead than Red.' . . . Not to think morally about the morality of nuclear weapons is immoral."

A feature of several of the new bishops' statements was support for a bilateral freeze on the development, testing, production and deployment of nuclear weapons. Those announcing their support of the freeze at Christmas included Archbishop Rembert Weakland of Milwaukee, Bishop Lucker of New Ulm and Bishop Straling of San Bernardino.

Bishop Paul Anderson of Duluth, who had been writing about peace in his diocesan newspaper column, urged support for a freeze in conjunction with his support for the New Abolitionist Covenant, a peace statement being circulated by Sojourners, a radical evangelical Christian movement based in Washington, D.C.

Generally liberal mainline Protestant denominations also escalated their rhetoric against the nuclear arms race during the fall of 1981; the United Methodist bishops and the moderator of the United Presbyterian Church in the U.S.A. issued statements in that period.

Catholic religious orders and individual parishes were also heard from. In Portsmouth, Virginia, 277 members of the 300-family Holy Angels Church signed an open letter to Congress urging "the unilateral destruction of our nuclear arsenal." The parish was no doubt influenced by the rhetoric of Bishop Walter Sullivan, who gave a speech in at least eight places in the Richmond diocese arguing that if it's immoral to use nuclear weapons, it's immoral to possess them, and therefore "it's immoral to produce them or be associated with them."

Sullivan's rhetoric prompted a letter from Bishop O'Connor to the Norfolk *Ledger-Star* challenging his conclusions. "I know of nothing in official church teaching that suggests that our military people are engaged in immoral activities in carrying out their responsibilities," he said, arguing that "it could be immoral" for a government to disarm unilaterally if it left the nation vulnerable. The Richmond Priests' Senate responded with a resolution backing Sullivan.

The debate continued in a somewhat different format when Cardinal Cooke issued a Christmas letter to military chaplains on December 7. Cooke replied to the two most frequent questions he said he was hearing from those in the military: "(1) Has the church changed its position on military service? (2) Must a Catholic refuse to have anything to do at all with nuclear weapons?"

He answered both questions in the negative. "As long as our nation is sincerely trying to work with other nations to find a better way, the church considers the strategy of nuclear deterrence morally tolerable; not satisfactory, but tolerable. . . . It follows clearly then that if a strategy of nuclear deterrence can be morally tolerated while a nation is sincerely trying to come up with a rational alternative, those who produce or are assigned to handle the weapons that make the strategy possible and workable can do so in good conscience."

Cooke added that "the church does condemn the use of any weapons, nuclear or conventional, that would indiscriminately destroy huge numbers of innocent people, such as an entire city, or weapons that would 'blow up the world.' " He also applauded a growing sense of urgency in the concern for peace; he defended the right and duty to question "all aspects of the national budget, including allocations for defense" as "one of the great values and obligations of living in a democracy"; he called for greater concern for the poor; and he announced the establishment of a House of Prayer and Study for Peace to be directed by O'Connor.

Cooke was immediately attacked by some sixty peace activists in New York and by Father Neil McCaulley, president of the National Federation of Priests' Councils. McCaulley also wrote a letter to O'Connor, defending Sullivan and urging O'Connor to speak out against nuclear weapons: "The scale of evil of nuclear weapons must be rejected . . . even if those weapons are aimed at combat troops."

The New York protesters, including the head of the archdiocesan Catholic Youth Organization and the Catholic chaplain at Columbia University, charged that Cooke "bases this moral tolerance on the fiction that 'our nation is sincerely trying to work with other nations to find a better way.' "

The most detailed episcopal rejection of that "fiction" came in a five-thousand-word statement issued December 30 by forty-five-year-old Bishop Roger Mahony of Stockton, California. Like Cooke, Mahony asked questions, and like Cooke, he answered them in the negative; but they were questions Cooke didn't ask, questions that examined not only church teaching but the way present U.S. policy measured up against it.

Using the position outlined in the Krol SALT testimony, Mahony asked whether U.S. nuclear policy is truly an "interim" one, whether it is being used to reduce arms, and whether "our goal is really a world free of nuclear threats and terror. We have moved beyond true deterrence to the production and use of nuclear weapons as an assertion of our national superiority," he said. "We are being urged to use our nuclear arsenal as 'bargaining chips,' in the language used by the defense establishment, which also speaks of 'a menu of flexible nuclear options.'

"We now need to distinguish between legitimate deterrence strategies and the rhetoric of a spurious 'deterrence' within which hawks on each side of the East/West Divide compete to increase arms and provocations, envision fictitious gaps and windows of vulnerability, enter unending inconclusive negotiations which do not really stop the arms race and accelerate our drift toward nuclear collision.

"It is my conviction," Mahony said, "that Catholics no longer have a secure moral basis to support actively or cooperate passively in the current U.S. arms policy."

Mahony, however, unlike some other bishops, did not jump from this conclusion to a call for unilateral disarmament, arguing that "the Soviet Union does represent a real threat to our national interests and security. But," he said, "unilateral disarmament is something quite different from serious, persistent, even unilateral initiatives toward bilateral disarmament." He urged a bilateral halving of nuclear arms stockpiles or a bilateral freeze as essential steps toward a "minimal deterrence policy."

Mahony, at six feet six the tallest bishop in the conference, was no stranger to political controversy. A year after being named an auxiliary bishop in Fresno, Governor Jerry Brown named him head of the new California Agricultural Relations Board; he served in the full-time job from July 1975 to December 1976.

As for the nuclear pastoral, Mahony says, "It was [Secretary of State Alexander] Haig that really got my attention when he said it was part of NATO strategy to consider firing a nuclear 'demonstration' bomb in Europe.

"That really was a turning point for me," he says. "I thought,

'These guys are serious about using these things—this isn't some big deterrence strategy.' "

In preparing the pastoral, Mahony spoke with John Coleman, a Jesuit theologian at Berkeley he frequently consulted for advice. He thanked Coleman and seven others he consulted for their help in drafting the pastoral, an unusual step for a bishop. "We're always hearing about bishops fighting with theologians," Mahony says, "so I figured, 'What the heck,' and gave them credit.

"I came very close to not issuing the letter," he says. "I was about finished when John Quinn gave his St. Francis homily, and I wondered about too many of us saying the same thing. But I talked to a few people, and after Thanksgiving I decided the heart of the letter was on deterrence; I added a couple of sections—one on the Third World—and decided to issue it."

Pope John Paul II returned to the question of nuclear war in his message for the World Day of Peace on January 1, 1982, saying "the church wishes her children to join the first ranks of those preparing peace and causing it to reign," and that "rulers must be supported and enlightened by a public opinion that encourages them or, when necessary, expresses disapproval."

But he expressed a cautionary note, adding, "Christians are aware that plans based on aggression, domination and the manipulation of others lurk in human hearts, and sometimes even secretly nourish human intentions in spite of certain declarations or manifestations of a pacifist nature."

The pope said self-defense by "proportionate means" against an unjust aggressor is "an elementary requirement of justice."

But speaking of the "nuclear terror that haunts our time," he said, "in view of the difference between classical warfare and nuclear or bacteriological war—a difference so to speak of nature—and in view of the scandal of the arms race seen against the background of the needs of the Third World, this right, which is very real in principle, only undermines the urgency for world society to equip itself with effective means of negotiation."

As the new year began, the West Coast continued to be a focus of episcopal antinuclear activity. On January 27, Archbishop Quinn again took the lead within the conference, telling a Senate arms control subcommittee hearing in San Francisco the United States and its NATO allies should conduct a "rigorous, explicit analysis and debate" on a pledge to not be the first to use nuclear weapons. Western Europe had long lived under the protection of the U.S. "nuclear umbrella," and the no-first-use-pledge movement offered a strong challenge to NATO policy.

Two days before Quinn's testimony, Archbishop Hunthausen announced in a Seattle TV interview that, after seven months of consideration, he had decided to withhold half of his federal tax as, he explained in a January 28 pastoral letter, "a means of protesting our nation's continuing involvement for nuclear arms supremacy." He said he'd give the withheld money to "charitable peaceful purposes."

He urged continued discussion of the nuclear arms issue "in a spirit of mutual openness and charity," adding that he wasn't asking others to imitate his action: "I prefer that each individual come to his or her own decision on what should be done to meet the nuclear arms challenge."

Hunthausen's decision left him vulnerable to having his assets attached to pay his taxes and penalties of up to five years in prison and $10,000 in fines for each year he withholds his taxes.

It also drew harsh words from Navy Secretary Lehman several weeks later. Speaking at the Chapel of the Four Chaplains in Philadelphia on March 7, he attacked "pacifist ideology" and said unilateral disarmament would lead to war.

Criticizing publicity for church pacifists, Lehman said, "In a particularly tasteless example of this unfortunate trend, the Catholic bishop of Seattle publicly called our new naval submarine base at Bangor, Washington, 'an American Auschwitz.' Such an ignorant and repugnant statement illustrates how far the abuse of clerical power has been taken by a few religious leaders. There is, I believe, something deeply immoral in the use—or misuse—of sacred religious office to promulgate extremist political views."

Lehman's speech was a classic example of the argument that Americans shouldn't abuse their freedoms by exercising them; Hunthausen's response was characteristically polite: "To think that I and other religious leaders have no right to speak out on social and political issues that touch the welfare of persons is to reduce the role of bishop and of Christianity to the realm of individual morality. It is to declare with the secularist mentality of recent centuries that religion is to be locked up in the sacristy and the home."

Lehman drew a more barbed response from Bishop Matthiessen,

who said, citing the bishops' 1976 pastoral, "If he believes that the teaching of the church is that the threat to use these weapons is moral, he hasn't done his homework."

Matthiessen had problems of his own that March. They began when he announced that Catholic Family Services of Amarillo would administer a $10,000 grant from the Oblates of Mary Immaculate in St. Paul, Minnesota, to help Pantex workers who quit their jobs on moral grounds. Ten percent of the twenty-four hundred Pantex workers and many others in the area threatened to withhold their contributions to the United Way, which gave money to Catholic Family Services. CFS agreed not to administer the grant, but refused to say it would not counsel Pantex workers who came for help. The United Way then dropped a $61,000 grant to CFS; the funds were to be used for youth and family programs, including help for abused children.

The National Conference of Catholic Charities continued to call the agency action "harsh and unfair" and "an intrusion by the United Way on the autonomy of Catholic Family Services." A year later, Catholic Family Services was considering legal action against United Way.

Matthiessen says one quarter of the funding had already been received when the United Way grant was cut, so the loss was actually about $40,000. CFS made a special appeal to the community for contributions to replace the lost funds and raised $75,000. "Even many people in disagreement with my own particular view were very upset at the high-handedness of United Way and contributed," Matthiessen says.

Another result of the fund cutoff was that CFS applied for and received a $250,000 grant from the federal office for adolescent pregnancy programs—the only Texas organization to receive such a grant.

By early 1983, only one Pantex worker had quit publicly because of conscience; at most, another half dozen left for similar reasons but didn't make public statements, Matthiessen says. Ironically, the worker who first came to Matthiessen for guidance continues to work at Pantex. Matthiessen told the man, who was poorly educated and nearing retirement age, not to quit unless he had another job, and the man had not found one.

Another Texas-based nuclear controversy was finally laid to rest in the spring of 1982 when Lehman relented on the name Corpus Christi. Mitch Snyder of the Community for Creative Non-Violence in Washington, D.C., went on a hunger strike "to the death" to protest the submarine's name. Snyder goes on hunger strikes the way other people write letters to the editor; Lehman sent a negotiator, and Snyder ended his fast after Lehman changed the sub's name to *The City of Corpus Christi.*

There was no victory for peace in the change; Lehman responded to an act of violence, which is the way most moral theologians view an action like Snyder's. The only victory was for the kind of meaningless symbolism so important to much of the Catholic left; U.S. policy was no more bellicose before the change and no less so afterward.

During the winter of 1982, the crescendo of antinuclear activity that had been apparent within the American Catholic community the previous fall reached the rest of society. *Time* magazine ran a special nuclear issue on March 29—four months after the Catholic weekly *Our Sunday Visitor* ran its special issue. The Catholic press, including the liberal *National Catholic Reporter,* had been far ahead of the secular media in its coverage of the nuclear debate, particularly its moral dimensions.

There were two major developments responsible for the upsurge in media attention to nuclear issues at this time. One was a series of articles in *The New Yorker* by Jonathan Schell; the three-part series, "The Fate of the Earth," combined exhaustive reporting on the medical and ecological implications of all-out nuclear war with a passionate vision of the new world order needed to prevent the earth's destruction.

The more substantive development was the emergence of the nuclear freeze movement, which was taken seriously when a handful of town meetings in Vermont endorsed the freeze, offering new evidence that the movement, which was being endorsed by a rapidly growing number of leaders and organizations did, in fact, have grass-roots support.

The concept of a bilateral nuclear freeze had been around in various forms for several years. President Carter proposed a freeze to the Soviet Union, which rejected it. Later, Republican Senator Mark Hatfield of Oregon suggested a freeze in 1979 as a proposed amendment to the SALT II treaty negotiated by President Carter. Hatfield hoped the amendment would gain support for the treaty among liberals who felt the treaty didn't go far enough.

The freeze idea also came from Randall Forsberg, a former editor at the Stockholm International Peace Research Institute. She developed the idea in 1979 because she was looking for an arms control proposal that was simple and easy for the public to understand. She discussed her idea in a 1980 book, *Call to Halt the Nuclear Arms Race.* The idea began to draw more attention after three Massachusetts state senate districts approved the concept by 59 to 41 percent in the November 1980 elections that also saw Reagan become President.

The freeze drew strong support from the religious community, particularly Catholic bishops. In early 1982, Gumbleton, Walter Sullivan and other bishops in Pax Christi suggested the group should promote the movement among the U.S. bishops.

Pax Christi, which by now had 57 bishops in its ranks, sent a statement on the freeze to all the bishops, along with a card on which to indicate their support. The first mailing drew an amazing 64 supporters by March; by late April, 132 bishops—almost half of the active U.S. bishops—had backed the freeze. Even that list was incomplete—it didn't include other bishops who had endorsed the freeze or local versions of it on their own but had not responded directly to Pax Christi.

Public opinion polls in early 1982 showed not only remarkable support for a freeze, but remarkable sophistication about it. A Washington *Post*-ABC News Poll found Americans supporting a freeze by 71 to 25 percent, despite the fact that 80 percent of Americans thought the Russians would cheat and 58 percent thought a freeze would leave the Russians with an advantage. The reason for such broad support for the freeze could be found in another finding— Americans believed by 79 to 16 percent that it doesn't matter which side is ahead because "both sides have more than enough to destroy each other, no matter who strikes first."

The freeze's appeal was ultimately more psychological than political—it was a vehicle through which people could say, "Enough!" And while the Reagan administration would never admit it, the freeze movement had its impact. On May 9, the President called for a reduction of one third in U.S. and Soviet land- and sea-based missiles and a ceiling on the number of warheads in each country; he suggested arms talks begin by the end of June. Soviet Premier Brezhnev rejected the U.S. position as one-sided and proposed that a freeze begin with the arms talks. There was no freeze, but the newly named START talks—Reagan's name for the Strategic Arms Reduction Talks—began June 29.

The spring of 1982 offered several opportunities for the continuing flow of bishops' statements: Easter; Ground Zero Week (April 18–25), a national educational campaign on the nuclear issue; the Second U.N. Special Session on Disarmament; and, finally, the heightened public debate itself.

Some of the bishops' statements issued that spring merit particular note:

—On March 23, the twelve bishops of New Jersey issued a four-page statement urging "our fellow citizens to press our government to take deliberate steps toward mutual disarmament."

—On March 29, Bishop Reilly of Norwich, a member of the Bernardin committee, spoke "On Priesthood, Peace and Poverty" at a ceremony honoring priests marking major anniversary years in the priesthood.

"We must promote peace through education," he said, "we must pray constantly for peace and move our leaders—and other world leaders—to unilateral initiatives that will lead to bilateral nuclear disarmament. Hopefully we will see in our day agreements among nuclear powers that will lead from a 'no first use' policy to a 'no use' policy to a 'no possession' policy."

—Cardinal Krol re-emerged in the debate with some of the strongest language seen within the bishops' conference at an Interfaith Witness to Stop the Nuclear Arms Race in Philadelphia. In addition to speaking, the seventy-one-year-old Krol, a bishop since 1953, used his communications office to promote the event—it produced thirty-second radio spots—and wrote every priest and religious institution in the archdiocese urging active support.

Krol told those at the event that "nuclear arms and their use exceed the limits of legitimate self-defense," arguing that "it is a primary moral imperative to prevent any use of nuclear weapons under any conditions. We must ask," he said, "whether the nuclear arms race is itself a threat to our security and whether nuclear disarmament might not directly enhance our national security."

A month later, speaking at St. Joseph's Preparatory School, he cited President Eisenhower's parting attack on the "military-industrial complex," which, Krol said, "in its zeal to provide security against a foreign aggressor . . . is becoming an internal aggressor, which threatens our national security through mounting national debts and the threat of insolvency."

In a particularly insightful comment, Krol said he was encouraged by the introduction of "moral reasoning" into political debate, but added, "Misused, moral argument can be subordinated to political ends so that it serves simply to support decisions made on the basis of other factors."

—At Easter, Cardinal Humberto Medeiros of Boston followed up a strong Christmas statement with a seventy-five-hundred-word pastoral and a strong local peace education program; he also urged the U.S. and the Soviet Union to consider a nuclear freeze. Before issuing his statement, Medeiros spent several evenings talking personally with medical and scientific experts.

—On April 21, in the middle of Ground Zero Week, Cardinal Cooke, citing a pastoral on peace he had written a decade before in the closing days of the Vietnam War, wrote to all the priests in his archdiocese urging prayer and study in preparation for the U.N. disarmament session, citing "the urgency—the moral necessity" for disarmament.

Cooke was the celebrant at a special Mass for the session June 6; he invited Bernardin to deliver the homily. Bernardin spoke in general terms about the church's teaching and said, "The church at both the international and national levels is particularly well-equipped to help build a strong constituency for peace."

One of the more unusual and important developments within the church occurred in Washington, D.C., where Archbishop James Hickey, sixty-one, launched an archdiocesewide educational program on the nuclear issue. Before publishing a June 3 pastoral letter announcing the program, Hickey and his top staff went through three days of study with experts including four Catholics with relevant expertise—former CIA director William Colby; SALT I negotiator Gerard Smith; Democratic Senator Patrick Leahy of Vermont, a major freeze backer, and General Edward Rowny, Reagan's START talks negotiator. Some of the same experts spoke again at a one-day session for archdiocesan priests and at a September 16 convocation which drew fourteen hundred people—twice the number expected.

Hickey, a bishop since 1967, says he began his program because he felt a unique responsibility as bishop in Washington; many of his people were active in government and the military and Washington was surely the first target of any possible Soviet attack. Hickey said he wanted to prepare his people so the pastoral—whatever it said—wouldn't cause sharp division.

He began his own study, Hickey says, so he would know the facts in order to help others make moral judgments. But shortly before announcing his local program, Hickey had backed the freeze movement, endorsing a congressional resolution introduced by Hatfield, Leahy and Senator Edward Kennedy. Hickey said in his pastoral that the new process was not an attempt to convince anyone to join him. "I'm still a citizen," he says, explaining his decision to back the freeze. "It was a strategy . . . to get something going. All we were doing was talking about increasing our nuclear armaments, nobody was blowing any whistles, everybody was almost mesmerized. At the same time, we were beginning to see the effects of those astronomical defense budgets on the poor."

Hickey was in his last year at Catholic University when Hiroshima and Nagasaki were bombed, and he remembers his moral theology professor condemning the nuclear attacks, as he had condemned the saturation bombing in Europe. That lay "dormant" within him for years, Hickey said.

That concern was revived partially by Hickey's growing awareness of the danger of conventional arms. In early 1981, as the Reagan administration tried to make a major foreign policy issue of El Salvador, Hickey became the point man for the U.S. bishops. He had visited the country several times and was personally involved because while in Cleveland, he had sent two church women to work with the poor in El Salvador—two of the four who were murdered December 2, 1980.

The U.S. Catholic Church, followed closely by mainline Protestant churches, led the way in fighting U.S. military (not economic) aid for El Salvador's junta. Opposition didn't reverse U.S. policy, but it tempered it.

Hickey's experience in El Salvador meshed with his experiences of ten years living in Europe, four of them as the Marshall Plan was being implemented; it strengthened both his belief that economic aid, not arms, was the way to build peace, and that U.S. leaders are unaware of the distrust with which they are viewed in other countries.

While in El Salvador, he had asked hungry peasants why they

didn't eat the scraggly cattle he saw. "They're being raised for pet food for the United States," he was told.

"Whether it's true or not," he said, "that's the perception."

As archbishop of Washington and chairman of the bishops' Doctrine Committee, Hickey had a certain amount of influence within the hierarchy; that was apparent when he was chosen to speak on "The Bishop as Teacher," one of six presentations at an unusual event that came to be known as "Collegeville."

The U.S. bishops met from June 13 to 23 at St. John's University in Collegeville, Minnesota, for what was basically a retreat. The session, planned by Bishop Malone, had been in the works for more than a year; there were no resolutions, no position papers—just prayer, reflection and small group discussions on the general theme of the bishop's role in church and society.

The "Collegeville experience" was another step in the growing collegiality and self-awareness of the post-Vatican II American bishops; by putting them in touch with one another and with themselves, it had a subtle impact likely to have greater impact on the church in the long run than most episcopal statements.

Collegeville was important for another reason; it was the first time the bishops got a look at the draft on war and peace in a nuclear age being prepared behind the scenes by the Bernardin committee.

V. THE COMMITTEE

When Archbishop Quinn's three-year term as conference president ended at the November 1980 meeting, the bishops elected the NCCB vice-president, Archbishop John Roach of St. Paul-Minneapolis, to succeed him. One of Roach's first tasks was to decide how to handle the bishops' obvious interest in the question of war and peace in the nuclear age.

"In hindsight," Roach says, "it was difficult to assess how ambitiously or seriously the bishops wanted to address it. But my instincts told me they were serious, and didn't want it handled as a committee document or task, but as an ad hoc conference position."

Roach and Bishop Kelly decided to bypass the large USCC Committee for Social Development and World Peace, now headed by Bishop Mark Hurley, to create a small, ad hoc committee similar to the one that had produced a pastoral on Marxist communism that had passed resoundingly in 1980.

Father J. Bryan Hehir particularly backed that approach; after the Marxism pastoral was approved, Auxiliary Bishop Rosazza had recommended that the bishops make a similar critique of capitalism. The capitalism and nuclear pastorals both seemed destined to land on Hehir's desk—a monumental task in addition to his already crowded schedule.

Kelly and Roach agreed to create two ad hoc committees, with Hehir serving as top staff person for both pastorals. Kelly—now archbishop of Louisville—says "you need a small group that can work well together for that kind of project."

The next task was choosing committee members. For the War and Peace Committee chairman, Roach said, "Because of the significance, I simply wanted the most respected person I could get who really didn't have an identifiable position on the issue, someone with a great deal of respect and skill."

That choice was Archbishop Joseph Bernardin of Cincinnati, the only person ever to serve as both general secretary and conference president. Kelly, a Bernardin protégé, points out that Bernardin had a recognized talent for mediation that was invaluable for the committee. Bernardin's skills include self-discipline. He rarely loses his temper and prays for an hour each morning; he recently lost more than thirty pounds, despite the fact he cooks as a hobby.

After he was appointed to Cincinnati, Bernardin conscientiously worked with all the consultative bodies ushered in by Vatican II; he notes he's sometimes been accused of doing too much consulting before he acts.

Bernardin expanded his influence during his 1974–77 term as bishops' conference president, beginning terms on the commission revising the Code of Canon Law and the Vatican committee in charge of the triannual Synod of Bishops; his activity and style in those posts and at the synods won him a large international following and recognition of his skills as a listener and a consensus builder.

Bernardin had long been regarded as a liberal hero and a future cardinal—rumors that he would one day succeed Cardinal John Cody of Chicago began to spread almost as soon as he left his staff position at the conference to go to Cincinnati in 1972.

Bernardin was born in Charleston, South Carolina, to Italian immigrant parents. His father, a stonecutter, died when Bernardin was six, and he grew up poor. He recalls that he often went to the Baptist Sunday school because it gave out free ice cream.

After college, Bernardin went to medical school before deciding to enter the priesthood. He was named auxiliary to Archbishop Paul Hallinan of Atlanta, a leading church liberal, in 1966 at the age of thirty-eight. That appointment marked him as a coming progressive leader; the image was reinforced when Cardinal Dearden brought him to Washington a year later to serve as NCCB-USCC general secretary.

Bernardin's church career was punctuated by controversial dealings with American Presidents; in that sense, controversy surrounding the War and Peace Committee was nothing new to him.

In January 1973, President Richard Nixon invited Bernardin, along with evangelist Billy Graham and Rabbi Edgar Magnin of Los Angeles, to preach at a Sunday White House service following Nixon's second inauguration. In those pre-Watergate days, Nixon was at his peak and feeling his oats: the Vietnam War still raged, he had fired Father Theodore Hesburgh as chairman of the U.S. Commission on

Civil Rights and, in preparing an attack on domestic social programs, he told Americans in his inaugural address, as Archie Bunker paraphrased it, "You're on your own."

Graham and Magnin seemed to see their assignment as offering thanks to God for Richard Nixon. Bernardin took a different approach, as described by John Osborne in his "Nixon Watch" column in *The New Republic:*

Archbishop Bernardin seemed to have set himself to answer the President's complaint in his Inaugural Address that "At every turn we have been beset by those who find everything wrong with America and little that is right."

The archbishop said to Richard Nixon and the others in his presence that "our loss of self-confidence and self-assurance"—a loss that the president had recovered from if he had ever suffered it—should be taken as "a sign of growing maturity, stemming from a greater sense of realism" rather than the challenge Mr. Nixon perceived to "our faith in ourselves and in America."

The real and compelling challenge, Archbishop Bernardin said, was "to strive, without respite, for justice and peace here and now, justice especially for the poor and oppressed here and abroad." Reporters who were there said that the president heard this with every show of respect and humility.

Bernardin's next major presidential contact came during the 1976 presidential campaign. It was the first presidential election since the 1973 Supreme Court abortion decisions and the bishops' subsequent decision to make a constitutional amendment to reverse those decisions a priority. The Democratic Party approved a platform plank opposing efforts to pass an antiabortion amendment, and many Catholic leaders were furious, partly because so many of them viewed the Democratic Party as home.

Bernardin, then president of the bishops' conference, issued several strong condemnations of the abortion plank. In between the Democratic and Republican conventions, Carter gave a wide-ranging interview to National Catholic News Service. During the interview, he stuck to his own position—opposing abortion, federal funding for abortion, and a constitutional amendment to reverse the court's decisions—but disowned the language of the plank, which had been written by his own staffers. Carter rejected any implication that people could not work for an amendment.

The interview drew national headlines and considerably eased tensions between Carter and the bishops' conference. A few days after the interview, the bishops announced that Carter would meet with the

Executive Committee, which included Bernardin, Cooke, Malone and Bishop James Rausch, the conference general secretary.

The meeting seemed to go well for both sides, although Carter was surprised when Bernardin began by reading a prepared statement. But when Bernardin held a press conference afterward, the media ignored his comments on the many areas of agreement between Carter and the bishops and zeroed in on his comment that the bishops were "disappointed" in his opposition to an amendment.

The media coverage provoked a furor, because the bishops' statements were seen as a partisan attack on Carter. The bishops were taken aback by the coverage of the Carter meeting; they had no excuse a few weeks later when they met with President Ford and Bernardin said the bishops were "encouraged" by his support for a states' rights amendment even though it didn't go as far as they would like.

The words "disappointed" and "encouraged" sparked the sharpest turmoil within the American Catholic Church since Pope Paul VI's 1968 birth control encyclical. Not a few bishops were among those screaming the loudest about the "perception" that the bishops had endorsed Ford on the abortion issue.

In September, the bishops' forty-eight-member Administrative Committee—including the Executive Committee—unanimously approved a statement emphasizing Catholics' right to conscience and making it clear they endorsed no candidate and wanted Catholics to consider a broad range of issues before voting.

The incident is revealing; in the light of the publicity surrounding Bernardin today, it's easy to get the impression his ecclesiastical career has been flawless. It hasn't, and that makes his success more impressive—it shows that his many skills include knowing how to survive. When Roach asked Bernardin to chair the War and Peace Committee, he said he wanted Gumbleton and O'Connor to serve on it. "I wanted articulate people at the extremes, and I don't mean that pejoratively," Roach says now.

Gumbleton was by far the best-known activist in the conference. In addition to his duties as a regional bishop in Detroit, where he was responsible for ninety parishes and several diocesan offices, and his work in the peace movement, he also serves as president of Bread for the World, a respected and effective Christian hunger lobby.

Gumbleton was also well-known for his emphasis on simplicity: in the early seventies, he began staying at the local YMCA instead of hotels during bishops' meetings. He still swims daily at the Y in Detroit to keep in shape, although he no longer has the time to play hockey as he once did.

It was Gumbleton who ultimately got the U.S. bishops to oppose the Vietnam War. In 1966, the bishops' Administrative Committee, while urging peace efforts, concluded that U.S. involvement was "justified," a judgment with which the bishops became increasingly uncomfortable. After several floor comments in intervening years, Gumbleton called in 1971 for a re-evaluation of the war.

Cardinal Dearden allowed a longer time than usual for debate and created a committee to draft a statement. The resolution, which passed with more than the two-thirds vote needed—and over strong objections from Archbishop Hannan—said, "At this point in history, it seems clear to us that whatever good we hope to achieve through continued involvement in this war is now outweighed by the destruction of human life and of moral values which it inflicts."

Gumbleton was so moved by the Vietnam issue that the following year he took the extraordinary step of publicly endorsing a presidential candidate, George McGovern, who opposed the war.

Gumbleton made national headlines at Christmas 1979, when he was one of the three American clergymen invited by the Ayatollah Khomeini to visit the American hostages in Iran. In sharp contrast to some other clergymen who went to Iran, Gumbleton didn't spout anti-American rhetoric and reported what the hostages told him, including the fact that some had been led to what they thought was a firing squad and had empty guns shot at their heads.

But Gumbleton never started out to be an activist. He described his development in a talk to the Collegeville meeting on "The Bishop in the American Political and Economic Context." He grew up, he said, in a large Catholic family during the Depression and entered the seminary in the ninth grade. He never saw a social dimension to his ministry until the Second Vatican Council: "I began to see a church which was identified with the poor and oppressed, and committed to share in their efforts to overcome the injustices that were destroying them."

But there were also personal experiences. Gumbleton recalls a visit to Cairo in 1962 in which he came face to face, for the first time, with absolute poverty. Standing in the midst of half-naked and starving children and old people, while he himself was clean, fed and with money in his pocket, he confesses: "I began to feel that I was being terribly cruel to them in a way that I hadn't thought of before."

A few years later, Gumbleton came to grips with the Vietnam War in a roundabout way as he was called on to help young Catholic men trying to claim conscientious objector status in Vietnam. Their major problem was dealing with draft boards who didn't believe a Catholic could be a CO.

"Almost no other experience in my life was so moving as to read those deeply probing and very honest statements of these young men as they searched into their own life, their own feelings, their own history, to discover why they knew they could not ever kill anyone else, even in a war that some thought to be just."

Further reading on pacifism, scripture study, awareness of the work of Latin American bishops on social justice, and a growing appreciation of "social sin"—the notion that structures can create sinful situations—followed.

"It is just one person's journey—nothing more," Gumbleton told the bishops at Collegeville. "However, I expect that the various influences that have affected me and the changes in my life that I still find very surprising are not all that different from what many others have experienced."

At about the time that Gumbleton was learning about the Catholic pacifist tradition, O'Connor, a tall, lanky man with dark, slicked-back hair, given to touching people as he talks to them, was serving as divisional chaplain to the 3rd Marine Division in Vietnam—service that won him a Legion of Merit award in 1965. It was his second such award—he received the first in 1958 for developing the Navy Moral Leadership Program.

O'Connor was ordained in Philadelphia in 1945. He has degrees in ethics and clinical psychology from the Catholic University of America and in political science from Georgetown University. He tried to become a chaplain during the Korean War. After some confusion and delay, he became a chaplain in 1953, leaving a post where he worked with retarded children.

O'Connor was greatly affected by his experiences in Korea. He recalls seeing men who were not wounded all that severely dying for no apparent reason. A doctor explained, "Those who believed in nothing died of nothing at all."

During his career, O'Connor also visited the remains of the concentration camps at Dachau: "I know nothing that has had more impact on my own life."

O'Connor's military career was distinguished; he was regarded as pious, extremely bright and a workaholic. In 1972, he became the first Catholic to serve as chief chaplain at the Naval Academy at Annapolis. In 1975, he was named the Navy's chief chaplain and promoted to rear admiral, although he said at the time he was reluctant to accept the new rank because, "as a priest and as a person, I am not used to the pomp and trappings" that come with the post.

Kermit Johnson, who served as Army chief of chaplains while O'Connor led the Navy chaplains, recalls that O'Connor had incredible staying power; he would argue a point long into the night and never give up. Johnson, who now works for the liberal Center for Defense Information, says, "All the decisions were two to one, the Army and Air Force against the Navy."

In April 1979, O'Connor, then fifty-nine, was named an auxiliary bishop to Cardinal Cooke in the Military Ordinariate. His home archdiocese offered a Mass of Thanksgiving for his appointment; Cardinal Krol gave the homily which condemned the arms race as "folly," a "treacherous trap" and "a form of insanity." He went on to say: "In the wake of the signing of the SALT II Treaty, some may wonder about the role of a priest in the military. The church was mandated by Christ to teach all men and to lead them to salvation. Even when serving the military forces, the church must affirm the program of the Prince of Peace."

O'Connor is highly sensitive about the stereotype that military chaplains are hawkish; he takes every opportunity to deny the charge, or anything that remotely makes that suggestion. One of his first tasks in his new job was to begin preparing for an October 1980 meeting of military chaplains from around the world. He prepared a report on the church's teaching on war and peace that was published by the Daughters of St. Paul in the spring of 1981 as a paperback book entitled *In Defense of Life*.

The heart of his summary is contained in this passage:

Is it possible to have a just war today? Yes.

Can the use of nuclear weapons ever be justified? "Strategic" nuclear weapons if understood as weapons of mass destruction: No. "Tactical" nuclear weapons or other nuclear weapons if understood as not weapons of mass destruction: Perhaps.

"The 'perhaps,' of course, reflects the fact that the church as described in this paper has not really addressed tactical or nuclear weapons as such," O'Connor said. He noted that the Vatican Council and the U.S. bishops' 1976 pastoral emphasized weapons of mass destruction.

"At the same time," he said, ". . . the ambiguities and technical complexities of questions related to nuclear weapons are such that it could not be said . . . that the Church has explicitly stated that tactical or other than strategic nuclear weapons may be used, although by implication, at least, such could be argued to be the case."

O'Connor's assessment of church teaching was accurate—but his suggestion that tactical nuclear weapons might be morally used heartened the most politically conservative elements within the church and increased the concern of the growing peace movement. It sparked the 1981 Pax Christi letter to Bernardin—O'Connor's "perhaps," the loophole left by the Second Vatican Council, offered a basis for condoning the notion of limited nuclear war.

O'Connor, who wears a red rose lapel pin, a symbol for some right-to-life groups, argued that the message of the popes was that the only road to peace was the defense of life—at all levels. In particular, he drew a parallel between opposition to abortion and support for peace:

In a day when so many who once protested so vehemently the alleged American violations of a people in a far-off land remain mute before the violation of life in the womb, in the hospital bed, in the homes of the aged, what is more critically needed than to teach life? In a day when many who are rightfully fearsome of military weapons that could destroy countless lives, offer no protest against surgical weapons that do destroy countless lives, can there really be any hope of peace unless the world is taught life? . . . How can you allow life to those you can see, if you destroy those you cannot see?

Roach asked Bernardin to recommend other bishops to serve along with Gumbleton and O'Connor. Bernardin suggested seven, including Rausch, a long-time rival of Bernardin's and a friend of Roach's. Bernardin suggested four names if the committee was to have seven members, the maximum for an ad hoc committee. But Roach and Kelly wanted to keep the group small.

Roach, Kelly and Bernardin wanted two bishops who didn't have official constituencies, but who would in themselves be representative of the conference's broad middle ground, and who didn't have identifiable positions on the issues to be studied. The three men settled on two names from Bernardin's list—Bishop Daniel Reilly of Norwich and Auxiliary Bishop George Fulcher of Columbus.

Fulcher, a neighbor of Bernardin's in Ohio, was a moral theologian and a member of the bishops' Doctrine Committee. Reilly, a friend of Roach's, was chairman of the bishops' committee overseeing Catholic Relief Services, a post for which Bernardin had recruited him. Kelly says Reilly's experience with "public morality" through the CRS connection was an important factor in his selection.

The choice of Reilly and Fulcher put Bernardin in the position of having an excellent chance—without prejudging what the finished pastoral should say—of gathering three of the committee's five votes if Gumbleton and O'Connor couldn't be brought into a consensus.

Fulcher and Reilly both feel they were selected partly on the basis of temperament. Though Reilly is more outgoing and Fulcher more mellow, both have an easy, relaxed, ironic sense of humor that provided a needed balance to Bernardin's slow, deliberative, process-oriented style and Gumbleton and O'Connor's intensity. "I've never seen anyone go at things with quite so much intensity," Fulcher says of O'Connor.

Fulcher and Reilly had several other things in common. Both had attended school abroad, Fulcher at the Pontifical University of St. Thomas Aquinas in Rome, Reilly at St. Brieuc Major Seminary in Côtes-du-Nord, France. And both had major weapons systems being built in their backyards—Fulcher the B-1 bomber, Reilly the Trident submarine. Both men were also appointed bishops during the tenure of Archbishop Jean Jadot, the popular Belgian apostolic delegate to the United States who earned a reputation for his role in appointing young, progressive, "pastoral" bishops. Both men fit that model.

Many, though certainly not all, of the bishops leading the way on the nuclear issue were "Jadot bishops." After Jadot was given a Curia post, many liberal Catholics assumed that Pio Laghi—an Italian and a career church diplomat—had been sent to crack down on the American church. But a comparison of the bishops appointed under Jadot and those appointed under Laghi reveals no discernible difference.

One factor in the continuity of type of bishops appointed under Jadot and Laghi is that the consultation process used to choose a bishop after the Vatican Council was in fact implemented—the input of church members and other U.S. bishops did have an impact on new appointments.

Fulcher, who jokes about all the bald heads on the committee—his, Bernardin's and Hehir's—was not widely known, even among the bishops, outside of Columbus, but he was tremendously popular in his native diocese. In the early seventies, he ran the diocesan Personnel Board and was elected the first president of the Priests' Senate. When he was made an auxiliary to Bishop Edward Herrmann in 1976, Herrmann said, "Nothing in which I have participated here has been received with greater acclamation and 'Amen' than the appointment of George Fulcher to the Episcopacy."

Fulcher, who was born in 1922, had served as a pastor, and he was editor of the diocesan newspaper from 1958 to 1967. When he was named to the War and Peace Committee, his diocesan appointments included serving as vicar general and vicar for spiritual life; chairman of the diocesan Ecumenical and Interfaith Commission; member of the Metropolitan Church Board of Directors; member of the Ohio Council of Churches General Board and member of the Metropolitan Human Services Commission.

In early 1983, Fulcher was named head of the Diocese of Lafayette in Indiana, a progressive rural diocese. The move was a shock in Columbus, because Fulcher was widely expected to succeed Bishop Herrmann, who had retired. The philosophic Fulcher shrugged it off. "Sometimes," he told a Columbus paper, "Rome likes to remind you who's in charge."

Reilly, a tall, barrel-chested man with a constant smile, sometimes creates the impression of a hale and hearty Boston politician. He is a New Englander, coming from Providence, where he served in traditional chancery roles—assistant chancellor, secretary to the bishop, chancellor and vicar general—before being appointed to Norwich in 1975. But the turning point in his church career was the Second Vatican Council, which he attended with Bishop Russell McVinney of Providence. It's almost impossible to spend a few minutes with Reilly without hearing him talk about the council—something he does with unblushing enthusiasm.

He spoke one day about his diocesan program encouraging lay ministers: "The local paper said it's because of the priest shortage. But we've got more priests in Norwich than we ever had before—it's Vatican Two, that's what it's all about."

At the local level, Reilly has been active on a number of fronts. He held the diocese's first Mass for divorced and remarried Catholics in 1978. "We won't compromise our values," he said, but "we won't abandon our brothers and sisters." In 1980 he signed an ecumenical "covenant" with the Episcopal bishop of Connecticut pledging increased cooperation between the two denominations.

Reilly, who has the reputation of a rising star in church circles, has also been active at the national level. While he was involved in the Bernardin committee deliberations, he also oversaw a major change and redirection of Catholic Relief Services which saw the replacement of its director, Bishop Edwin Broderick, with a layman and increased independence from U.S. foreign policy.

Throughout the process, Reilly says he followed the lead of another committee member, Auxiliary Bishop John McCarthy of Galveston-Houston, a veteran social action leader (and perhaps the best story-teller in the bishops' conference). McCarthy speaks highly of Reilly, noting that while personal confrontation doesn't come easily to him, he handles it well when it needs to be done.

The committee worked closely with two USCC staffers, Hehir and Ed Doherty. Hehir is a short, slight man, who may be a test case for determining whether caffeine is ultimately helpful or harmful—he drinks six cups of coffee for breakfast and guzzles Cokes for the rest of the day until dinner.

In addition to performing his USCC tasks, Hehir teaches Mondays at St. John's Seminary in Boston. Instead of living at the staff house in northwest Washington where other priests working for the USCC live, Hehir lives in a parish, St. Anthony's, in northern Virginia, where he shares pastoral duties. Another priest living at the same parish is Donald Shea, who has worked for the Republican National Committee since 1976. In one display of priestly camaraderie, Shea agreed to substitute for Hehir at a 7 A.M. weekday Mass so Hehir could appear on the "Today Show"—to criticize the Reagan administration's El Salvador policy. (The appearance was canceled for other reasons.)

Almost every story about Hehir notes that he was a student of Henry Kissinger at Harvard, but Hehir says the connection was minimal. Hehir does cite Stanley Hoffman of Harvard, another political scientist, as a major influence.

Hehir has been the prime target for conservative Catholic critics; while there is no substance to the charge that he has somehow led the bishops around by their noses, he has had a tremendous influence based on the bishops' respect for his talents and fairness. No one has shaped the bishops' foreign policy views in the last decade more than Hehir, and he has also helped shape an emerging philosophy of the church's involvement in public life. Hehir sees the church as one mediating institution that is a vital part of society apart from the state, with a right to enter into public debate on moral issues and a responsibility to do so in terms the rest of the society will understand.

Hehir guided the bishops' emphasis on human rights in foreign policy, helped shepherd through support for the Panama Canal treaties, led support for SALT II, and was a leading figure in the church's criticism of U.S. Central American policy. It's easy to tell when congressional testimony or a speech given by someone else was written by Hehir—it will be clear, logical and highly organized, usually divided into three sections, with each section divided further into neat subsections.

Hehir has worked closely on nuclear issues with Ed Doherty, who came to the USCC in the mid-1970s after retiring from the State Department. Doherty, in his late sixties, is a tall, ruddy-faced man whose features conjure up some of the adjectives—such as "craggy"—habitually used to describe Ed Muskie. His expertise is in European affairs, although he has served in Asia as well as West Germany.

Working on a pastoral was nothing new for Doherty, although this time the form was different. He was working in the State Department's office of policy and planning in 1968 when Hehir's predecessor, Msgr. Marvin Bordelon, invited Doherty and other experts around town to the University Club.

Bordelon was looking for ideas to incorporate into Part II of the pastoral "Human Life in Our Day," the American response to Pope Paul's encyclical *Humanae Vitae*. Bordelon asked for notes. "Since I was doing a lot of speech writing at the time," Doherty says, "I figured I'd just write a draft."

Bordelon used most of the draft verbatim; the bishops approved it that way. Father Robert Gregorio, a Camden priest who did a doctoral dissertation on the pastoral, credited Doherty with the "textual parentage" of Part II. The one major section of Doherty's draft that wasn't used was on nuclear weapons. Doherty says that section was too progressive for the time—it sounded a lot like the kind of things the bishops were saying today.

VI. FIRST DRAFT

The bishops' Ad Hoc Committee on War and Peace held its first meeting in Washington on July 26, 1981—a month after Hunthausen's call for unilateral nuclear disarmament and a few weeks before Pilla's pastoral and Matthiessen's letter appeared.

The bishops and staff were joined, in line with NCCB policy, by two representatives of the Conference of Major Superiors of Men and the Leadership Conference of Women Religious, the organizations representing the heads of U.S. men's and women's religious orders. The CMSM representative was Father Richard Warner, head of the Indiana Province of the Holy Cross Fathers, who had spent eleven years as a missionary in Chile. The LCWR representative was Sister Juliana Casey, head of the Immaculate Heart of Mary in the Detroit area, and holder of a doctorate in Scripture.

Bernardin summarized the committee's genesis and its mandate—to take a new look at war. He described the procedure of an ad hoc committee working with an outside author. Bernardin and Hehir said discussions had already taken place with William V. Shannon, the former New York *Times* columnist and ambassador to Ireland in the Carter administration who was now teaching U.S. history at Boston University.

The choice of Shannon was well received by all but O'Connor, who wanted Hehir to write the pastoral. Hehir argued that he and Doherty had been so involved in the nuclear debate that some people might claim bias in any draft they wrote. Gumbleton and Fulcher praised Shannon and, despite another dissent from O'Connor, Bernardin said Shannon would be acceptable if he could commit the time needed for the project. Turning to the subject at hand, Bernardin described the committee's task as "grave and urgent."

Doherty then offered a list of suggested specialists in government, arms control, the military and weapons systems, political science and moral theology for the committee to call on as needed.

Gumbleton noted the absence of scripture scholars; O'Connor noted the absence of women and suggested two, including Sister Mary Evelyn Jegen of Pax Christi. Bernardin said committee members should suggest people they wanted to hear.

He noted that the committee wasn't "starting from scratch" because of the depth of church teaching. Hehir summarized bishops' statements since 1968; Bernardin said the Krol testimony might not be regarded as "official" because it hadn't been approved by the full body of bishops.

Doherty, who helped write the Krol testimony, ever mindful of his unsuccessful effort to challenge Russ Shaw's new language in the 1976 pastoral, noted that the section on nuclear war in that document hadn't received very thorough discussion either. Bernardin said there was very little discussion of Part II of "Human Life in Our Day"—mostly Doherty's work—because of the attention focused on the first part which, like the 1976 pastoral, dealt primarily with sexual ethics.

O'Connor returned to the Krol testimony, noting that Krol had confirmed for him that the testimony did not speak for the body of bishops.

Reilly noted the distinction between church teaching, which was general, and its application, which was more specific. Which, he asked, was the committee's responsibility? Bernardin said the committee must apply existing teaching and—if possible—develop new doctrine.

Hehir emphasized the emergence within the church of "nuclear pacifism," which he said differs from pacifism in the same way selective conscientious objection differs from conscientious objection to all wars. Hehir said "Human Life in Our Day" implicitly endorsed nuclear pacifism because it endorsed selective conscientious objection to the nuclear branch of military service. (The 1968 pastoral used Doherty's language on this point.) The committee's work will be "cast upon the waters" if it doesn't acknowledge this kind of responsible moral judgment, Hehir said.

Bernardin set one firm ground rule for the committee—it would not, under any circumstances, support unilateral nuclear disarmament. He said Doherty's list of experts was pretty technical, noting that the letter he'd received earlier from Pax Christi had urged emphasis on a moral vision. Both elements should be present, he said.

O'Connor said the document must take the tone that the bishops believe "peace is possible"—although, he added, he questioned how this can be done "in the world as presently constituted." He also questioned how specific the document should be; Warner countered that it was certainly appropriate for the American bishops, living in a nuclear power, to address public policy issues—other countries would be looking for their leadership.

Gumbleton urged that it be addressed to American Catholics, and Bernardin noted that pastorals are normally addressed to the Catholic people. Reilly argued that the best way to influence public policy is by influencing the thinking of Christians as citizens.

Bernardin noted that the bishops of Ohio had opposed capital punishment, but their people opposed their position in the state legislature; he wondered whether the bishops would have been better off if they had spent more time talking to their people and getting them to influence the legislature. Fulcher agreed.

Reilly urged the committee to emphasize a "vision" of peace, but O'Connor warned that if the committee began with assumptions that were "too noble for our people," their work would be futile.

Reilly said the bishops should also deal with difficult issues like the one he faced with the construction of the Trident in his diocese. Doherty said the committee must deal with the fact that Americans have a broad and deep belief that their security depends upon nuclear weapons whose use would violate Vatican II's teaching.

O'Connor, citing the "universality of the faith," asked if it was possible to consult with other bishops' conferences; Bernardin said it might be done on an informal basis.

After the first meeting, Hehir spoke again with Shannon, who concluded he wouldn't have the time to handle the project. Hehir then approached Bruce Martin Russett, a professor of political science at Yale, a Catholic and a prolific author who was also editor of the *Journal of Conflict Resolution*. The two had met several years earlier when Hehir gave a lecture on campus; they discovered common interests, though not always common positions, and stayed in touch.

Russett signed on, although he was uncomfortable with the title "author," believing he was more a consultant to the committee writing process and fearing that identifying anyone as the author would detract from the fact that it was a bishops' document. He was eventually listed in the pastoral's appendix as principal consultant.

After the first meeting, committee members sent Hehir and Doherty names of people they would like the committee to hear; O'Connor's lists were often almost as long as all the others' put together. The process of broad consultation and public debate the committee launched eventually became at least as important as the pastoral letter itself. Warner, for one, thinks it would have been impossible even a decade earlier. "We hadn't thought of the process as unique," O'Connor says. "It just seemed the natural thing to do."

Fulcher said the process "seemed to flow" from the committee's task. And while that flow wasn't always smooth, the naturalness with which it developed was a subtle, but important, legacy of the Second Vatican Council. The process grew in length as the committee got into the issues; when Russett was hired, he was told to expect to attend four to six meetings and spend two weeks writing.

The process was also moved along by the interest the subject sparked in a broad array of people. Reilly says the committee was surprised by the high level of people who were willing to talk to the committee—including high-ranking Administration officials, former Defense Secretaries James Schlesinger and Harold Brown, and SALT I negotiator Gerard Smith.

The most important testimony—because of its influence on the "swing men," Reilly and Fulcher—probably came in early 1982 from Schlesinger, who had served under President Ford, and Brown, who had served under President Carter.

Reilly recalls the two were "so forceful in resistance to nuclear war, in saying that nuclear war has to be avoided at all costs as unthinkable madness. They were very affirming of the committee's work," Reilly continued. "They said the Catholic bishops' conference was perhaps the one group that could bring this forward. They gave me and the committee a sense of 'let's hang on—we're being taken seriously by important people.'"

Fulcher called the sessions with Schlesinger and Brown, whom he called "gifted, talented, sensitive people," a turning point for him. "Here are these men," he said, "who have had to make these decisions, who were put in the position of having to justify the use of the bomb. What a horrifying thing that is. . . ."

The meeting with Brown was particularly dramatic for the committee. As Brown discussed various missile systems and the damage they could do, O'Connor interjected, "Aren't we really talking about rationalizing insanity?" Brown paused for a minute, then said, "Yes."

Testimony from Reagan administration officials also influenced Reilly and Fulcher, although it came later in the process. O'Connor had pushed from the beginning for presentations by Administration officials; there was no disagreement in principle, but Bernardin was somewhat reluctant to involve government officials in the pastoral's preparation. Working on the assumption that Administration officials would stick to official positions, he tried to hold off Administration testimony until the committee was further along in its own thinking.

It wasn't until late January 1982, after the committee had heard Schlesinger and scheduled Brown, that the committee decided—after more prodding from O'Connor—to ask for Administration witnesses. The committee agreed that rather than trying to decide who to ask, it was better to ask the President to choose a representative. Bernardin wrote to Reagan on February 5; Secretary of State Haig, Defense Secretary Caspar Weinberger, and Arms Control and Disarmament Agency head Eugene Rostow replied within about a month.

The committee also arranged a meeting with members of Congress by asking majority leaders to recommend a group, but the meeting fell through when all of the members of Congress involved bypassed the meeting to vote on a major budget measure.

The committee met with Administration officials on May 13. They began at the State Department. Since Haig was in Turkey, they met with Under Secretary of State for Political Affairs Lawrence Eagleburger, who appeared nervous about having to set the tone for the day's meeting. "When they saw the Roman collars in the State Department," Reilly laughs, "they looked at us as though we were backing unilateral disarmament."

Eagleburger was called out of the room on business several times; while he was gone, several of his younger aides chided the bishops for being too idealistic. When Eagleburger sent a formal follow-up letter to Bernardin, he added a handwritten postscript apologizing for his aides' behavior.

The meetings with Rostow and Weinberger were more cordial. Rostow noted that Reagan's May 9 call for deep reductions in U.S. and Soviet nuclear forces would have been given earlier but was delayed because of the worsening situation in Poland. From his point of view, Weinberger may have been a little too candid. What he said wasn't new to Hehir and others familiar with various Administration statements, but it was new to Reilly and Fulcher, who particularly remember two points.

First, despite Administration rhetoric about the possibility of limited nuclear war, Weinberger confirmed what others had told the committee—there was no such thing. Fulcher remembers Weinberger conceding the risk of "spillover" into all-out nuclear war.

Reilly later recalled the second point this way: "Weinberger said we couldn't have substantial negotiations until we reached parity with the Russians. So we asked how long it would take to reach parity. He said about eight years. And they wonder why we don't praise the START talks."

But Reilly says the frankness with which Schlesinger and Brown spoke encouraged him to ask Weinberger how he felt as a person; the Defense Secretary said he tries to be a moral person and a Christian, and these matters weigh heavily on him. "That's why I'm not totally discouraged," Reilly says; ". . . we're dealing with people who are seeking to be moral."

As the committee began its discussions, a number of patterns emerged. One was that the committee regularly prayed together and celebrated liturgy at its meetings. Committee members also seemed to play out their predefined roles. Bernardin was the consensus builder, the facilitator, sometimes talking about the process used at the Vatican Council and the Synods of Bishops. "He never loses control," Fulcher says. "Just when you think it's all over, he says, 'Now this is what we've decided,' and he's right."

To emphasize his process role, Bernardin says, "I volunteered that I would take no position of advocacy on any group or movement, no matter how much I might agree with it. . . . Other members did not feel so obligated and have been more vocal." He looked forward to the day when the committee's work would be completed "and I will be freer to speak as an individual bishop."

Bernardin's approach involved more than an effort to pull together the broadest possible consensus; in a sense, the mediator became the message—the committee process became a model for dialogue and negotiations.

During discussion, Bernardin made sure that everyone was heard. He brought the staff, Russett, Casey and Warner into the discussions as full participants. He frequently went around the table asking for comment, although he usually went to Hehir for the final word. While the two had not always been on the same side of internal USCC disputes, Bernardin trusted Hehir completely and leaned on him heavily.

Conservative critics consistently charged that the bishops were being manipulated by "church bureaucrats," particularly Hehir. Hehir had considerable influence, but it was open and earned—the bishops had come to respect his insight and skills, as well as his caution. Within the committee, he was trusted completely by all members. "He was always saying, 'This is the issue, this is what you have to decide—but you have to decide,' " Gumbleton says. Doherty says, "That must have happened thirty times."

To outsiders, the match-up of Gumbleton and O'Connor was fascinating. O'Connor says the stereotype was that he would play Attila the Hun to Gumbleton's St. Francis, but that kind of clash never developed. Gumbleton says they approached discussion using conflict resolution techniques—not as debaters trying to score points, but as people bringing different perspectives to a shared effort to solve a problem. There were no up-and-down votes on the first draft—most of the time, members just talked until a consensus emerged.

Fulcher says Gumbleton and O'Connor were the hardest-working committee members, drafting and redrafting sections of the pastoral. Not unexpectedly, Gumbleton offered the most pacifist positions and O'Connor showed the most sensitivity to the concerns of military and political leaders.

But Fulcher notes that O'Connor often came up with contributions from a perspective the others didn't expect. And throughout, Gumbleton continued to distinguish between how far church teaching could go and how far he could go as an individual within the framework created by that teaching. Bernardin says one lesson he learned through the long process—both with outside experts and committee members—was "not to stereotype people as pacifists or warmongers."

Throughout most of the discussions, Reilly and Fulcher primarily reacted to the work of others—which, Roach says, was their role. Gumbleton says the two helped the committee "reach people where they are."

Bernardin used Reilly and Fulcher as a gauge, knowing that their reactions would reflect the bulk of the conference. The development of these two men was critical; Russett says their education took four or five months, but that by then, both knew more about the issues than most of the bishops' critics. Referring to Reilly, Fulcher and Bernardin, who hadn't been deeply involved in the nuclear issue before, Gumbleton says, "Once it gets to be real to people, you can't just back away—you can't let go."

There aren't three men in the country who know the American hierarchy as well as Bernardin, Roach and Kelly; they picked two men to represent the conference, and within a few months, both had backed the nuclear freeze movement and one—Fulcher—had joined Pax Christi.

Fulcher notes that one of his brothers, a priest, had been very active in Pax Christi. He says he hesitated before backing the freeze because of his role on the committee but concluded he still had a right to speak as an individual. At the same time, he said, "I felt I knew more about it" because of his committee work.

Reilly signed what he calls "the Pax Christi freeze" partly to show his support for the religious values behind it. He declined to endorse local freezes because he didn't know the people supporting them; but he says he would never try to undercut the freeze movement.

One of the most surprising things to outsiders was that there was a woman in the midst of the whole process. Casey said the men made her feel at home, although she said O'Connor sometimes felt uncomfortable.

There were some comic moments. When the committee met at a retreat house in Spring Lake, New Jersey, Casey stayed at a motel. O'Connor took another room at the motel so she wouldn't feel so left out, and the others joked about "John and Julie going off to a motel." Casey also recalls the first time the committee met in Chicago after Bernardin's appointment there: "You don't know what it means for a woman to make a phone call sitting on [Cardinal] Mundelein's bed."

But there were less comic dimensions to being the only woman in the group. Casey stopped taking notes during the testimony after one former government official mistook her for a secretary. She also felt some truth to the notion that men talk about issues like war in terms of abstractions, while women see them in terms of people.

And she was also struck by the internal committee process. Meetings weren't preplanned, the way women religious plan things; Bernardin always set the agenda at the start. And she says, "We never stopped after some of the testimony to talk about how we felt about what we had heard, even when everyone was visibly moved. Women would have talked about how they had changed."

As the committee's hearings moved along, Russett prepared a three-page outline for discussion at the meeting of January 27, 1982. He offered "a more-or-less 'centrist' position." Russett says that from the beginning he hoped to show the just-war tradition and pacifism merging in the form of nuclear pacifism.

Russett says his reading of church teaching found no absolute ban on the use of nuclear weapons. But, he says, emphasis on the absence of an absolute ban "runs the risk of playing into the hands of those looking for a nuclear 'war-fighting' capability." The solution, he felt, was to downplay the nature of a very limited deterrent and stress the need for negotiations and cuts.

The outline expressed "profound doubts" about the ability to keep nuclear war limited and to discriminate military from civilian targets. It concluded that nuclear weapons could not be used against population centers, even in retaliation for a nuclear attack against the United States. Russett also recommended a "no-first-use" policy before it was backed in a famous *Foreign Affairs* article by former presidential advisers McGeorge Bundy, George Kennan, Robert McNamara and Gerard Smith. The outline called for acceptance of increased spending for conventional weapons—and even the return of the draft—if necessary to make a no-first-use policy possible.

"If nuclear weapons may be used at all," the outline said, "it may be only after they have already been used against oneself (including one's allies) and, even then, only in an extremely limited, discriminating manner." The outline expressed little confidence in the ability to do even that. It also said that if a specific use of a nuclear weapon is forbidden, "so is intention or threat to so use."

Russett raised the question of whether the committee would condemn "limited" second-strike use in the absence of any church teaching on the subject. He urged accelerated arms control and disarmament, reduced nuclear arsenals, an end to testing and further deployment, and unilateral U.S. initiatives along with bilateral efforts. "Even temporary toleration of nuclear weapons is dependent on these efforts," he said.

Russett's second outline, dated February 12, shows some expansion, but no substantive change, following committee discussion. The committee inserted a section on the scriptural basis of peace and relevant quotations from the Pastoral Constitution on the Church in the Modern World; it fleshed out the discussion of the just-war tradition; it emphasized the need to move progressively toward disarmament; it urged all Christians to be open to nonviolence and asked the development of nonviolent conflict resolution techniques.

The draft was put together during three days in late May and completed during the committee's fourteenth meeting. Its title was "God's Hope in a Time of Fear." Russett had used it as a section title; O'Connor liked it and the committee agreed to use it for the whole draft.

The draft was reminiscent of the horse that was built by a committee and came out a camel. It was hard to follow, with the same point often repeated several times and two halves of a point separated by fifteen pages. But the draft did reflect the basic message the committee was trying to get across: the present arms race can't go on unchallenged, but it can't be ended overnight; so intensified efforts toward serious arms control and disarmament negotiations are crucial.

The introductory section relied heavily on a New Testament description of peace, recognized the complexity of the issue, and said, "We must keep alive the hope and conviction that peace is possible—a present possibility in our day."

The draft then described the practice of nonviolence found in the Gospels and, citing figures like Francis of Assisi, Dorothy Day, Gandhi and Martin Luther King, Jr., said, "Nonviolence is an option that calls powerfully to Christians today." It also emphasized that "a right of defense has traditionally been a part of church teaching. The right is an extension of the commandment of love. The first use of the right was to defend others."

The draft then outlined the Just War Tradition, which, it emphasized,

begins with an assessment of war as evil, imposing great harm on participants and non-combatants alike. Under the best of circumstances, Christians may take part only reluctantly. We must remember what is fundamental in the Just War Tradition: the presumption in favor of peace. It is too often forgotten that the "theory" of just war elaborated through the centuries was an evolving effort to discourage war.

Gumbleton notes that the Just War Tradition has not been taught well over the years and that it has frequently been used to provide a rationale for an unjust war. If all people get out of the final pastoral, he said in the summer of 1982, is an understanding of what the Just War Tradition really means, the pastoral will have been a success.

The section on the just-war tradition, in describing the requirement that war be declared by a competent authority, made a passing reference to the " 'just-revolution' argument," noting the question of competent authority was particularly critical in such a framework.

The draft tackled what it called "the paradox of modern deterrence"—the fact that possession of nuclear weapons can deter the use of such weapons but still provide a threat in themselves:

Use or threatened use of weapons of mass destruction pushes the conditions for a just war to their limits or beyond, raising the most severe doubts as to whether the horrors inflicted could be discriminating or proportionate to any desired good. These realities require us to think about war in an entirely new way.

As the draft inched toward substantive recommendations, it said;

We offer some first approximations to an ethically acceptable defense policy. . . . We honestly believe our conclusions flow from our moral and spiritual tradition, yet recognizing the complexity of the issues, we offer them as an invitation to moral direction, dialogue and growth.

The five points in Russett's draft had grown to six. While working on the draft, Hehir and Russett had concluded that the five points led to a hypothetical position and that something else was needed to address present realities. But it wasn't clear to most readers that the sixth point didn't flow from the other five but stood alongside them.

The draft said:

—Under no circumstances may nuclear weapons or other instruments of mass slaughter be used for the purpose of destroying population or other predominantly civilian targets. . . . We also cannot reconcile our principles with the use of any weapons aimed at military targets, however defined, where the targets lie so close to concentrations of population that destruction of the targets would likely devastate those nearby populations. . . . No Christian can rightfully carry out orders or policies deliberately aimed at killing noncombatants.

—We do not perceive any situation in which the deliberate initiation of nuclear warfare, on however restricted a scale, can be condoned. Non-nuclear attacks by another state must be deterred by other than nuclear means.

The draft said no one can be certain that escalation of limited nuclear war to all-out nuclear war will not occur. The draft said "initiate nuclear warfare" instead of "use nuclear weapons first" at O'Connor's urging; he thought it was possible to use nuclear weapons first without initiating a nuclear war.

—The draft repeated the 1976 condemnation of the threat to use strategic nuclear weapons. It elaborated by saying such a threat produces "anxiety" in those being threatened and leads those making the threat to accept violence too easily:

Threats to use nuclear weapons first, or against predominantly civilian targets even in retaliation, cannot therefore be justified. We urge all governments to abstain from all such threats and to take concrete steps to insure that such uses do not occur. We urge the United States to do this even if all other nuclear powers do not.

—In attempting to address the question of whether nuclear weapons may be used under any circumstances, the draft said:

It is difficult for us to see how what may be legitimate in theory may indeed be justifiable in practice. In all candor, we have no confidence whatever that retaliatory and restricted usage could be kept limited.

If nuclear weapons may be used at all, they may be used only after they have been used against our own country or our allies, and, even then, only in an extremely limited, discriminating manner against military targets. A declared intention to use nuclear weapons in this way could continue to serve as deterrent to a nuclear attack without incurring the condemnation applied to deliberate use against civilians. . . . We do not intend to legitimate here, however, what is often conventionally described as a counter-force strategy, if by that is meant an effort or ability to deprive our adversary of his own strategic forces.

—The fifth point addressed the possession of nuclear weapons and argued that rejecting any conceivable use of those weapons would raise a "very difficult question" about continued possession:

Abandonment of nuclear deterrence might invite an attack upon the United States. . . . We cannot lightly demand abandonment of possession of all nuclear weapons at this moment.

Rapid, abrupt and one-sided abandonment of all nuclear deterrence might create dangerous political and military instabilities in the world. Soviet nuclear weapons provide fully as great a threat to humanity as do our own. We are strongly advised that if the United States were to renounce its own weapons unilaterally, it would greatly diminish any incentive for the Soviet Union to negotiate reduction or elimination of its weapons. But a temporary toleration of some aspects of nuclear deterrence must not be confused with approval of such deterrence.

With the first five points, the draft seemed to be allowing only the legitimate possession of a nuclear hand grenade—a nuclear weapon so limited it could be used against a military target without any damage to civilians. Gumbleton says Gerard Smith remarked, "What you're saying, in effect, is that you could use an elephant to walk through a field as long as it never trampled the grass."

But the sixth point looked to reality as opposed to an ideal. "We have hereby outlined," it began, "what would be at most a marginally justifiable deterrence policy. We find ourselves at odds with elements of current deterrent policy. . . ."

The draft quoted the key paragraphs from the 1979 Krol testimony and, in several pages written by Hehir, elaborated on the use of the principle of moral "toleration" to live with deterrence:

Toleration is a technical term in Catholic moral theology; in the case of deterrence, toleration is based on two judgments. First . . . if nuclear weapons had never been made, we could not condone their creation; second, the role of the nuclear deterrent in preserving "peace of a sort" gives it a certain utility. Hence, the mixed nature of deterrence produces the moral judgment of toleration, a judgment that to deny the deterrent any moral legitimacy may bring about worse consequences than we presently live with under conditions of deterrence.

The deterrence relationship which prevails between the United States, the Soviet Union and other powers is objectively a sinful situation because of the threats implied in it and the consequences it has in the world. Yet movement out of this objectively evil situation must be controlled lest we cause by accident what we would neither deliberately choose nor morally condone.

The draft cited an urgency in moving out of deterrence:

Toleration of deterrence is not meant to be a comforting moral judgment, but an urgent call to efforts to change the present relationship among nuclear powers. . . . We fear, however, that "gradual" disarmament has become a relatively meaningless term, in that the discernible pace of efforts suggests that some political leaders seem to believe the status quo may be safely maintained for many years. We cannot accept this assumption, nor can we accept what is perceived to be a lack of urgency bordering on apathy in the pursuit of this crucial goal.

The draft said, "Our toleration must be conditional upon sincere, substantial efforts to modify current policy as well as ultimately to eliminate these weapons."

Next came a section called "Toward the Waging of Peace: An Appeal," containing recommendations. The first called for "active and accelerated work for arms control, reduction, and disarmament." It said:

> We urge the immediate end, by all states, of the further development, production and deployment of major new nuclear weapons and delivery systems. Not only should development and deployment of new weapons cease, the numbers of existing weapons must be reduced in a manner that reduces the danger of war.

While neither this passage nor the whole first draft mentions the nuclear "freeze," this passage was explicitly designed to back the essential elements of the freeze. Fulcher says committee members wanted to avoid political "red flag" words like "nuclear freeze" and "no-first-use" that would distract attention from the committee's support of the substance of those proposals.

The draft called on the United States to make some "unilateral initiatives" toward disarmament. It also said that "in the absence of nuclear deterrent threats," many analysts believe more spending on conventional arms would be necessary. They acknowledged that possibility, but said, "We do not in any way want to contribute to a notion of 'making the world safe for conventional war.' "

The committee similarly acknowledged the possible need for a draft. But they repeated a 1980 USCC statement saying the draft was acceptable only in time of "a national defense emergency" and echoed support for both conscientious objection and selective conscientious objection.

Other recommendations included the need to develop nonviolent means of conflict resolution and a "compelling vision of peace, justice and a positive world order."

The section on pastoral practice, written by Bernardin, began:

> The spectre of nuclear war, as seen in the escalating arms race and talk of "winning" nuclear war, demands many things of Christians. These demands include formation of conscience, prayer and penitential practice.

The draft said issues of war and peace involve a moral dimension "which the responsible Christian cannot ignore."

It said the fact that such matters are also political doesn't deny the church the right to help its members form their consciences:

> We reject, therefore, criticism of the church's concern with these issues on the ground that it "should not get involved in politics." We are called to move from discussion to witness to action. At the same time, we recognize that the church's authority does not carry the same force when it deals with technical solutions involving particular means as it does when it speaks of principles or ends.

The section complained that some people all along the spectrum have not understood the church's teaching:

> Some would place almost no limits on the use of nuclear weapons if they are needed for "self-defense." Some . . . insist on conclusions which may be legitimate options but cannot be made obligatory on the basis of actual church teaching.

The section called for respect for life at all stages:

> Violence has many faces: oppression of the poor, deprivation of basic human rights, economic exploitation, wretched prison conditions, religious, ethnic or sexual discrimination, sexual exploitation or pornography, neglect or abuse of the aged and the helpless. . . . Abortion in particular blunts a sense of the sacredness of human life. If the innocent unborn are killed wantonly, how can we expect people to feel righteous revulsion at the act or threat of killing innocent non-combatants in war?

The draft called for including a prayer for peace in the prayer of the faithful at Mass, for making the kiss of peace at Mass an authentic sign of reconciliation, and pledged the bishops to observe Friday as a day of abstinence from meat as a sign of penance.

The draft's final section addressed various groups of Catholics—educators, parents, political leaders, and so on.

Russett boiled O'Connor's sixteen-page single-spaced draft down to thirteen double-spaced pages, leaving a still formidable chunk of material. He also strengthened a few sections, including the one reminding members of the military of their obligation not to take directly the lives of noncombatants.

Parts of the section drafted by O'Connor later drew criticisms from peace groups, who charged it was patronizing toward pacifists and nasty in urging those in the peace movement not to "engage in bitterness and recrimination while urging others to pursue the vision of peace."

But O'Connor also wrote the section that told those who work in the nuclear weapons industry:

We cannot at this time require Catholics who manufacture nuclear weapons, sincerely believing they are enhancing a deterrent capability and reducing the likelihood of war, to leave such employment. Should we become convinced that even the temporary possession of such weapons may no longer be morally tolerated, we would logically be required to consider immoral any involvement in their manufacture. All Catholics in weapons industries should evaluate their activities on a continuing basis, forming their consciences in accordance with the general principles enunciated in this pastoral letter.

Gumbleton regarded the statement calling for a continuing review of conscience a major advance.

As the committee neared completion of the first draft, Bernardin insisted that members go over it line by line; they did, twice, and all signed off on it—at least to the extent that they agreed it should go to the bishops for discussion. From the beginning, O'Connor remained vague about how he really felt about the document even though it contained his own words.

The committee had originally planned to complete its draft by August, but it ran ahead of schedule. That turned out to be fortunate, because they were asked to have the draft ready for distribution at the Collegeville meeting. Some bishops wanted it distributed there, but Malone didn't want it added to the agenda, so a compromise was reached and the draft, which was printed in Collegeville, was distributed at the end of the meeting. As it turned out, the bishops had a pretty good idea of what was in the draft, because they read about it first in the newspaper.

Gumbleton had discussed the draft's contents at a meeting of the Catholic Theological Society of America in early June. Word reached reporters, and Marjorie Hyer of the Washington *Post* broke the story on a Saturday. The bishops in Minnesota saw it in a local paper that carried the *Post*'s wire service. The full draft text and commentary also appeared in the issue of the *National Catholic Reporter* that came out as the Collegeville meeting ended. "I did a stupid thing," Gumbleton says about discussing the draft at the CTSA meeting.

Hyer's story emphasized the bishops' emphasis on avoiding the use of nuclear weapons, a lead that, from the committee's standpoint, was useful.

On May 25, Doherty sent Hehir a memo offering some predictions about the way the draft would be received. He said, "The most controversy will be provoked by the draft letter's qualified approval of retaliatory counterforce use" and that the draft would be seen as a regression from the Krol testimony, saying "possession, yes, use, maybe," while Krol had said "possession, yes, use, no."

Doherty also predicted that the draft's opposition to the first use of nuclear weapons—at odds with NATO policy to use nuclear weapons to deter conventional war in Europe—would cause "the most serious problem" for the Reagan administration and other governments.

VII. SECOND DRAFT

After the first draft was written, but before it was distributed, Pope John Paul II made back-to-back statements on war and peace which were to have a profound impact on the second draft.

The first came on June 10, during the pope's visit to Great Britain. Speaking at Coventry, "a city devastated by war but rebuilt by hope," while England and Argentina were fighting a short, costly, bizarre war over the Falkland Islands, he said: "Today, the scale and the horror of modern warfare—whether nuclear or not—makes it totally unacceptable as a means of settling difference between nations. War should belong to the tragic past, to history; it should find no place on humanity's agenda for the future."

On June 11, the Vatican Secretary of State, Cardinal Agostino Casaroli, delivered an address in the pope's name to the Second U.N. Special Session on Disarmament. The talk echoed Vatican attacks on the arms race and contained this section on deterrence which was to be quoted endlessly during the ensuing debate: "Under present conditions, deterrence based on balance—certainly not as an end in itself, but as a stage on the way to progressive disarmament—can still be judged to be morally acceptable."

The introduction to the second draft described the talks as examples of the church talking to different audiences—one Christian, one secular. But popes, like politicians, run the constant risk that one audience will hear the words intended for another; the juxtaposition of those two paragraphs uttered only hours apart suggested that the American bishops weren't the only people having a hard time reconciling the church's various teachings on peace and war in a nuclear age.

As the church began to digest the first draft, Bernardin gave a rare public talk on the subject at a symposium sponsored by the Boston archdiocesan Justice and Peace Commission. An aide describes the talk as "the most Bernardin" he'd heard so far on the subject.

Bernardin didn't discuss the draft's text, but he emphasized the need for implementation once it was completed and praised Boston's educational program as a model for other dioceses. He also praised the freeze and no-first-use movements without quite endorsing them and said the combination of a new public awareness and shifts in the policy debate had created "an 'open moment' in the history of the nuclear arms race."

He said the Catholic Church could offer hope and moral analysis and guidance to the public debate. "Today there is a tangible public desire to raise the moral, human and religious dimensions of the nuclear threat." But, he said, "The creation of a constituency for peace may be the most important contribution we have to make to the public debate at this time." That constituency, he said, is "potentially as broad as the Church itself in this country."

"Negotiations are pursued by governments," Bernardin said, "but it is clear that governments will not move fast enough and at times cannot move at all unless there is a visible and vocal constituency committed to changing the dynamic of the arms race.

"Complex technical debate over specific proposals is absolutely indispensable, but it must proceed at such a pace as not to paralyze the political process. When no one can make an absolutely decisive case that the agreement clearly should be supported or clearly is flawed, and where the issue hangs in the balance, there is a need for a public voice willing to take risks on the side of reversing the arms race rather than reinforcing it."

The committee held its first meeting to discuss the reaction to the first draft July 28–30 at a retreat center at Spring Lake, New Jersey. The center was then run by the Military Ordinariate, and O'Connor had suggested a retreat setting.

The first thing that struck the committee as it came together was the sheer bulk of the material before it. Fulcher recalls that when the meeting ended, the bishops made a comic sight, each lugging a shopping bag full of responses to the airport.

"It was overwhelming," Gumbleton recalls. "I personally had received a stack of material about a foot high. I tried to read all of it and got through most of it. When I got to the meeting, I discovered there was another stack of material equally as high."

Gumbleton said there was no way to meet the committee's deadline and be honest to the process. The deadline was August 14, one month before the meeting in which the bishops' Administrative Committee had to approve the pastoral letter for debate in November.

The others pretty much agreed but decided to spend the morning going through the material before making a final decision. After a few hours, they reached a consensus to seek a delay.

Bernardin called Roach and Msgr. Daniel Hoye, the bishops' new general secretary to tell them the committee's conclusion. The decision would leave a major vacuum in November because not much else was scheduled, but Roach and Hoye agreed to go along with the delay. They said the bishops would decide in November whether to put off a vote on the pastoral until November 1983, or hold an unusual special meeting in the spring.

As the committee discussions continued on the evening of the twenty-eighth, it became clear that O'Connor—who had apparently been surprised by the level of criticism from his conservative and military friends—had developed real problems with the first draft. He spoke for more than an hour, calling for a thoroughly new approach to the theology of peace and complaining that the committee had not consulted sufficiently with conservative theologians.

Bernardin fidgeted during the presentation; Russett describes it as "painful . . . he didn't just want to go back to 'square zero,' he wanted to go back to 'square minus-six.' " At one point, O'Connor privately offered to resign if he was "an embarrassment" to Bernardin. "Of course not," Bernardin responded.

By the next morning, O'Connor had changed again, now apologizing for his performance. He later apologized to Bernardin again for his "importunings" at Spring Lake and any offense he might have given again in an August 5 letter explaining some of his theological concerns.

On the second day at Spring Lake, the committee began to focus on specific criticisms and how to deal with them. Since Russett was to be out of the country during the key period, the major rewriting job fell to Hehir. The committee met again August 11 and 12 in Washington and on September 22 in Chicago.

The pope never commented directly on the first draft. But on July 8, the Vatican Justice and Peace Commission sent Bernardin a generally favorable critique. The commission praised the bishops for their tone, honesty and fidelity to both Catholic teaching and intellectual tradition; it particularly praised the sections on pastoral guidance and the "exhortations." The commission urged that the pope's U.N. speech be integrated throughout the document, seeing no contradictions between the two.

The commission expressed concern about the document's length and clarity and preferred moral generalities to specifics. It also made a number of minor recommendations, including the suggestion that the "just-revolution" argument was a distraction. But the committee rightly saw the commission comment as an endorsement of its efforts. "I was very pleased when I saw it," Bernardin says.

The responses to the first draft from bishops and outside experts came to about seven hundred pages. Some seventy bishops commented. About a third of those submitting written comments mentioned their own consultation on the draft—some with one or two experts; some, as in the Archdiocese of Baltimore where Frank Murphy was cochairman of the Justice and Peace Commission, with a broad range of people. Many other bishops who didn't comment formally on the first draft also held local discussions.

Most of the bishops made comments for editorial changes in the draft, and most of those called for strengthening the document; only about a half dozen questioned the basic direction.

As the committee prepared for its first meeting after the draft's release, Hehir sorted through the responses and sent the committee a handful that involved "substantial challenges to the text (from diverse points of view) or call for substantial change (either in content or style and size of the pastoral)."

The strongest criticism came from Archbishop Hannan, who, echoing his public statements, argued that the draft would hurt the U.S. negotiating position and was at odds with the pope's U.N. speech; he wanted to scrap the whole pastoral and simply distribute the U.N. address.

Hehir sent out two comments calling for stronger criticism of U.S. policies. The most influential came from Archbishop Quinn, one of the most important shapers of the pastoral outside of the committee itself.

Quinn argued in an eight-page letter that "neither production nor possession [of nuclear weapons] can any longer be said to have moral legitimacy." Like the committee, he acknowledged the risks of unilateral disarmament and cited the principle of toleration. "Still," he said, "we have clearly stated that toleration is based on the fulfillment of certain conditions; namely, that there be sincere and substantial effort toward disarmament, mutual, verifiable, at an equal pace, and so on.

"But the Vatican Council already stated that fifteen or more years ago. Cardinal Krol repeated it powerfully in his testimony three years ago. How long do we have to wait to make a judgment that the efforts are not substantial and that toleration cannot be given any longer?

"What guidance do we give our people on this question, of when, how to judge whether the efforts are sincere and substantial and thus merit some toleration? I believe we have to tackle this question in the document. Have we reached the point where toleration is no longer possible?"

Quinn generally argued for making the letter stronger, with more specific moral judgments on facts and an explicit call for a nuclear freeze. He also said "the document oscillates between being tentative and preemptory in its moral judgments."

The second comment Hehir sent out urging a stronger document came from Father Francis X. Meehan, a moral theologian at the Theological Seminary of St. Charles Borromeo in Philadelphia. In his thirteen-page letter, he went beyond Quinn's criticism of the draft's tentativeness, describing its reference to "some first approximations to an ethically acceptable defense policy" as "pusillanimous."

The draft's tentative tone can be explained on two levels. First, much of it was written by Russett, who took pains to offer a "centrist" position and not to unduly influence the committee. Second, the committee itself didn't want to be too far in front of the rest of the conference. It was characteristic of Bernardin's style that he wanted the pressure for a stronger document, if it was to come, to come from the bishops, not the committee itself.

Meehan pressed for stronger language and more specifics, including condemnations of the MX and Trident II as first-strike weapons. He also called for specific rejection of the nuclear bombings of Hiroshima and Nagasaki and of the saturation bombing of Dresden and Tokyo. "A sin unnamed and unrepented," he said, "will reproduce itself."

Concerns ranged from the simple to the complex. Several bishops didn't like the title, "God's Hope in a Time of Fear." Some thought it was too vague or confusing; some noted it seemed to be saying that God hopes. Committee members threw out other titles until they found one that was acceptable—"The Challenge of Peace: God's Promise and Our Response."

In general, the second draft reflected a major jump from the hypothetical to the realistic. The immediate context which had spurred the pastoral's creation was made more explicit, as were related problems.

Two related concerns were confusion over the pastoral's intended audience and its dispassionate tone. The committee agreed to have an introduction to explain that "Catholic teaching on war and peace has two purposes: first, to help Catholics form their consciences; and second, to contribute to the public policy debate about the morality of war."

The first page of the new draft reflected a more urgent tone:

> Today the apprehension about nuclear war is a tangible, visible element of our time. . . . We have experienced this terror in the minds and hearts of our people—indeed we share it ourselves.

The draft cited the Pontifical Academy of Sciences report and said the moral task, like the medical, was prevention. It also said:

> The "new moment" which exists in the public debate about nuclear weapons provides a creative opportunity and a moral imperative to examine the relationship between public opinion and public policy.

The section on Scripture was expanded, particularly with more references to the Old Testament.

The second-draft section on nonviolence reflected pressure from Pax Christi and other peace groups urging a fuller development and higher priority for the theme. "From the earliest days of the church," the new section began, "we have evidence of Christians, moved by the example of Jesus, committing themselves to a nonviolent lifestyle." It concluded, "Today in the Catholic community, when any issue of peace or war is addressed, the nonviolent tradition must be part of the discussion."

The following section called the just-war tradition "the alternative moral response to the pacifist tradition," a phrase that was later to cause problems for the committee. The section retained a reference to the just-revolution argument and described the just-war tradition in more detail, citing the requirements of competent authority, just cause, right intention, last resort, probability of success, proportionality and just means of waging war. The second draft added a reference to the bishops' 1971 statement opposing the Vietnam War on grounds of proportionality.

Part II of the second draft, "War and Peace in the Modern World: Problems and Principles," reflected a tougher tone and references to the "new moment" in public debate.

The first draft's six points had been reduced to three, including a repetition of the condemnation of nuclear attacks on civilian centers and of the initiation of nuclear war.

Doherty had been right that the first draft's section on possible nuclear second strike against a military target would bring strong criticism. As the committee reworked this point, Russett, who, with a writer's eye for significant events and turning points, says Bernardin made his first major contribution, and a forceful one, on a substantive issue.

By this point, Bernardin was more sure of himself on technical issues. But Russett and others noted that his appointment to Chicago had left him more relaxed and sure of himself. It wasn't simply that Bernardin had gotten something he wanted; he also must have been relieved by the lifting of the pressure caused by the fact that so many others expected him to get the assignment.

As the committee wrestled with the question, Bernardin went around the table asking, "Is there anything in our Catholic faith that rules out the use of nuclear weapons under any circumstances?" The answer was no, the result of Vatican II's loophole. The church's hierarchical nature required that if the council or a pope hadn't already done it, the American bishops couldn't do it now.

Given the committee's conviction that any use of nuclear weapons would escalate into all-out nuclear war, Bernardin decided the task was to create "barriers" to the use of nuclear weapons. The second draft eventually put it this way: "The issue is the real as opposed to the theoretical possibility of a 'limited nuclear exchange.'"

The new draft approached the question of a "limited" retaliatory strike against military targets by posing a set of questions:

—Would leaders have sufficient information to know what is happening in a nuclear exchange?

—Would they be able, under the conditions of stress, time pressure and fragmentary information to make the extraordinarily precise decisions needed to keep the exchange limited if this were technically possible?

—Would military commanders be able, in the midst of the destruction and confusion of a nuclear exchange, to maintain a policy of discriminate targeting?

—Given the accidents we know about in peacetime conditions, what assurances have we that computer errors could be avoided . . . ?

—Would not the casualties even in a war defined as limited by strategists still run in the millions?

—How "limited" would be the long-term effects of radiation, famine, social fragmentation and economic dislocation?

"This cluster of questions," the draft said, "makes us skeptical about the real meaning of 'limited.' "

Another major criticism concerned the moral theology used in the first draft's treatment of deterrence. In a brief letter, Auxiliary Bishop Lawrence Riley of Boston said the draft, by justifying an evil means for a good end, was practicing "consequentialism," an ends-justifies-means approach to moral theology rejected by the church.

A far more detailed critique came from Germain Griesez, a well-known conservative Catholic moral theologian, who argued that the draft had developed a totally new use of "toleration." Traditionally, he said, we may tolerate another's evil without actually willing it; for example, he said, a government may tolerate the spread of false religions as a side effect to a policy of protecting religious freedom.

But, he said, no one may tolerate his own evil. Griesez argued that since Americans have a say in determining their nation's policies, they would be both tolerator and doer of evil. He noted that the draft called the arms race an "objectively sinful situation," but he said that identifying something as a sin and choosing to maintain it turns it into subjective evil. He charged that leading someone to continue to consent to a sinful act is "to lead them to commit sin. To lead a person to commit sin is formal cooperation in his or her sin; moreover, to do this is to commit the specific sin of scandal."

Griesez charged that "the principle of the argument in the present draft is: Moral evil might be done that good might follow from it. . . . No matter what the bishops say or do not say about nuclear deterrence, they must not both condemn it as morally evil and approve it as tolerable."

Speaking for himself, Griesez said he believes nuclear deterrence is morally evil and intolerable—a position which led him to support unilateral disarmament, although he acknowledged there was no consensus on this within the church.

"Many people," Griesez concluded, "surely would take the approach of this draft to the problem of deterrence as a model for dealing with their own problems—ones less threatening to human-kind at large, but no less excruciating for them. . . . Businessmen working to support their families often excuse fraudulent practices by pointing out that in their business one cannot survive in any other way. Women who have an abortion often do so very reluctantly, recognizing its moral evil but seeing no acceptable way out.

"Even if the 'theology of toleration' underlying the present draft were somehow defensible, it would be very dangerous: Everyone would find this newly approved way of handling difficult problems preferable to the hard, old way."

The debate over "toleration" and "consequentialism" was one the committee had not foreseen. While the subject at hand was nuclear war, the real issue in the new debate was the authority of the church's teaching on sex—particularly birth control, sterilization and abortion.

The debate provided more than its share of strange bedfellows. Reilly points out that Griesez is the kind of theologian someone like Hannan would cite on abortion; instead, Bishop Matthiessen of Amarillo was inviting him to debates to support unilateral disarmament. At the same time, O'Connor, who had little use for liberal theologians like Father Charles Curran and Jesuit Father Richard McCormick because of their opposition to the church's teaching on birth control, was surprised to find out they weren't pacifists.

Curran describes three major premises in moral theology. The first, which is official church teaching, is that one may never do or intend to do evil. Consequentialism, Curran says, holds that only consequences count. Curran says he favors a middle view he calls proportionalism—both means and consequences must be considered.

The orthodox approach creates a number of problems. Take the "use-intent-threat-possession" spectrum Russett mentioned in his outline. Many Catholic activists were arguing that church teaching says that if it's evil to use nuclear weapons, it's evil to intend to use them. In 1976, the bishops had accepted the next logical step proposed by Russ Shaw—who coauthored a book on ethics with Griesez—that it is morally wrong to threaten to use them. The next logical step is that it's evil to possess them.

But what do you do after you decide that possession of nuclear weapons is morally wrong? Many argue that the only response is to get rid of them. But how? Over how long a time? Even Gumbleton acknowledges that getting rid of them precipitously poses a great risk.

But the orthodox moral theology proposed by Griesez would bar consideration of that risk. Even O'Connor, the most concerned about consequentialism on the committee, argues that "important though intention is, it's only one aspect of human action and moral assessment."

The pope had given the committee a way out of the "toleration" debate. While the toleration argument had been used by people as orthodox as Krol, Quinn and Cooke, it was becoming a distraction. The committee also saw that, on a practical level, there was no difference between what it had called "morally tolerable" and what the pope had called "morally acceptable" under certain conditions.

The problem was that critics of the first draft had jumped on the words "morally acceptable" as a final answer. START negotiator Rowny quoted the passage as virtual carte blanche for the Administration's arms buildup.

Led by Gumbleton, the committee reached a compromise: use "morally acceptable" but spell out the conditions required. But even with this basic decision made, things didn't go smoothly. As the committee neared the end of its deliberations, Hehir offered a draft that called the pope's U.N. speech the most authoritative statement on deterrence since the Vatican Council.

Gumbleton balked, arguing that that was too much weight to give to an almost offhand comment in a speech. O'Connor also had some problems with the section.

Bernardin, in what Russett called a classic "process" approach, said that if Gumbleton and O'Connor could agree on new wording, the others would be glad to consider it. If not, they already had a text in hand.

Gumbleton rewrote the section; O'Connor offered only a few minor changes, and the committee approved it in an hour-long conference call on October 7, just under the wire to send the new draft out for the November meeting.

The draft called deterrence a "sinful situation" and cited its negative impact. But, it said, "As clearly unsatisfactory as the deterrent posture of the United States is from a moral point of view, use of nuclear weapons by any of the nuclear powers would be an even greater evil."

That lesser-evil argument eventually heightened the charges of consequentialism.

Citing other parts of the pope's U.N. speech and a later talk to scientists in August, the draft developed three criteria for evaluating deterrence policy:

1. If deterrence exists only to prevent the use of nuclear weapons by others, then proposals to go beyond this objective to encourage war-fighting capabilities must be resisted. We must continually say "no" to the idea of nuclear war.

2. If deterrence is our goal, "sufficiency" to deter is an adequate standard; the quest for superiority must be resisted.

3. If deterrence is to be used as "a step on the way toward progressive disarmament," then each proposed addition to our strategic system or change in strategic doctrine must be examined precisely in light of whether it will render steps toward arms control and disarmament more or less likely.

The draft used these criteria to develop seven specific recommendations. The committee opposed:

—The addition of weapons which are likely to invite attack and therefore give credence to the concept that the U.S. seeks a first-strike, "hard-target kill" capability; the M-X Missile might fit into this category.

—The willingness to foster strategic planning which seeks a nuclear war-fighting capability.

—Proposals which have the effect of lowering the nuclear threshhold and blurring the difference between nuclear and conventional weapons.

The draft recommended:

—Support for immediate, bilateral, verifiable agreements to halt the testing, production and deployment of new strategic systems.

—Support for negotiated bilateral deep cuts in nuclear arsenals of both superpowers, particularly of those weapons systems which have destabilizing characteristics.

—Support for a Comprehensive Test Ban Treaty.

—Removal by all parties of nuclear weapons from border areas and the strengthening of command and control over tactical nuclear weapons to prevent inadvertent and unauthorized use.

By the time the second draft was completed, it had a waiting audience, thanks largely to the attention the Reagan administration had given the draft over the past few months. Doherty had correctly predicted that the Administration wouldn't like the first draft's no-first-use section, but he didn't predict the Administration's strong reaction to the draft's freeze language.

While he didn't mention the bishops directly, Reagan attacked the freeze in an address on the 150th anniversary of the Knights of Columbus in Hartford, Connecticut, on August 3. In front of an audience that included more than a hundred bishops from the U.S. and overseas, including Cardinal Casaroli, Reagan called the freeze "sterile" and "obsolete." He charged that a freeze wasn't as good as the deep reductions he had proposed and that passage of a freeze resolution in the House would send Moscow a signal that it could settle for less.

The committee's decision to postpone final action on the pastoral became public the day of Reagan's speech; some critics tried to credit Reagan with producing the change, but he wasn't a factor at all.

Other Administration officials had already begun responding to the first draft. William P. Clark, the President's national security adviser, had criticized the first draft in a July 30 letter to Clare Boothe Luce, a member of the board of the peace center run by O'Connor. Clark criticized the no-first-use section and complained that the draft didn't give the Administration credit for its arms reduction proposals. He said the U.S. didn't target civilian populations as such and argued that Administration policy was "a better and wiser position than that suggested" in the pastoral letter draft.

Eagleburger's letter sent to Bernardin over the summer criticized the draft's support for a freeze. "A freeze," he said, "would lock in a Soviet advantage in two critical areas: land-based intercontinental ballistic missiles—the most destabilizing of the nuclear weapons—and intermediate range nuclear weapons." He said the Russians "will not talk seriously until they believe we can either equal or surpass them."

ACDA director Rostow and Defense Secretary Weinberger made similar criticisms of the no-first-use section. Weinberger said he had been "heartened" by the pope's reference to deterrence as "morally acceptable."

The exchange between the Administration and the bishops was the subject of a New York *Times* article on October 4. On October 23, a few days before the second draft's release, Michael Getler of the Washington *Post* ran a front-page story—which also ran on front pages across the country—emphasizing the challenges to U.S. nuclear strategy in the document.

When the draft was formally issued, the New York *Times* and other papers ran front-page stories headlining the bishops' rejection of first use of nuclear weapons. With the publication of the second draft, the

American Catholic bishops as a body clearly emerged as the major moral critic of American—and, for that matter, Soviet—nuclear policy.

One sign of the bishops' impact: *Origins,* the NC News Service documentary service, got an order for a copy of the issue with the second draft from the office of one Richard M. Nixon.

VIII. DEBATE

The bishops' large-scale entry into the nuclear debate didn't pass unnoticed all along, but the release of the second draft and the front-page coverage it attracted raised public scrutiny to a new level. It also fed the growth of new conservative groups organized to fight the bishops.

Michael Novak, a Catholic academic who wore love beads and denounced the Vietnam War in the 1960s and now hobnobs with corporate executives while developing a "theology for capitalism," became almost hysterical in his opposition to the "peace bishops"— whom he dubbed "the war bishops," charging their policies made war more likely.

Novak, the Reagan administration's ambassador to the U.N. Human Rights Commission, denounced the bishops in every publication that gave him the opportunity: the *Wall Street Journal, Commentary, National Review* and others. He also joined a new group—the American Catholic Committee—formed to oppose the bishops on Central America and the nuclear issue. The organization's board included a number of lower-echelon Administration figures: Thomas Pauken, head of ACTION, Joseph Dugan of Jeane Kirkpatrick's U.N. staff, and Robert Reilly of the U.S. International Communication Agency. (O'Connor addressed a day-long symposium on the nuclear issue sponsored by the ACC in October 1982; he says he knew nothing about the group when he accepted its invitation.)

Philip Lawler of the ultraconservative Heritage Foundation launched the Catholic Center for Renewal; and the Ethics and Public Policy Center, which had focused most of its earlier criticisms on liberal Protestant churches, zeroed in on the bishops. The center is run by Ernest Lefever, best known as Reagan's unsuccessful nominee to head the State Department's Human Rights Office.

In November 1982, Lefever's center received a $192,000 grant from the International Communication Agency—its first government grant

—to hold four conferences for European church leaders to discuss morality and nuclear weapons. The man who oversaw the ICA office in charge of grants for conferences to voluntary organizations was Robert Reilly of the American Catholic Committee.

On the eve of the 1982 bishops' meeting, Lefever published a book critical of the U.S. bishops' social justice statements with an introduction by Jesuit Father Avery Dulles (son of John Foster) supporting the conclusions of the author, J. Brian Benestad, a University of Scranton professor.

The Benestad book echoed many of the criticisms coming from the right—it attacked the bishops' competence to speak out, charged they were manipulated by their staffs, and said their statements on political issues sparked divisiveness. Most of those criticisms were primarily smoke screens, which served the purpose of diverting attention from the substance of the issue to the bishops' defense of their right to speak out.

Bernardin told *Time* magazine that the charge about the bishops' lack of competence "makes me smile. There are many people who write about these issues, newspaper editors, for example. Are they really experts in a technical sense in every field they write about? They write on the basis of study, on the basis of their conversations with people. The same is true of us bishops."

The bishops also had their defenders. Msgr. Ellis argued that on the nuclear issue in particular, the bishops are not ahead of their people: "It's the most important moral issue of the day. If they didn't speak out, they could be accused of dereliction of duty. . . . Future historians of the church looking at this period won't have to be embarrassed the way I was in writing up the history of the Catholic Church in America before the Civil War when it failed to condemn slavery."

There's always a certain carnival atmosphere around bishops' meetings—occasional demonstrations, book promotions, lobbying by right-to-lifers or women's ordination advocates.

But the November 1982 meeting practically reeked of color. There was the Bethlehem Peace Pilgrimage, sixteen people including Father Zabelka; General Daniel Graham pushing the "High Frontier," a space-borne missile intercept program; various right-wing groups opposing the bishops' pastoral—including Phyllis Schlafly with a counterpastoral denouncing communist "neo-pagan" governments;

three hundred reporters, including French and German crews, and glaring TV lights that flooded the meeting room.

It could even be said that events had literally changed the shape of the bishops' conference. The Capitol Hilton ballroom where the bishops met is usually arranged in long, straight tables; this year, the bishops sat in groups of eight to ten at round tables to facilitate the kind of small group discussions that had proved so popular at Collegeville. They used that format to discuss the pastoral as well as preparation for the 1983 Synod of Bishops on the theme of penance.

Bishop Raymond Lessard of Savannah, who led the discussion of penance, laughed after a sparsely attended press conference where a reporter asked how "an outside bishop" felt about the draft pastoral; Lessard had begun his report to the bishops by noting that his topic was not unrelated to the pastoral.

In all, six of the meeting's nineteen hours were formally devoted to the pastoral—not counting references like those in Roach's presidential address. As he had the previous year, Roach confronted a relevant cliché—this time, "The Catholic bishops in the United States are conservative in doctrine and liberal in politics." The cliché, he said, implies "that there is a conflict, even a contradiction, between our doctrine and our view of public issues, as if in the one sphere we were authentically Catholic but not quite American, while in the other we were American enough, but perhaps not entirely Catholic."

He said the bishops are more consistent than either liberal or conservative critics allow: "Indeed, we are usually a good deal more consistent than the critics."

Rejecting "selective reverence for life," he said the bishops' concern with "abortion and the bomb" is grounded in their doctrinal concern for "the sanctity of human life." He went on: "Not to be pro-life is to set oneself against the fundamental good of life and in this way to do moral injury to oneself."

Similarly, he said, "We must also consider whether a particular deterrent strategy, in and of itself, does or does not involve us individually or collectively in an immoral commitment. Not only are there moral limits on what can be done in waging war; there are also moral limits on what can be accepted in the name of deterrence."

Roach's speech was partly a tactical effort to disarm both conservative critics of the bishops' nuclear stand and liberal critics of their abortion stand. One group that wasn't impressed was Catholics for a

Free Choice, a group lobbying for acceptance of the Supreme Court's abortion decisions. CFC jumped on the speech almost immediately, arguing that the nuclear pastoral involved extremely broad consultation, including consultation with people who disagreed with the bishops, and that "no such thoughtful or nuanced consideration of the abortion issue has taken place."

The criticism came from a group not likely to be taken seriously by the bishops, but it was accurate and a sign that the model provided by the war and peace pastoral process had become the standard by which all other major undertakings were to be measured.

Even though the process was technically not new—the bishops have consulted before—it was unprecedented in its broadness and visibility. It set the stage for higher visibility for the upcoming pastoral on capitalism, and Roach said in response to a question at a press conference that it would be used as a model for the pastoral on women's issues launched by the bishops at the 1982 meeting. "We've learned a great deal in doing this pastoral," he said. ". . . We've found the enthusiasm of people with some particular expertise on several sides of the issue to be helpful to us . . . so I think what we've learned here we will translate into other experiences."

Shortly after Roach's speech, the apostolic delegate, Archbishop Pio Laghi, gave his annual talk to the conference. He told the bishops their concern with peace "coincides remarkably well" with the pope's commitment to peace and church doctrine. Laghi praised the bishops' courage in deciding to address the issue. "Given the place of the United States in the world, not only your words, but even your silence would speak eloquently."

He also praised their "prudence" in delaying a final document to allow further debate. "For when the time does come for you to speak," he said, "it is important that you speak with clarity and the greatest possible unanimity. Teaching on these issues which was either muted or fractionalized would not serve the best interests of either the church or the world.

"Perhaps the need for clarity and unanimity will lead to less specific teaching than some would wish. On the other hand, perhaps it will lead to teaching which is more specific than some would like."

Laghi's encouragement was important given the upcoming meeting between the American and European bishops who had been invited to discuss the pastoral at the Vatican. The French and Germans were particularly concerned that the U.S. pastoral's opposition to first use of nuclear weapons would weaken the security of Western Europe. Roach and Bernardin emphasized at the November meeting that while they wanted to talk with the other bishops, they were conscious of the integrity of their own conference and America's unique role in the world. Laghi told the committee privately, "It's your meeting, not their meeting, not a Vatican meeting."

As the Monday morning session broke up, reporters gathered for a press conference with Gumbleton and Reilly that produced two important developments. The first was Reilly's emergence as the "point man" for the committee. He moved right in on a question about the bishops' competence to address the issue.

"I think one of the ways that people who do not agree with what we're saying try to attack the document is by saying the bishops are talking about something they know nothing about," he said. "That happens to be the nuclear bomb, but sometimes it's marriage and family life . . . so I think there's some unfairness in that particular objection. Because if you look around this nation today, I would like to know, who are the experts that can talk to us on this particular matter? Do we turn simply to the politicians, do we turn simply to scientists, do we turn to militarists?"

Reilly was interrupted by applause—some from the press, some from observers who had crowded into the room.

"The bishops," he continued, "speak as moral teachers. And as long as we have someplace to stand on any issue that has a moral dimension, the bishops are going to speak about it, the church is going to speak about it, and we have a right to do it, and thank God we are doing that, so please do not be misled."

The second development was the surfacing of the ambiguity surrounding the second draft's wording. The previous year, Bernardin had caused a stir by saying a retaliatory nuclear strike against civilians was immoral. This year, the questions reflected a shift in the national debate that had already taken place: could the United States, reporters asked, morally retaliate with nuclear weapons against a military target?

"I think that if you read the pastoral closely, it really doesn't answer that question," Reilly replied. ". . . That's still open to further discussion."

Gumbleton, citing the pastoral's emphasis on avoiding limited nuclear war, said he understood the document to bar retaliatory nuclear strikes.

"You see," Reilly added, "what we're entering into here now is interpretation of the document, not necessarily what the document says. . . . Bishop Gumbleton and I are not disagreeing, but we're really at the nub of this whole predicament—in the document itself, and that's what we're talking about, it says the issue at stake is the possibility of a limited nuclear exchange. And then rather than giving principles here, we give a series of questions.

"Can a war really be kept limited? We doubt it, and that's really what Bishop Gumbleton was saying, but we do it in the form of questions."

Bernardin addressed the same general issue in his report to the bishops that afternoon: "We have tried to be sensitive to complexity and ambiguity but not be paralyzed by either." He said the committee was not "totally satisfied as yet with the theoretical argument" on deterrence but was comfortable with its conclusions, including its intention—"to draw a strong, clear line politically and morally against resort to nuclear weapons." He then said the issues needing further work included the elements of possession of nuclear weapons, threat to use them and the "intention which undergirds the policy."

Bernardin said the pastoral should be assessed in terms of both the "process" and the "product." "The process of discussion, writing and witness which already has been generated by the statements of bishops and particularly the pastoral may be the most important long-range consequences of our efforts. The product," he said, referring to the pastoral itself, "should be at once a pastoral guide, a policy statement and a word of hope spoken in the face of fear generated by the nuclear threat."

Bernardin's talk was followed by an extraordinary set of "interventions" from what Roach called "some of our very respected members": Cooke, Hannan, Hunthausen, Krol and Quinn.

Hehir had prepared the list at the staff level, with Bernardin's clearance. The selection was designed to provide a forum for bishops with presumed constituencies and to provide a spectrum of opinion for the press at the start of the meeting.

The five spoke in alphabetical order. Cooke offered somewhat disjointed remarks reflecting his diverse constituencies. For the military, he warned of the draft's potential for divisiveness, urged that the pastoral recognize both the contributions of those in the military and the reality of the communist threat, and called for dialogue with other bishops' conferences "anxious about their own defense."

For his prolife constituency, he said, "A sound theological base, well defined and free from consequentialism and false 'ends justify the means' reasoning is needed."

Cooke slid into urging that savings from slowing the arms race be spent to help the poor without quite calling for such a slowdown. But he also called for the creation of a permanent, international committee with the power to "monitor and verify multi-lateral disarmament" and prevent the outbreak of war. He ended by repeating his comments at the 1980 Synod of Bishops: "Can anyone doubt that in this nuclear age we have reached a crossroads of history, a point of no return, where war is no longer an acceptable alternative."

Hannan began his plea to scrap the pastoral and replace it with the pope's World Day of Peace and U.N. talks by saying, "If I hurt anybody's feelings, I apologize beforehand." He said the pastoral had "so many defects," primarily that it is "minimally concerned with the horrible suffering, physical and spiritual, of those enslaved now by communists and other dictatorships.

"The argument against the threat of using nuclear weapons," he said, "fails to mention the proportionality of the aggression and the oppression right now of the Reds." The pastoral, he argued, ignores the duty to defend Western Europe and the Reagan administration's arms control proposals.

And, he said, "the issuance of the letter now would undercut our present negotiations . . . and the issuance of this letter at the proposed time next year [May] would involve the NCCB directly in a presidential campaign," making "a divisive issue among our people."

Hannan concluded with a parting shot: "I was at a meeting of bishops and theologians this fall, and most of them opposed the document."

The meeting to which he referred was the annual colloquium of bishops and scholars sponsored by the bishops' Doctrine Committee. Commenting on Hannan's description of the meeting, Hickey, the committee chairman, says, "I thought it was peculiar that that's the way he remembered it. It's not the way I recall it."

The meeting offered a balanced discussion similar to that found in Washington archdiocesan settings, Hickey says. Hannan and Frank

Murphy of Baltimore were among the speakers. Fulcher and Gumbleton attended the meeting—which had the highest turnout in the colloquium's history—and challenged Hannan when he complained about staff writing pastorals; the two committee members said every bishop on the committee stood by the document, and Hannan apologized.

Hannan was followed at the bishops' meeting by Hunthausen, offering the starkest contrast of the day. The Seattle archbishop spoke with a soft voice and a frank manner. "To many," he said, "my message seems like foolishness. But to many others and to me, it is simply the gospel of Jesus Christ."

Hunthausen praised much of the pastoral, but said it should say that the strategy of deterrence is "a root cause of the arms race." He went on to say that accepting the gospel "in practice . . . means that we call on our people and our government to begin to lay down our nuclear arms now regardless of what others may do." He urged the bishops to support "noncooperation" with "the millions of acts of cooperation which you and I and our people do today that will make the nuclear holocaust a reality tomorrow."

Krol, speaking "in the hope of perfecting an already very good pastoral letter," called for a stronger attack on the arms race's diversion of resources from the poor and inclusion of a "précis"* that will clarify that the bishops are aware of the Soviet threat and the legitimate right to self-defense.

Just as Cooke must make a bow to his military constituency each time he addresses the issue, Krol must make one toward his, the Eastern European Catholics in America. But the strength of his anticommunist rhetoric makes his position more powerful. When he backed a local freeze referendum in Philadelphia, a reporter asked about the President's charges that freeze supporters were aiding Moscow. Krol smiled and said, "I am not a Soviet front."

"The possession of nuclear weapons does not absolutely and finally commit the possessor to their use," Krol told the bishops. That, he said, is why Pope John Paul II could say deterrence "may still be judged morally acceptable." But, Krol said (as only he could say): "With due deference to His Holiness, I would suggest that we might use a more precise term than 'acceptable,' the word 'tolerable.' Toler-

* Subsequent to the Chicago meeting, the committee changed "précis" to "summary," which it felt was a more accurate description.

ance of an error . . . or an evil, for the sake of a greater good, is an admitted reality. Once you accept something, you make it positive."

After the afternoon session broke up, a reporter obviously new to covering the bishops and equipped with the standard stereotype of Krol asked, "Is this a change in position for you? You're generally regarded as an establishment figure."

Krol stood a little straighter, looked down at the reporter, and said majestically, "I never said that. I'm for the truth. We have to be a witness for the truth." "Oh," the reporter said. "Well, does that represent a change in position for you?"

Krol was followed at the podium by Quinn, who argued that "the strengths of the pastoral far outweigh its weaknesses." He praised the pastoral's recognition of "the utter importance of creating a psychology of peace based on the conviction that peace is really possible." One weakness, he said, was that the pastoral "does not clearly rule out" nuclear retaliation after an attack.

If deterrence is acceptable only when conditions such as serious negotiations are met, he said, "it would be helpful to have some indication of the criteria on which one would make a judgment that the conditions for tolerating deterrence have or have not been fulfilled."

Quinn also called for stronger language on the MX, arguing that experts question its "strictly deterrent utility" and that deployment "could well increase first strike tendencies on both sides of the arms race."

When the speakers concluded, reporters provided an informal applause meter, and the consensus was that Hunthausen had received the most applause, followed by Krol and Quinn in a dead heat, followed by Cooke, with Hannan last, although with more than a merely polite reception.

The reception for Hunthausen was surprising, because if there was one thing certain about the final pastoral, it was that it would not back unilateral nuclear disarmament. Several bishops said the reaction was a sign of personal respect for Hunthausen, who had come to his position prayerfully and who offered it humbly, with respect for those who disagree with him. Reilly, perhaps thinking of some whose approaches don't measure up to Hunthausen's, said the applause level was partly a recognition that Hunthausen wasn't "a hateful pacifist."

After the five presentations, the bishops broke up into small groups to discuss the draft. They worked from an informal survey sheet prepared by a team of "professional facilitators" who set up the discussions without consulting with the Bernardin committee.

After the discussion, the facilitators picked four tables at random to report on their discussions. A quick tally found about thirty bishops polled almost evenly split over the pastoral—a stunning development given earlier talk of widespread support for the pastoral, and a puzzling contrast to the enthusiastic response to Hunthausen.

Bernardin said afterward that he wasn't concerned about the straw vote; it reflected, he said, the committee's own discussions at a similar stage of its work. Reilly in particular dismissed the straw poll, but Tuesday began on a low note for the committee as media coverage focused on the poll and the Hannan-Hunthausen contrast to emphasize division among the bishops.

But the day's major surprise came when the full straw poll was released. It showed 195 bishops in "basic agreement" with the draft, 71 with "major reservations," and only 12 in "basic disagreement." Reporters gathered around Hehir looking for a reaction. He tried to duck an interpretation and finally broke away, saying, "Look, you guys can read the numbers as well as I can."

"The numbers" showed two thirds of the bishops voting—the amount needed for passage—already approving the pastoral. While the vote wasn't definitive, Bernardin was ecstatic—he could see the broad consensus he sought taking shape. It was also clear from conversations with the bishops that many of those with "major reservations" about the draft wanted to make it stronger. The vote was further broken down by category, and a clear pattern was apparent:

On the draft's "socio-political analysis," the vote was 234 in basic agreement, 44 with major reservations, 6 in basic disagreement.

On use of Scripture and Catholic teaching—202, 64, 4.

On theology—141, 114, 2.

On "practical strategies for peace"—191, 68, 3.

On "purpose, tone, style, length, intended audience"—110, 139, 6.

The full straw vote made it clear some major editing and refinement of theology were needed, but it also reflected the bishops' seat-of-the-pants confidence in their basic conclusions and suggested that the final draft could well gather 235 or more votes.

The discussion of the draft took another turn late Tuesday when the bishops were tipped that there would be a surprise for them in the next day's New York *Times*—a leaked letter from William Clark to Bernardin criticizing the second draft.

Clark's letter was only the latest Administration effort either to shape the pastoral as a blessing of U.S. policy or undercut it:

—Two weeks before the meeting, columnists Evans and Novak ran a column claiming that the Administration was pressuring the pope to stop the U.S. bishops from committing "heresy" over the nuclear issue. The column said Bernardin had been summoned to Rome for criticism and that State Department troubleshooter Vernon Walters had met secretly with the pope to urge him to block the pastoral.

The only problem with the column was the facts: Walters' meeting wasn't secret, it was printed with the rest of the pope's schedule in the Vatican daily, *L'Osservatore Romano;* Walters said that while he had mentioned the pastoral, he didn't attempt to pressure the pope; Bernardin's trip to Rome was for a long-scheduled meeting of the Committee on the Synod of Bishops; the only time Bernardin saw the pope was with the rest of the committee. "The only thing I said," Bernardin reported, "was, 'Holy Father, everything is going well in Chicago.' "

—On the opening day of the November meeting, the *Wall Street Journal* ran a lengthy article by Navy Secretary Lehman criticizing the bishops. He said the bishops' recommendations "could lead directly to immoral consequences" and argued, "One cannot complain about the immorality of nuclear war because of its unlimited impact and then oppose the development of a strategy or a technology that seeks to limit its impact."

—The Administration had sought a high-level meeting with the bishops since the second draft was released, but was told the bishops' schedule was too tight to allow for such a meeting. USCC officials suggested a meeting later in the month. The Administration made an exploratory suggestion that the new Secretary of State, George Shultz, would like to address the bishops to defend U.S. policy, but nothing developed, partly because conference policy allows only bishops to address bishops' general meetings.

Administration officials and their supporters had accused the bishops of trying to influence the various freeze referenda on the November ballot by issuing the second draft shortly before the election. (One theologian sympathetic to both the pastoral and the freeze said, "I wish they were that smart.")

Many bishops, including Reilly, and veteran church observers believed—correctly—that the Administration's lobbying would be counterproductive, more likely to make the bishops close ranks than become divided. (Columnist Mary McGrory quoted one unnamed bishop as saying, "Clark? Isn't he the one who didn't know where Europe was a year ago?"—a reference to Clark's total lack of experience in foreign affairs before going to the State Department.)

In his letter, Clark referred to the earlier administration correspondence with the committee and said, "We understood then that our comments would be fully considered by the committee as it continued its important work," suggesting he couldn't understand why the draft hadn't been changed accordingly.

Clark praised the draft's rejection of unilateral disarmament and acceptance of deterrence, and argued that U.S. arms policy had a moral basis compatible with the bishops' position. But he complained that the draft "continues to reflect fundamental misreadings of American policies, and continues essentially to ignore the far-reaching American proposals that are currently being negotiated with the Soviet Union."

The White House distributed copies of the Clark letter and the earlier administration letters at the bishops' meeting on Wednesday. As the bishops gathered for small group discussions that morning, Shaw told O'Connor, "It's your turn" to handle the noon press conference, and read a brief committee response prepared by Bernardin.

But when the full committee gathered, the other members urged Bernardin to hold the press conference, since the letter was addressed to him. (Fulcher notes that Bernardin didn't answer Clark's letter to Clare Boothe Luce because it wasn't addressed to him.)

In the two-paragraph statement, Bernardin called the letter "another link in the dialogue invited" by the committee. "The committee welcomes Mr. Clark's letter," Bernardin said, "although [we were] somewhat surprised to read it first in the New York *Times.*" He said the committee would be glad to talk again with Administration officials, adding, "We . . . are not unfamiliar with the points contained in Mr. Clark's letter."

Bernardin remained typically "calm"—to use one of his favorite words—during the press conference. Patty Edmunds of the *National Catholic Reporter* began a question by saying, "This morning you told some of us that you were not intimidated by the letter. . . ." "That was your word," Bernardin interrupted—calmly. "You asked if I was intimidated, and I said, 'No. . . .'"

Bernardin's aplomb proved a little much for McGrory, who had won a Pulitzer Prize by making issues come alive through people's personal stories and reactions. She asked how Bernardin felt about the President's charge that those supporting the nuclear freeze were tools of the Kremlin.

"I don't think I've been manipulated or duped," Bernardin said. ". . . If we take our signals from anyone," Bernardin said, "it's from the popes."

"But how do you feel about it, Archbishop?" McGrory insisted. "Your loyalty and intelligence have been questioned. . . ."

"Oh, I don't worry about those things," Bernardin replied, to laughter.

"It's inevitable," he said, "that when you discuss matters of this kind, matters that are so important, matters that impinge so greatly upon our well-being, both individually and collectively, there will be a great deal of emotion, a great deal of feeling.

"I think that's all right. It makes the whole process a little more interesting. You have to make sure that you're not swept away by the emotion. You have to keep coming back to the facts and the realities in a very calm and effective way. I'm learning this in my new position in Chicago."

But Bernardin's continued calm was hard for some reporters to take. One, noting that there was a great deal of talk about searching for "the truth" at the meeting, said, "Some of us are looking for substance as well," and pressed for a more detailed response to Clark's charge that the draft reflected "fundamental misreadings" of U.S. policy.

So prodded, Bernardin began to drop the kind of one-liners sure to make reporters' leads. "Obviously, there is a difference of opinion on a number of issues. That's why this exchange has taken place. We will see who is misreading whom in due time."

Asked if he thought Clark was trying to influence American Catholics, Bernardin said, "You'll have to ask the author if that was his intention. All I can conclude, and it's a very simple conclusion, is, obviously, he wanted as much attention for his letter as we are getting for our pastoral. I think he's gotten it."

The bishops got some more publicity—and support—on Wednesday with the release of a public letter signed by twenty experts, including former CIA director William Colby, SALT I negotiator Gerard Smith, SALT II negotiator Paul Warnke, Senator Hatfield and Nobel Prize winner Hans Bethe.

"Before issuing their draft document," it said, "the bishops took council with a substantial number of well-informed civilian and military leaders, and we suspect that as a result, they are better informed technically than most of their critics.

". . . The current draft realistically recognizes that the armed forces of America are essential for the national security. The bishops prudently do not propose that their findings be binding on the individual consciences of those who look to them for guidance. And they explicitly oppose unilateral disarmament."

While reserving judgment on the final pastoral, the letter said, "In the meantime, the undersigned want to express their full support for the bishops' right, in fact their obligation, to speak out on what is unquestionably the most urgent and difficult moral problem that mankind has ever faced. If nuclear war were to come, present silence on their part would be unforgivable."

The letter originated with a discussion between Msgr. Geno Baroni, a veteran activist now working for Archbishop Hickey, and Sargent Shriver after the Evans and Novak column appeared. They felt that Shriver—as George McGovern's running mate and Teddy Kennedy's brother-in-law—might not be the best person to send the letter. They turned to Smith, a Republican, and Colby, who had served Republican administrations. Baroni led the gathering of additional signatures from military, political, scientific and religious leaders.

The bishops also received supportive letters from a group of American Baptists meeting in Washington on the peace issue and from the United Methodist bishops, who said, "We thank God for your courageous witness on behalf of peace with justice." A key figure among the Methodists was Bishop James Armstrong, president of the National Council of Churches, the umbrella group for mainline Protestant and Orthodox organizations. NCC General Secretary Claire Randall signed the Smith letter and issued a short statement of support of her own. In fact, the NCC was preparing a statement for its Governing Board to issue backing the Catholic bishops' final statement.

This support reflected both the ecumenical nature of the new peace movement, particularly at the local level, and marked the first time in

American history that Protestant churches had turned to the Catholic hierarchy for leadership on the peace issue.

The bishops also received several dozen Mailgrams and letters—all but a handful supportive and many from non-Catholics—during their Washington meeting; author Paul Horgan hailed the "moral splendor" of their stand and a group of nuns, borrowing Reagan's slogan for the 1982 midterm elections, urged them to "Stay the Course."

On Thursday morning, attention shifted to the planned two hours of floor discussion, the first opportunity for the body of bishops to comment on the draft pastoral. Tension was heightened slightly by the fact that the bishops' ballroom was honoring a national "Smokeless Thursday" campaign—a few bishops left briefly to take a few puffs at their cigarettes or pipes in the hall outside.

In preparing for the discussion, the committee asked bishops interested in commenting to sign up, indicate the section of the draft they wanted to address and whether their comment would be positive or negative. More than thirty signed up. The committee planned to allow each one two to three minutes to speak. But Roach said he was committed to some discussion from the floor; he allocated half the time for those who had signed up and half for free debate. The committee picked seventeen bishops at random from those who signed up, and Roach seemed to keep the rest in mind as he recognized requests for time from the floor.

In all, more than thirty bishops spoke up; easily 90 percent of them had something substantive to offer to the debate, providing further indication that concern about the issue was both broad and deep within the conference.

A sampling of the discussion shows the range of the comments:

—Auxiliary Bishop Richard Skilba of Milwaukee, president of the Catholic Biblical Association, supported the pastoral's conclusions, but said it used Scripture selectively and didn't integrate it throughout the document.

Then he added a comment sparked by the pastoral's tone. Referring to a "disparity" in the way the church has handled different sections of the Sermon on the Mount, he said, "We have been much more scrupulous about the means of sexuality and marriage than about peace and love of living. Perhaps some of the same political sensitivity must be brought to both areas of life. Those of us who wish to see peace as an ideal beyond the reach of frigid human society must be prepared to view the ideal of marriage with the same respect."

—Several bishops asked for a clear statement on the teaching authority behind the pastoral. Malone said it must have at least a "derivative" binding authority on principles because it restates church teaching.

"If we cannot clearly state certain principles of war and peace and give some examples of how they apply in practice," he asked, "what kind of direction can we really give as shepherds of our flock?"

—Archbishop Oscar Lipscomb of Mobile said the continued existence of the planet was not an absolute good: "Should this world and our species remain in such a way that life in the Father is not possible to the generations that would follow, then we have threatened not just the sovereignty of God over the world, but the victory of Christ over sin and death."

—Bishop Kenneth Untener of Saginaw, Michigan, said he had distributed eighteen thousand copies of the second draft within the diocese. Far from being a source of division, he said, "most people saw it as a moderate document, a document they are proud of." And, he added, "alienated Catholics see in this a call to come home to a church of which they are very proud."

—Bishop McNicholas of Springfield, Illinois, called for a little "flag waving" in the pastoral and asked, "Why are we afraid to say to our people that we love this country even when we criticize its military policies?"

—Bishop Mahony called for an "explicit connection between the world-wide arms race and world hunger and deprivation."

—Archbishop Weakland, Bishop Rosazza, Bishop Lucker and Auxiliary Bishop Joseph M. Sullivan of Brooklyn, echoing Quinn's intervention on Monday, called for some criteria to use in judging the seriousness of U.S. arms control negotiations.

—Archbishop Frank Hurley of Anchorage called the draft's distinction between "possession" of nuclear weapons and "intent" to use them artificial, and called the reference to military chaplains "condescending."

He also said that if the bishops were going to ask the country to express sorrow for the 1945 bombings, "it is even more necessary that we bishops do so first for not having raised our voices then as we have now."

—Walter Sullivan produced a low chuckle by ending his remarks by quoting "a famous American" and urging the committee to "Stay the Course" for peace.

—John Quinn said the second draft had already accomplished one of the bishops' major goals—it had "raised the moral issue in the midst of this public debate" in such a way that it could never again be dismissed.

He also noted that some of the draft's specific conclusions had been questioned by bishops and others, and recalled a "great principle" of Catholic moral analysis: "We do not require metaphysical certitude in order to reach moral conclusions."

As the discussion ended, the bishops voted—with only four "nays" —to hold a special meeting in Chicago May 2 and 3 to discuss the third draft of the pastoral. At his solo press conference, Roach described the vote on the May meeting as support for the draft's direction and "a vote of hope for the passage of the final pastoral."

Asked about comments indicating some bishops don't believe the Administration is serious about arms control, Roach said, "I think that you could probably make a case . . . that there is significantly more effort being made to develop the power capacity—as you equate that with deterrence or military buildup—than there is with the various kinds of energies devoted purely to the peace cause.

"Now, I recognize that people who feel deterrence is the way to go and the only way to go to preserve peace would say that is a peace effort. But I think what these people were saying this morning is that we have become so preoccupied with developing even a language of war and a language of power that we've become almost feeble in developing a language of peace."

Roach noted the ecumenical dimension of the new peace movement.

"One of the things that I think has happened in this war and peace discussion is that because the public discussion has become so, in a sense, grass-rootsy, and because the church was involved in that discussion so early in the game . . . the church has taken, and is now rather comfortable with taking, a very public posture on a very public question as that public discussion and that debate affects public policy.

"I've got a kind of a theory about that, which you may or may not be interested in," he said, "but I think it also may represent a little footstep, a little move ahead in the kind of nice maturing which is going on in the churches, not just in the Catholic Church, but in other churches. It may be one more little step away from the kind of immigrant mentality which I think we've kind of labored with for a long time. . . . We've always known we had something to say, we were just a little cautious, a little tentative, about saying it."

Roach was asked about the controversy over the treatment of deterrence as a "lesser evil."

"That's the heart of the moral issue," he said. ". . . I've really been wrestling with this in my own mind, and I've finally come to the conclusion that ambiguity has been a legitimate, treasured part of the whole moral tradition of the church. It's the way, over a period of time, that we develop moral positions. We tolerate some ambiguity as we go along, and I would have to say that that's the stage where we are in the pastoral right now. I think that ultimately as we wrestle with the ambiguity, ultimately we will come up with more refined, precise teaching."

IX. THIRD DRAFT

On the Monday after the bishops' meeting concluded, *Time* magazine ran a cover story on "God and the Bomb," complete with a painting of Bernardin on the front. The generally favorable story drew negative mail to the magazine, but it also produced a flood of mail to Bernardin.

"About two thirds of it was positive, one third negative," he says. "Of the one third negative, some of the people disagree with some of our conclusions and tell us why. That's very helpful, very constructive. Then you have another segment that says we have no business talking about such matters. . . . Of course, it's a matter of whose ox is being gored. If we were saying what they wanted us to say, we would have not only every right, but every obligation to speak out."

The *Time* cover was only one example of the celebrity status the bishops obtained as a result of the pastoral. Bernardin received a mention in "Doonesbury" in a strip about the cartoon's William Sloane Coffin character writing a pastoral letter on nuclear war.

The bishops even made "Saturday Night Live"; the show's mock news broadcast reported that the bishops were having trouble reconciling their possession that it's all right to possess nuclear weapons with their position that it's not all right to use them; a commentator said that shouldn't be a problem for the bishops, who, after all, have been practicing celibacy for centuries.

The bishops' celebrity status and high visibility on the nuclear issue helped produce a major setback for the Administration's plans for the MX missile in the House. While the bishops didn't lobby as a conference and, for that matter, didn't have an official position, the second draft's reference to the MX, added to the large number of attacks by individual bishops, the passage of most nuclear freeze initiatives in the November elections, and the elections' overall message of opposition to the Reagan arms buildup created the climate for a House vote temporarily blocking funding for the missile.

The Administration continued to give the bishops a high priority. Weinberger called on Archbishop Hickey in Washington to explain the Administration's position. Rowny wrote a letter to Bishop O'Rourke praising an editorial he had written criticizing the second draft.

On December 16, the New York *Times* ran a story by Richard Halloran describing an "intricate minuet" between the Administration and the bishops over the pastoral. He described the Administration's efforts to meet with the bishops during their November meeting and noted that the Bernardin committee had said it was now ready to meet with the Administration. The article also mentioned the French and West German bishops' criticisms of the second draft and noted that the Administration seemed to be looking to the pope to pressure the Americans to back down.

A few days later, an Arizona *Republic* columnist reported that Reagan planned to invite several bishops to the White House to discuss the pastoral, although such a meeting never came off.

The Administration and the Bernardin committee reached a compromise calling for two private meetings. One involved Hehir, Doherty and Russett and Administration officials; then, on the morning of January 7, the second day of its first meeting after November, the committee met with several Administration officials at the State Department.

The day before the State Department meeting, the committee met to discuss the third draft. Bernardin worked from a list of nine questions he had gleaned from the floor discussion at November's meeting: the handling of deterrence, revisions in the Scripture section, the relationship between the just-war tradition and pacifism, how specific the document should be, the right to legitimate self-defense, the document's moral authority, more concrete strategies for peace, guidelines for implementation, and stronger criticism of the Soviet Union and more praise for the American system.

Bernardin said deterrence would be the tough one, but the others would be easy enough to handle. On the question of moral authority, he said, "Let's be a little more careful to distinguish general principles and their application."

Casey volunteered to consult with Bishop Skilba on Scripture; Hehir, Doherty and Russett were to work on the section on deterrence, Gumbleton on strategies for peace, O'Connor on the just-war tradition and pacifism, Russett on superpower relations and Reilly and Fulcher on pastoral implementation.

At this meeting, the committee also approved Bernardin's response to a December 15 letter from twenty-four Catholic congressmen—twenty-two Republicans and two Democrats, none regarded as movers and shakers—led by Republican Representative Henry Hyde of Illinois, sponsor of the amendment restricting federal funds for abortion.

Hyde, a right-to-life hero, had earlier challenged the bishops' opposition to the death penalty, claiming support for the death penalty was the real right-to-life position. He again led the right-to-life charge against the bishops on the nuclear question.

"Our real threat," the letter said, "is not embodied in weapons—however gruesome modern weapons might become. Our real threat comes from an ideology that challenges our fundamental faith in human dignity. Forgive us if we speak too bluntly, but we do so because we take your Excellencies' efforts with the utmost gravity and respect. But we would expect the view that no values are worth defending if a nuclear war might ensue to be espoused by materialists—those who are at best agnostic about the existence of the immortal soul and the nature of good and evil. When we read such pessimism from some of our bishops who are dedicated to the propagation of the faith, we cannot but wonder, 'What faith?'

"In all the burgeoning literature of apocalypse surrounding this issue, we have never encountered such a startling statement as the second draft contains, when it says: 'Today the destructive potential of the nuclear powers threatens the sovereignty of God over the world he has brought into being. We could destroy his work.' The notion that mere creatures could do anything to 'threaten the sovereignty of God over the world' strikes us as one definition of original sin."

Bernardin answered Hyde a month later and subtly, but neatly, turned the tables, implying that Hyde and his colleagues were guilty of one charge leveled against the bishops—letting the ends justify the means. He noted that the committee had already considered the points raised in the letter and was as aware as the congressmen of the difference in "ends" of the United States and the Soviet Union.

But, Bernardin wrote, "Catholic ethics, which has always been concerned with questions pertaining to means, must ask whether all means and measures presently contained in the arsenals of the superpowers could be used even to resist the end we know is possible in the world today."

Bernardin noted that Hyde had quoted Pope Pius XII: "There are human goods of so high an order that immense sacrifices may have to be borne in their defense." The same pope, speaking of the right to self-defense, Bernardin wrote, said, "When the damages caused by war are not comparable to those of 'tolerated injustice,' one may have a duty to 'suffer the injustice.' "

"The tensions expressed by Pope Pius XII between the right of a state to legitimate self-defense and the limitations imposed on that right by an 'ethic of means' has been intensified in the thirty years since he spoke," Bernardin wrote.

Bernardin's diplomatic response hit at the heart of the right-wing opposition to the bishops' stand on nuclear war—the critics placed no limits on what they would do to prevent Soviet domination.

Several times during the meeting on the sixth, O'Connor was called to the phone. During dinner, he took a call from the Pentagon and announced that that evening the chairman of the Joint Chiefs of Staff would make a speech of interest to the bishops; he repeated a sentence saying it wasn't U.S. policy to attack civilian populations per se, although the others didn't offer much reaction.

U.S. targeting policy was a concern to Bernardin and was the issue to be discussed the next morning at the State Department. Before the group went to Foggy Bottom, O'Connor said his sources had told him the bishops wouldn't get precise targeting plans but U.S. "targeting philosophy."

The committee and the others met with a group which included Robert McFarlane, deputy assistant to the President for national security affairs, Joseph Lehman of the Arms Control and Disarmament Agency, Ronald Lehman of the Defense Department and Elliot Abrams, head of the State Department's Human Rights Office.

Bernardin came right to the point: what was the fundamental misreading of American policy Clark had described?

The reply was that the bishops apparently thought it was U.S. policy to target civilian populations, but it wasn't policy to target civilians per se. But the Administration officials said civilian casualties from attacks on military and industrial targets would be high. Russett noted that there were forty military targets in Moscow alone.

"The end result may be the same," Bernardin said.

The other point emphasized by McFarlane in particular was that the President was thoroughly committed to arms control and disarmament. While Reagan had never been seen as deeply committed on the issue, several incidents had intensified concern.

In December, the new Soviet premier, Yuri Andropov, had made a counteroffer to the U.S. "zero-zero" option plan in Europe—lowering the number of Soviet medium-range missiles to the number of French and English missiles in exchange for nondeployment of the U.S. Pershing II missiles in Europe and reducing long-range missiles and bombers by 25 percent if the U.S. cut by 10 percent.

Reagan dismissed the offer as one-sided and a propaganda ploy. Some of the sharpest criticism of that decision came in a homily delivered by Cardinal Krol at his World Day of Peace Mass on January 1. If Andropov's offer was a propaganda ploy, Krol asked, "did not the out-of-hand rejection concede to him a propaganda victory?"

Krol offered a course in elementary diplomacy, noting that it's normal for each side's first offer to be tilted in its favor; but, he said, "every offer should be explored and made the basis for a serious dialogue." He asked whether "so-called 'doctrinaire cold warriors' in the Administration are delaying serious dialogue for disarmament and peace until after the United States achieves military parity or superiority."

Not long after the Bernardin committee met at the State Department, Administration arms control policy was thrown into further confusion when ACDA director Rostow was fired and Paul Nitze, negotiator for the Intermediate-Range Nuclear Forces talks, criticized for seeming to back away from the zero-zero option. The situation was further complicated by Reagan's choice of Kenneth Adelman to succeed Rostow. The thirty-six-year-old aide to U.N. Ambassador Jeane Kirkpatrick, Adelman had earlier called arms control negotiations a "sham."

The next hurdle for the War and Peace Committee was a consultation in Rome with Vatican officials and bishops from France, West Germany, Great Britain, Belgium, Italy and the Netherlands. The pastoral got a boost in early January when the pope elevated a new group of cardinals—including Bernardin. The conventional church wisdom was that if the U.S. pastoral was way off base, that wouldn't have happened.

Hehir worried about the meeting; at any given point throughout the two-year process, Hehir was the most pessimistic figure among those involved. It was part of his job to spot obstacles to completing the project, but friends say he's a worrier by nature. He envisioned a scenario for the Vatican meeting in which the pope and Casaroli called Roach and Bernardin aside and told them to cool it, especially on no-first-use, because of problems it would create for the French and German bishops with their governments.

When the meeting actually took place, the tone was cordial and "collegial." Roach says some of the European bishops praised the Americans for their courage in addressing the issue. Roach and Bernardin added in a memo to the rest of the committee that "the Holy See also complimented the NCCB on its pastoral concern for this problem and the courage and humility to agree to this open exchange in Rome."

Roach and Bernardin each made a statement at the meeting, describing the pastoral's genesis and the process used; Bernardin summarized the latest draft and the changes that were being made as a result of the November bishops' meeting. In summarizing the draft, Bernardin said it called for the "immediate cessation" of the arms race. Both men emphasized that while they could not develop the pastoral in isolation, they also could not abdicate their specific responsibility as American bishops. They also both argued that the American bishops felt it was necessary to make specific policy and pastoral recommendations in order to have their pastoral letter understood, or even heard.

Much of the Vatican discussion revolved around the American bishops' concept of a pastoral letter. They had a tradition of addressing specific issues as well as general principles in pastorals, but in the European tradition, pastorals deal with principles only. Vatican officials and some European bishops were concerned that the U.S. bishops' specific recommendations would be seen as binding church principles that differed from those of the universal church.

Msgr. Jan Schotte, secretary of the Vatican Justice and Peace Commission, gave an overview of comments the Vatican had received on the pastoral. Casaroli made some general comments about the pope's U.N. speech and deterrence. Casaroli said that at the level of applying moral principles to deterrence, "one must deal with true principles in the moral order," and not technical issues, and must deal with principles that are "certain, surely and gravely binding."

Speaking of the teaching authority of bishops and episcopal conferences, Casaroli said, "In the latter, there can easily appear majority and minority opinions, even on doctrinal points, or at least in regard to the application of doctrine to concrete cases and situations even where the principles are accepted by everyone."

It was this last point that apparently served as the basis for a *National Catholic Reporter* article which said the implication of Casaroli's remarks was that national bishops' conferences "are free to go further than Vatican pronouncements or to disagree with recent papal statements." The article continued: "Some Catholics might interpret Casaroli's gesture as precedent-setting. They might even begin to pressure their national conferences to march ahead of or fall behind Rome on abortion, women's ordination or liberation theology."

At Bernardin's behest, Hoye issued a press release attacking "inaccurate reports" on the January 18–19 meeting, partly to assure the Vatican that the American bishops hadn't been the source of the story. Hoye said anyone who could interpret Casaroli's remarks that way "was not present at the meeting."

"It is true," Hoye said, "that episcopal conferences were told they are free to expand on Vatican pronouncements on peace. It is consistent with the nature of the church to expect bishops in their own country to apply principles articulated in papal teaching to local conditions. One should expect this to happen."

In their January 25 memo to the committee, Roach and Bernardin outlined the major areas of discussion and the steps the committee needed to take because of them; they noted that almost all the questions raised had been raised by the American bishops earlier.

First, they said, the committee would have to make clear what was a binding general principle and what was a specific application. "Father Hehir presented an analysis of how the NCCB saw the different levels of authority in the letter and Cardinal Joseph Ratzinger (Prefect of The Sacred Congregation for the Doctrine of the Faith), when asked by Cardinal Bernardin, indicated his tentative agreement with the analysis."

Roach and Bernardin said the work already being done by the committee on Scripture would take care of the questions raised and that questions raised on theology could be handled by rephrasing a few paragraphs. (Ratzinger was concerned about a few phrases he felt didn't distinguish clearly enough between the eschatological peace of salvation and the possibility of peace on earth.)

They emphasized an expected concern about the relationship between the just-war tradition and pacifism. There aren't two traditions, Schotte had said; there is the just-war tradition within which pacifism is a legitimate option for individuals, not governments.

Then Roach and Bernardin summed up the discussion about no-first-use and deterrence:

No First Use: While differences of view on the specific question exist between some European conferences and NCCB (as we had known prior to the Rome meeting) the specific concerns of the Rome meeting can be met by making two points about first use: (1) This is a section of the pastoral where the bishops are making concrete applications of principles involving specific prudential judgments and this should be made clear; (2) there should be a recognition that the implementation of a "No First Use" pledge will take time, cannot be done immediately and will require specific changes in NATO strategic doctrine and planning.

On deterrence, Roach and Bernardin said the Americans must make clear that the pastoral's commentary on the pope's U.N. speech is their own.

"Finally," they said, "the specific conclusions we have drawn about deterrence policy (page 58, line 7 through page 60, line 25)"—the section including the three criteria and specific recommendations, including the freeze—"were not questioned, criticized or addressed. These can remain, but again, they are to be acknowledged as specific conclusions and have the moral authority proper to such judgments."

Although it wasn't mentioned in the memo, the Rome meeting also reinforced the view of the American bishops who had called for stronger criticism of the Soviet Union.

At the end of the meeting, Roach, Bernardin and Hoye met with the pope, but they discussed other conference business and the pastoral wasn't mentioned.

The pope did discuss the pastoral, however, in an hour-long lunch with Bernardin during the consistory. His major concern was that different national hierarchies not appear divided on moral principles, particularly since some people were already trying to use the debate for the wrong ends. Bernardin said the American bishops wouldn't rest with general principles, but would have to make their own moral analysis and deal in specifics. John Paul generally didn't ask for specific changes; he said he was concerned that the church not be seen as pacifist and that he knew the Americans weren't calling for unilateral disarmament. The pope said the Soviets didn't subscribe to the same moral principles as the church, but he emphasized the need for both superpowers to come together.

The pope told Bernardin that taking care of the pastoral letter was his—Bernardin's—responsibility.

When Bernardin returned from Rome, he was concerned about the publicity the second draft had received and the impact it would have on the reception of the third draft. "We're out there in full view," he said. "Every change that's made now is going to have to be explained. Why did you go from this point to that point? Once a document has become so well known, changes that are in themselves relatively insignificant can take on major proportions in terms of the perception of other people."

Bernardin also noted that so much of the publicity had focused on the freeze: "The document was one hundred and five pages long and the nuclear freeze was in one paragraph, and it was there in a rather nuanced way."

When the committee met again February 17, Hoye sat in as Bernardin described the Vatican meeting and his consistory visits. Reilly asked if it was necessary to wait for Schotte's summary of the meeting before proceeding. Bernardin said it wasn't; he'd already talked with the pope, Casaroli and Ratzinger, and the Schotte memo was "only a staff report. . . . We have to go on the information we have now. I don't feel uneasy."

After the review, the committee discussed and accepted Hehir's draft on the document's moral authority and Casey's revision of the Scripture section. Then it turned to the section on deterrence, which had become a bigger problem than it had ever been.

O'Connor, assigned to revise the section on just war and pacifism, had ignored the second draft's framework and completely redone the section on deterrence. He sent Bernardin a forty-seven-page redraft with a cover letter saying: "It essentially reflects the position that in conscience I believe we must take. As always, I hope I am completely open to discussion and improvement. In integrity, however, I am not sure that I can deviate far from the basic position I attempt to express herein. And in honesty I must observe that I believe the format, structure and style of the enclosure better suit the issues treated than does the section in the Second Draft as currently presented."

The others interpreted O'Connor's letter as an implied threat to at least dissent, possibly resign, if he didn't get his way. (In an interview in November, O'Connor said that if he ever came to a point where he couldn't reconcile his concerns within the committee, he would ask Bernardin and Roach whether they wanted to replace him or have a minority report.) Russett told Hehir that if the committee accepted O'Connor's draft, he would resign, and not quietly.

O'Connor's draft left out the key section of specifics on deterrence that was at the heart of the second draft, as well as the no-first-use section. And while the draft included condemnation of indiscriminate and disproportionate use of nuclear weapons and warnings about the danger of escalation, it gave at least as much weight to finding possible uses of nuclear weapons:

> The danger of escalation and the uncontrollability that goes with it clearly makes offensive nuclear warfare immoral, but it is not at all clear that such danger outlaws a nuclear defense against nuclear aggression. Or if it does, it would outlaw an effective defense with conventional weapons as well, since this would provoke a continuation of the nuclear attack, the danger of escalation, etc. The only alternative would be obligatory surrender. Besides being highly questionable, this would make papal and conciliar insistence on the right to self-defense meaningless.

None of the intrigue was mentioned during the meeting itself. Gumbleton had also done a redraft of the deterrence section. Bernardin said that both drafts contained some good material but couldn't be integrated into the existing framework. He said O'Connor had left out things the committee had already accepted.

Bernardin said he thought the second draft had moved a little too far to the left and needed to be moved back toward center, giving the U.S. more credit and firming up the just-war-pacifism section. Now, he said, "my concern is that John has moved too far to the right and Tom too far to the left."

Gumbleton conceded his draft went beyond what the majority might accept; he said he was willing to give and take and noted that sections of his draft could be worked into the existing framework.

O'Connor argued that his writing style was better than that of the draft; he stepped up his criticism of the references to the freeze, the

MX and no-first-use, arguing that the media focused on them and created problems for the bishops.

He particularly criticized the proposed new freeze language—suggested by Russett—which broadened the coverage from "strategic" to "nuclear" weapons systems. That change, he said, would block the development of smaller, more accurate, less deadly nuclear weapons; despite the pastoral's emphasis on avoiding steps that blur the distinction between conventional and nuclear weapons, O'Connor consistently backed the production of nuclear weapons which he said could be both discriminating and proportionate.

Bernardin said the third draft had to contain no-first-use; he'd just cleared it with Rome. He said he wasn't wedded to mentioning the MX, because it had just been used as an example. The committee later agreed to drop the reference to the MX from the text and move it into a footnote, adding the Pershing II, and saying many experts see them as first-strike weapons.

"More problematic is the question of the freeze," Bernardin said, "precisely because of the attention given it by the media—the 'pastoral on the freeze,' some people call it. We have to say something about it. Over half the bishops have endorsed the freeze. We were not mandated to omit it."

O'Connor saw daylight in Bernardin's response and asked if he could propose alternative wording; Bernardin said it would have to be done carefully. For the rest of the afternoon and evening, O'Connor argued with the others, offering a relentless attack on the second draft. The others insisted that the bishops expected them to be working from that draft and defended specific sections. "We don't want everything up for grabs," Reilly said.

The committee began working with O'Connor's draft, looking for sections to incorporate in the next revision. When they got to a section in which O'Connor had explained the relationship of pacifism and the just-war tradition by using the analogy of celibacy and marriage, Reilly asked, "Can we drop that?" They did.

During the lengthy discussions, Bernardin revealed a result of the Vatican meetings that hadn't come up before: the committee couldn't commit church teaching to a condemnation of any conceivable use of nuclear weapons, because the church hadn't already done so. "In terms of wanting to be severe critics, we can go as far as we want if we are speaking for ourselves, as long as we make it clear," he said. "The same point on deterrence. We don't say it's intrinsically evil, but beyond certain limits we can't go, and we say so."

The next morning, Bernardin began by announcing that it was time to put everything in the hands of one writer—Hehir—using the second-draft framework. He said the committee would spend the day deciding what he should use from the O'Connor and Gumbleton drafts; at the end of the day, Hehir would summarize his understanding of what he was to do.

When the committee was addressing U.S. targeting policy, O'Connor announced that he had raised three questions privately with Weinberger and distributed copies of a letter he had received from him.

As the discussion dragged on, O'Connor again focused on the freeze language. He proposed changing the call for a "halt" to the testing, production and deployment of strategic weapons to a call for a "curb." "This is crucial for me," he said, complaining that by using specifics the committee was "opening up a Pandora's Box."

Bernardin said he sensed that, for the first time, they had reached a point where they didn't have a consensus. He favored going with the existing language and candidly telling the bishops that there was dissent within the committee, adding, "We've got a Pandora's Box in any case."

Bernardin again said that Hehir would consider O'Connor's draft in rewriting. "My absolute minimum," O'Connor said, "is that the drafter take my proposals into serious consideration." "We asked him to do that," Bernardin said.

The committee agreed to meet again on March 8 and 9. On March 1, Doherty and Hehir gave a briefing on the Vatican meeting to about 130 diocesan justice and peace directors in Washington for their annual meeting with the USCC.

While most of those present were more involved with poverty issues and community organizing, there was broad support for the pastoral. "Who would ever have thought," one veteran activist said, "that we'd be sitting around trying to figure out how to catch up with the bishops."

The directors sent an informal delegation to Hoye to ask for the USCC to set up a temporary clearinghouse for information to help dioceses implement the pastoral. Hoye said an in-house committee studying implementation was already looking at that and that he expected an answer in a few weeks.

When Hehir spoke, several people noted a massive letter-writing campaign against the pastoral aimed at the bishops and asked if it would help if they generated letters of support. Hehir said it would, but added, "At this point, I don't think it would be useful to tell the bishop 'I wanted you to go three miles and you only went two' when he's hearing from people saying 'you went two miles when I only wanted you to go a half.'"

A few days later, Archbishop Laghi sent the committee the summary of the Vatican meeting prepared by Schotte, noting that it would ultimately be sent to all the bishops. The memo summarized the meeting, sometimes in a biting tone.

Schotte noted that bishops' conferences do not have a mandate to teach—only local bishops and all the bishops in concert with the pope have that. He quoted Casaroli's comments and reported that participants made comments like these:

1. When bishops propose the doctrine of the church, the faithful are bound in conscience to assent. A serious problem arises on the pastoral level when bishops propose opinions based on the evaluation of technical or military factors. The faithful can be confused, their legitimate freedom of choice hindered, the teaching authority of bishops lessened and the influence of the church in society thus weakened.
2. When differing choices are equally justifiable, bishops should not take sides. Rather they should offer several options or express themselves hypothetically.

The memo weighed heavily on the minds of many of those gathered for the March 8 meeting. O'Connor insisted on a page-by-page comparison of Hehir's new draft to his own, and the day dragged on.

O'Connor continued to press for substantive changes in sections he had either already agreed to or written himself in the first place—including language on no-first-use. While he was always vocal in denigrating the bishops' competence to speak out on technical issues, he also frequently drew on his own military background to talk about specific weapons systems. And while he opposed using specifics in the text because he didn't want it to be political, it was obvious that dropping specifics would be seen as political.

That evening, after O'Connor left the group to make another appointment, the others worried over the Schotte memo, which Bernardin had earlier dismissed as a "staff report." On one hand, Bernardin still felt secure in his understanding of his conversations with Ratzinger, Casaroli and the pope. On the other hand, there was concern that if the Vatican sent the Schotte memo to the bishops close to the time of the May meeting and if O'Connor jumped ship over specifics in the pastoral, the document could be in real trouble. (At this point, Gumbleton says, if the committee had gutted the pastoral of specifics, he would have said "No thank you" and quit.)

Hehir was particularly upset by the memo; he recalled that Casaroli had said at a press conference at the U.N. in June that the church shouldn't get involved in the freeze issue, even though he didn't say it again at the Vatican meeting. Hehir was also worried by the Schotte memo's quoting of Casaroli emphasizing the need to deal with "moral principles" when dealing with deterrence, although this was merely from the Casaroli talk at the Vatican meeting which they had already heard and of which they already had a transcript. Bernardin and Hehir felt that with the Schotte memo, they had to give O'Connor something to keep him from dissenting. Hehir said "curb" was the best they could get; most of the others agreed to give O'Connor "curb" to save the other specifics in the deterrence section.

The next morning, Bernardin arrived with a brilliant strategy for handling the Schotte memo—in effect, a preemptive first strike. He and Roach would get permission from Laghi to send the Schotte memo to the American bishops themselves. They would also send their own memo on the meeting and a cover letter explaining that they were confident that they had met all of the Vatican's concerns. It was clear that the memo would be leaked as soon as it was distributed; the theory was "better early than late."

When the discussion came to the freeze language again, O'Connor pushed for "curb" and a deal was struck. The remaining three specifics were kept, although O'Connor immediately tried to get more changes in those passages. He finally agreed to language calling for an early, successful conclusion to negotiations for the Comprehensive Test Ban Treaty. He had wanted to call for "a" comprehensive test ban and development treaty. There was no such thing, and the statement would have pulled the bishops out of the debate over the existing reality, the Reagan administration's abandonment of that treaty process.

As far as the freeze was concerned, "curb" was a respectable-sounding word that had solid church roots—the Second Vatican Council talked of "curbing the savagery of war." And it was argued that the change was also more realistic—any "freeze" that came about would have to be negotiated and would take time.

But the committee was ultimately trying to have it both ways—to make the call for a generic freeze less specific to placate O'Connor and to argue that it hadn't changed. The third draft eventually ran twenty-five thousand words, and O'Connor had found the one word that would change the interpretation of the entire document in a politically charged, media-heavy climate. The dictionary difference between a "halt" and a "curb" was the difference between a "freeze" and a "chill."

One reason O'Connor won on this point was the internal dynamics of the committee itself. As the bishops continued to grapple with their day-to-day responsibilities, the long committee process became a drain. The further away the committee got from November, the more it seemed to become a world of its own, more and more isolated from the consensus the bishops had shown in November and more and more absorbed with the committee itself. Within this framework, the need to keep O'Connor within a consensus assumed far greater proportion than the influence of O'Connor—who had lost approximately 250–6 in opposing the 1981 statement on Central America—within the whole conference would merit.

And, ironically, the "curb" deal was cut on the day the New York *Times* said in a front-page story on the President's speech to the National Association of Evangelicals that White House aides had said that his call for the evangelicals to avoid setting themselves above the battle and treating the United States and the Soviet Union as moral equals was a slap at the Catholic bishops.

Reagan's use of the speech to imply that freeze supporters were un-Christian as well as un-American came at about the same time Vice-President Bush and Secretary of State Shultz had made comments raising questions about the connection between the Catholic Church and Marxism in Central America. Roach eventually met with Bush to ease tensions; Bush did an interview with *Our Sunday Visitor* in which he made news by saying it was possible to disagree with Administration policy on Central America or the freeze and still be a good American.

The committee process still wasn't complete, however. The committee was supposed to finish up by March 15, but O'Connor's proposed changes dragged on. His proposals consistently left the door open for limited use of nuclear weapons and gave the Administration every possible benefit of the doubt.

A final meeting was scheduled for Chicago on March 21, the day before the bishops' Administrative Committee was to meet in Washington; that committee had to have a final draft in hand to approve its transmittal to the bishops. Reilly had to miss the unexpected meeting in Chicago because he had already scheduled an important Mass for that day. Weather was bad in Chicago—Gumbleton arrived late and Fulcher had to leave early.

O'Connor arrived with yet another stack of proposed changes— sixty "nonessential" changes and forty-eight "changes with a substantial impact." The committee went over them for clarification, but didn't deal with them. Bernardin called another meeting for two days later in Washington when the whole committee could be present to wrap things up. After O'Connor had left, Bernardin asked Russett, "Was there any more I could have done?" Russett said, "No."

When Reilly, a member of the Administrative Committee, arrived in Washington Tuesday, he was surprised to see Bernardin, who told him there was another meeting the next day. That meeting ran smoothly, although it took from nine in the morning until six in the evening. The others gave O'Connor as many changes as they could without gutting the draft, which finally reached the Administrative Committee at the last possible minute.

At the final go-around on the freeze language, O'Connor changed once again. Even with "curb," he couldn't accept it because it included "testing." But the others stayed with "curb," partly because they had already said they could accept it and partly because Bernardin, while not opposing a freeze, had had some serious questions about it. They did, however, change "strategic" to "nuclear," a major strengthening of the section—as long as "curb" wasn't interpreted as a retreat from the freeze.

Some of the changes O'Connor had proposed on Monday amounted to a claim that Vatican II had not endorsed conscientious objection; on Wednesday, Gumbleton was prepared with a two-page memo that countered O'Connor's, and no changes were made.

The last meeting on the third draft finally ended on the same note as the last meetings on the first and second drafts: the committee agreed unanimously to forward the pastoral to the bishops, with the note that not every member agreed with every sentence. O'Connor had made it clear that he would dissent on the freeze, no-first-use and parts of conscientious objection, but, as all through the process, no one could predict what O'Connor would do next.

During the November discussion, one bishop said he hoped the third draft would be as great an improvement over the second as the second was over the first. All in all, it was. It was still overly long—it ran 150 pages—and parts of O'Connor's work that had been grafted on often provided a clash of tone. But each succeeding draft reflected both political and ecclesiastical reality better than what had gone before; the third draft acknowledged criticisms and responded to them well, at times by strengthening its original point.

In response to a number of requests, the committee put together an eight-page précis of the document. "That's so the New York *Times* gets it right," Hehir had told the diocesan social action directors.

An expanded introduction dealt with the moral authority question right away:

> In this pastoral letter, we address many concrete questions concerning the arms race, contemporary warfare, weapons systems and negotiating strategies. We do not intend that our treatment of each of these issues carry the same moral authority as our statement of universal moral principles and formal Christian teaching. Indeed, we stress here at the beginning that not every statement in this letter has the same moral authority. At times we reassert universally binding moral principles (e.g., non-combatant immunity). At still others we reaffirm statements of recent popes and the teaching of Vatican II. Again, at other times, we apply moral principles to specific cases.
>
> When making applications of these principles we realize—and we wish readers to recognize—that prudential judgments are involved based on specific circumstances which can change or which can be interpreted differently by people of good will (e.g., "No First Use"). We shall do our best to indicate, stylistically and substantively, whenever we make such applications.

The scriptural section was more comprehensive, with, as Ratzinger wanted, a deeper sense of Jesus as Messiah and of a distinction between peace on earth and "eschatological peace." It dealt more explicitly with the image of the "warrior God" in the Old Testament, noting it came from a small, oppressed people and provided them with

a sense of security; they had a God who would protect them even in the face of overwhelming obstacles. . . . The images of war and the Warrior God became less dominant as a more profound and complex understanding of God is presented in the texts.

The theological section, which began with nonviolence in the second draft, now began with a strong assertion of a nation's right to legitimate self-defense:

The Christian has no choice but to defend peace, properly understood, against aggression. This is an inalienable obligation. It is the how of defending peace which offers moral options. . . . The Council and the popes are explicit, consistent and definitive concerning the obligations of governments. A government threatened by armed, unjust aggression must defend its people. This includes defense by armed force if necessary as a last resort.

In the discussion of the just-war tradition, the just-revolution paragraph, taken from O'Connor's work, took on a snide tone:

Some who normally argue that no war can ever be justified seem to exempt certain "wars of liberation" from this prohibition and even support and praise wars waged by revolutionary forces, while denying established governments the right to wage wars against revolutionaries. Such a position is clearly unacceptable. While the legitimacy of revolution in some circumstances cannot be denied, Just War teachings must be applied as rigorously to revolutionary-counterinsurgency conflicts as to others. The issue of who constitutes competent authority and how much authority is exercised is essential.

The just-war section had been expanded with the addition of another O'Connor passage which added a whole new category to the teaching—"comparative justice." The passage was at best redundant, given the presumption that the issue is defense against unjust aggression to begin with. It concluded:

The facts simply do not support the comparisons made at times, even in our own society, between our way of life, in which most human rights are at least recognized even if they are not adequately supported, and those totalitarian and tyrannical regimes in which such rights are either denied or systematically oppressed.

The section on nonviolence, at the Vatican's request, didn't trace a pacifist tradition from church fathers through Francis of Assisi to Dorothy Day and Martin Luther King, Jr.; but it mentioned the last three, saying Day and King had had "a profound impact upon the life of the Church in the United States."

The section on modern warfare continued the second-draft theme of building barriers to nuclear war. The section condemning use of nuclear weapons against civilians remained. The section subtitled "The Initiation of Nuclear War" reflected the agreements reached in Rome. It emphasized that this was an application of principle, not binding principle, and acknowledged that it would take time to develop new NATO policies to allow for a no-first-use pledge. The language was also softened slightly. "We abhor the concept of initiating nuclear war on however restricted a scale," the draft said, calling it "an unjustifiable moral risk" and "an unacceptable moral risk."

The section on limited nuclear war was strengthened, partly by the introduction of another just-war criterion—the requirement of a reasonable hope for success:

> We must ask whether such a reasonable hope can exist once nuclear weapons have been exchanged. The burden of proof remains on those who assert that meaningful limitation is possible.

The section also added a paragraph on the "ethics of means" issue addressed in Bernardin's letter to Henry Hyde:

> A nuclear response to either a conventional or nuclear attack can cause destruction which goes far beyond "legitimate self-defense." In such a case, the use of nuclear weapons would not be justified.

In discussing deterrence, the draft dealt explicitly with Administration criticisms. It quoted a letter Clark had sent Bernardin on January 15, shortly after the committee met with Administration officials:

> For moral, political, and military reasons, the United States does not target the Soviet civilian population as such. There is no deliberately opaque meaning conveyed in the last two words. We do not threaten the existence of Soviet civilization by threatening Soviet cities. Rather, we hold at risk the warmaking capability of the Soviet Union—its armed forces, and the industrial capacity to sustain war. It would be irresponsible for us to issue policy statements which might suggest to the Soviets that it would be to their

advantage to establish privileged sanctuaries within heavily populated areas. . . .

During the Administration's exchanges with the bishops over deterrence policy, officials often created the impression that they wanted the bishops' *Good Housekeeping* Seal of Approval because of U.S. targeting policy; they didn't get it.

The draft said that while U.S. policy met the test of "discrimination," it must still face the test of "proportionality."

A narrow adherence exclusively to the principle of non-combatant immunity as a criterion for policy is an inadequate moral posture, for it ignores some evil and unacceptable consequences. Hence, we cannot be satisfied that the assertion of an intention not to strike civilians directly, or even the most honest effort to implement that intention, by itself constitutes a "moral policy" for the use of nuclear weapons.

A few pages later, the draft used a strong passage that had, ironically, come from O'Connor's draft:

It would be a perverted political policy or moral casuistry which tried to justify using a weapon which "indirectly" or "unintentionally" killed a million innocent people because they happened to live near a "militarily significant target."

The committee tried to deal with the "consequentialism" charge primarily by dropping the reference to deterrence as a "sinful situation" and emphasizing the judgment, based on the pope's U.N. talk, of strictly conditioned moral acceptance. At O'Connor's urging, the 1976 pastoral's reference to the threat to use nuclear weapons and the Krol testimony were vaguely mentioned, but not quoted. (Ironically, when the Americans asked about consequentialism at the Vatican consultation, no one responded—it wasn't exactly a major concern.)

The draft repeated the three criteria for evaluating deterrence used in the second draft, strengthening the language somewhat to say that efforts to develop war-fighting capability and so on "are not acceptable"; the second draft said "must be resisted."

The section on specific proposals, at O'Connor's urging, said the bishops "resist"—the second draft said "oppose"—deployment of likely first-strike weapons. It added a line opposing deployment of such weapons by the Soviets and cited the MX and Pershing II in a footnote.

The proposals recommended by the bishops included the new freeze language and the Comprehensive Test Ban Treaty. The section calling for deep bilateral reductions in nuclear arsenals acknowledged that that was the goal of the START talks and the talks on Intermediate-Range Nuclear Forces but added, at Russett's request, "Our hope is that they will be pursued in a manner which will realize these goals."

The section expanded the fourth recommendation in the second draft, now calling for

removal by all parties of short-range nuclear weapons which multiply dangers disproportionate to their deterrent value [and] removal by all parties of nuclear weapons from areas where they are likely to be overrun in the early stages of war, thus forcing rapid and uncontrollable decisions on their use.

Any claim, by any government, that it is pursuing a morally acceptable policy of deterrence must be scrutinized with the greatest care. We are prepared and eager to participate in our country in the on-going public debate on moral grounds.

The section on superpower relations, acknowledging criticisms from U.S. and European bishops as well as the Vatican, offered a much sharper criticism of Soviet society but also said "the irreducible truth is that objective mutual interests do exist between the superpowers," the most important being the avoidance of nuclear war.

The section criticized U.S. support for repressive governments and "repugnant covert operations," but said:

A glory of the United States is the range of political freedom its system permits us. We, as bishops, as Catholics, as citizens, exercise those freedoms in writing this letter, with its share of criticisms of our government. We have true freedom of religion, freedom of speech and access to a free press. We do not imagine that we could exercise the same freedom in contemporary Eastern Europe or the Soviet Union. Free people must always pay a proportionate price and run some risks—responsibly—to preserve their freedom.

One of the major changes in the section on pastoral practice was an expanded section on "Reverence for Life," particularly abortion. Bernardin had been piqued by Catholics for a Free Choice's criticisms and wanted more on abortion, although the committee resisted O'Connor's effort to label it "murder."

In a passage that seemed to deny even the element of tragedy in abortion, the draft said:

As we have discussed throughout this document, even justifiable defense against aggression may result in the indirect or unintentional loss of innocent human lives. This is tragic, but may conceivably be proportionate to the values defended. Nothing, however, can justify direct attack on innocent human life, in or out of warfare. Abortion is precisely such an attack.

The section chided those who agree with the bishops on peace but not on abortion; it didn't similarly chide those who agree on abortion but not on peace.

The section on penance restored a pledge for the bishops to

commit ourselves . . . and call the community of the Church to fast and abstinence each Friday in the name of peace. Such fast and abstinence should be accompanied by works of charity and service towards our neighbors.

There were two changes in the exhortations to those in military service and those working in defense industries:

It is surely not our intention in writing this letter to create problems for Catholics in the armed forces. Every profession, however, has its specific moral questions, and it is clear that the teaching on war and peace developed in this letter poses a special challenge and opportunity to those in the military profession.

Speaking of defense industry workers, the draft said:

Those who in conscience decide that they should no longer be associated with defense activities should find support in the Catholic community. Those who remain in these industries should find in the Church guidance and support for the on-going evaluation of their work.

The third draft was mailed to the bishops April 1. But before they saw the draft itself, they saw a package of documents on the Vatican meeting: the Roach-Bernardin memo, the Schotte memo and a cover letter from Roach and Bernardin. The cover letter noted Bernardin's conversations with Casaroli, Ratzinger and the pope. "The substance of the conversations in January was reviewed, and the principal points and the significance of their work for our ad hoc committee were confirmed."

Referring to the Schotte memo, Roach and Bernardin said, "While transmitted by the Holy See, this is only a summary of an informal consultation and, we are told, could not be cited in the pastoral itself as an authoritative source. Rather, it is intended for your personal information and help at this time, as it has already been of information and help to the ad hoc committee."

The cover letter was dated March 21; on March 25, Jerry Filteau of the NC News Service ran a story on the whole package, a modern indoor record for episcopal news leaks. *Origins* printed the texts of the three documents. "Open covenants, openly arrived at," Doherty laughed when he learned of the *Origins* publication.

The third draft was sent to reporters with an embargo for April 6 release. Reporters who wrote their stories based only on the draft and staff assurances that the committee would not interpret "curb" as a backing away from the freeze wrote stories crediting the bishops with either "standing firm" or strengthening their criticisms of U.S. policy; both were accurate readings.

But other reporters wrote different stories—with good reason.

The difference was a press conference Bernardin held in Washington April 5. He had been scheduled for a year to address the National Catholic Educational Association on the implementation of the pastoral letter; he also received the NCEA's award of merit for his work on the pastoral. He accepted in the name of the bishops and particularly the committee and staff.

At first, Bernardin said he wouldn't hold a press conference or give interviews after his talk, but he changed his mind. The talk went well. Bernardin described the committee process, called for strong follow-up, and highlighted the policy recommendations.

"We never say that any contemplated use of any nuclear weapon would ipso facto be immoral," he said. "But we are close to that position because of the severe risk factor involved."

A reference to the freeze was carefully phrased. "While not identifying with any specific political initiative for a nuclear freeze, the pastoral does support 'immediate, bilateral, verifiable agreements to curb the testing, production and deployment of new nuclear weapons systems.' " A normal reading of the English language in that sentence would interpret that call as a general support for the freeze concept. So far, so good.

But the press conference was a disaster. Bernardin, who had just given a thirteen-page speech, didn't see the need to read a prepared statement; he also had to serve as his own moderator, trying to answer questions fired by reporters trying to outshout one another.

Bernardin is unmatched as a church politician, but he has never been able to master the world of secular politics, the Washington land of "blue-smoke and mirrors" in which perception is all and careers and movements live or die by the headlines.

The very first question, from a television reporter, was about "curb." Others followed in rapid succession asking if this draft was "kinder" to the Reagan administration than others. Bernardin began a typical long explanation, noting that the committee had tried to be "sensitive" to the Administration as well as others who commented. He described the draft as more "flexible"—technically accurate, but a word reporters jumped on as a sign of retreat. The inability of Pentagon reporters to understand the newly highlighted distinction between general principles and application helped make matters worse. So did the dropping of most of the section on the negative aspects of deterrence in an effort to avoid the appearance of making a "lesser evil" argument.

Bernardin said the change to "curb" was made because some bishops wanted to be less specific; he offered the planned rationalization for the change—implementing a freeze would require negotiations—but it fell flat, and the general impression was that of a retreat from the freeze.

The more nuanced stories written after that press conference highlighted "flexible"; the tougher ones headlined abandonment of the freeze as a caving in to Administration pressure. "We'd have been all right if Roach had done the press conference," one USCC aide lamented.

The bishops' critics were also prepared. Michael Novak, who had been widely attacking previous drafts and had most recently been circulating a counterpastoral, now gave this one his blessing. The New York *Times* ran a front-page story on April 7 with the headline "Administration Hails New Draft of Arms Letter—Says Bishops 'Improved' the Nuclear Statement." The story was based on a statement by State Department spokesman John Hughes, who greeted the shift from "halt" to "curb" as no longer advocating a freeze and supporting Administration arms reduction proposals. The story gave the Administration a real boost at a low point for arms control: Paul Nitze had just told the Senate Foreign Relations Committee that the INF talks in Geneva were just about dead.

Virtually overnight, the public perception of the bishops had been turned upside down. They were no longer the nation's leading moral

critics of U.S. policy, but almost apologists for it, right up there with
Jerry Falwell, who had been using White House briefing materials to
launch a holy war against the freeze.

The timing was also crucial—a vote on the freeze resolution in the
House was scheduled for the next week. Henry Hyde moved in on the
opportunity, circulating a "Dear Colleague" letter using the third
draft to oppose the resolution.

Hyde cited newspaper headlines: "Bishops Back Off Freeze Idea"
(Baltimore *Sun),* "Pastoral Due Today Avoids Endorsing Nuclear
Arms Freeze" (Los Angeles *Times).* Then Hyde did something the
Bernardin committee never did—he looked up the words "halt" and
"curb" in the dictionary.

"After a careful, painstaking study of what a call for a halt would
mean in terms of impeding successful negotiations for arms reductions," Hyde said, "the bishops have wisely adopted the more prudential course of calling for a curb instead. . . . It is clear that after
careful deliberation, the Roman Catholic Bishops have refused to
endorse the nuclear arms freeze. As we enter the next phase of the
floor deliberation, I hope the wisdom of the bishops' second thoughts
on the freeze will guide the debate and serve as a model for us all."

"It's 1976 all over again," one hill aide wailed. And it was. "Curb"
and "flexible" had replaced "disappointed" and "encouraged." For
those who cared, the perception that the bishops had abandoned the
freeze because of administration pressure was intolerable. Columnist
Mary McGrory talked about "the poor freeze," almost as though it
were a living being—and in a way, it was. The freeze was always less a
political solution than a force, a symbolic no to nuclear war into
which scores of bishops across the country had helped breathe life.
For the bishops to be seen as abandoning it now because of administration pressure would be like seeing a father abort his own child in
the eighth month.

But at least the clarification didn't take as long as it did in 1976.
With the State Department comment, it was clear that the bishops
were being co-opted. On the same day the *Times* story ran, Melanne
Verveer, an aide to Democratic Representative Marcy Kaptur of Ohio
who had worked for the USCC until only a few months before,
showed the Hyde letter to Doherty. Doherty, who called it "scurri-
lous," showed it to Hehir, who was already being pressured by Geno

Baroni to issue a statement, and urged a clarification. Hehir agreed and went to Hoye, who talked with Bernardin, Roach and Russ Shaw.

When Russ Shaw saw the *Times* story, he sat down and began writing a memo to Hoye urging a clarification. "It was apparent to me, and to anyone with eyes in his head and functional literacy, that the Administration had finally gotten around to doing what I could have told them last fall—praise the bishops, pat them on the head and dismiss them."

Bernardin had already considered a clarification and Roach needed no convincing. Shaw and Hehir drafted a response; Hehir got comments from Bernardin, Shaw got comments from Roach through Hoye, and Shaw and Hehir put together the final product.

They came up with a two-page statement issued jointly by Roach and Bernardin. It was distributed on Friday for release on Sunday, April 10.

The statement welcomed comments on the drafts from the Administration and elsewhere, but said, "We could not accept any suggestion that there are relatively few and insignificant differences between US policies and the policies advocated in the pastoral." It said the draft must be seen as a critique of U.S. policy for the past four decades, not just for the present. The statement also noted that the bishops as a body had yet to act on the draft. "It would therefore be premature and risky for anyone—ourselves included—to say 'This represents the policy of the Catholic bishops.' "

Roach and Bernardin noted the broad consultation they had used, but said, "In the final analysis, however, the third draft is far more the product of reflection and dialogue within the Catholic community than of dialogue between the drafting committee and the administration."

(Reilly says the greatest influence on the third draft was the internal committee discussions.)

They continued: "Without wishing to be ungracious to administration spokesmen, we think it is important to note some of the areas in which the third draft takes stands significantly at variance with current US policy. These include, for example, advocacy of a policy of 'no first use' of nuclear weapons and support for early and successful conclusion of negotiations on the comprehensive test ban treaty.

"On the question of a nuclear freeze," they said, "neither the second draft nor the third draft advocates a 'freeze' as such. . . . In both drafts the clear intent is a call to cap the arms race and reduce the weapons on both sides as rapidly as possible, with particular emphasis on potentially destabilizing systems. As the second draft did not endorse a specific freeze proposal, so the third draft cannot and should not be used to oppose any specific proposal. Our purpose in both drafts has been to state a central moral imperative: that the arms race must be stopped and disarmament begun. The implementation of this imperative is open to a wide variety of approaches."

Roach and Bernardin emphasized the evenhandedness of the pastoral. "The basic moral judgment of the document is, we believe, summed up in these two sentences: 'A justifiable use of force must be both discriminatory and proportionate. Certain aspects of both US and Soviet strategies fail both tests. . . .'

"In sum," they said, "we welcome reactions to the third draft of the pastoral letter from administration spokesmen and all other interested parties. This exchange of views has been integral to the evolution of the document to date. Come May 2 and 3, however, the decision will now rest with the bishops and only with them."

(A personal aside is called for here. At the time the clarification was issued, I was facing a deadline for this book. I called Roach, who had earlier backed the freeze, making it clear he was to speak as archbishop of St. Paul-Minneapolis and not as NCCB president. I posed a hypothetical question: if the pastoral were approved with the word "curb," would it be sufficient authority for the USCC to testify or send a letter to Congress supporting a specific freeze resolution? Roach's answer: "Yes, with either 'halt' or 'curb.'" When the story on the Roach-Bernardin clarification didn't catch up with the original headline—clarifications never do—it was clear I had a piece of information that was vital to the story. I called Dave Anderson, who covers religion for UPI, a friend who had also gotten burned with an early story saying the third draft had been strengthened, and passed along the Roach quote. He wrote a story on it that was run in the New York *Times* and elsewhere.)

As the House freeze vote neared, Russett wrote an op-ed piece saying the bishops hadn't been co-opted. Several profreeze members of Congress, mostly Catholics, including Kaptur, sent a "Dear Colleague" letter quoting the clarification, arguing that the third draft couldn't be used to oppose a freeze resolution and containing Pax Christi's list of 142 bishops who had backed the freeze. Ironically, the list didn't contain the name of three influential bishops—Cardinal Krol and Archbishops Quinn and Hickey—who had backed the freeze but had not signed the Pax Christi petition.

On Tuesday, April 12, Bernardin held a conference call with committee members—except O'Connor, who was out of the country—and staff. He said he'd voted earlier in the day and now was free enough of local political problems—the controversy surrounding the mayoral campaign of Harold Washington, a black Democrat—to turn his attention back to the pastoral.

He read the clarification to Gumbleton, Reilly and Fulcher, who hadn't seen it before. Doherty mentioned the Kaptur-Markey letter. Russett suggested that the three committee members who had already endorsed the freeze issue a statement saying they still support it. Bernardin didn't like the idea; he said he didn't want to fractionalize the committee, and he didn't want people reading things into the fact that he and O'Connor hadn't publicly backed the freeze.

Russett said that if the House resolution lost, the bishops would be seen as having killed it. But Bernardin said he thought the clarification and the New York *Times* story (on Roach's comment) had taken care of that. Reilly asked if Bernardin wanted the others to stay quiet; Bernardin said they should use their own judgment in speaking out as individuals.

The following weekend, Reilly held a press conference before a speech in Providence and said there was no way the third draft could be seen as an endorsement of Reagan administration policies. (He also expressed a willingness to consider the President's "Star Wars" space defense system.)

The same weekend, Hehir complained in a speech in New York that some of the press accounts he had seen made it look like "the administration rewrote the draft while the bishops were out for coffee."

During the same period, Bernardin spoke to the Chicago Council on Foreign Relations; he stitched together parts of his NCEA speech with his Boston speech, calling on Catholics to build a constituency of peace.

As the Chicago meeting neared, other bishops began to comment on the third draft. Frank Murphy hit the "halt-curb" shift, noting the White House's support for Jerry Falwell's antifreeze campaign and saying it would be "a supreme irony" if the bishops were perceived as blocking the freeze. Bishop McManus of Fort Wayne-South Bend said he wouldn't be "a wallflower" in trying to get "curb" back to "halt."

Roach said in a talk at Macalaster College in St. Paul that he expected an effort to restore "halt"; he described the change as "a little too much horse-trading" within the committee, the closest thing to a public rebuke of a bishops' committee in memory.

In the House, meanwhile, the freeze debate dragged on as opponents staged what amounted to a filibuster by amendment. The debate that should have been over in March was now scheduled for conclusion the week of May 2—not until after the bishops completed action on their pastoral.

X. CHICAGO

Proposed amendments to the pastoral letter were due by April 20. While the right wing spent the middle of April patting itself on the back, Catholic peace groups spent the time trying to "reclaim" the pastoral.

A number of peace activists turned on Gumbleton, blaming him for giving in to O'Connor within the committee. The charge was unfair. Gumbleton had held out for "halt" all the way through and had probably contributed more than any other committee member to shaping the pastoral. He had worked with Julie Casey on the scriptural section, provided much of the section on nonviolence, contributed significantly to shaping the section on deterrence and policy, fleshed out almost single-handedly the "strategies for peace" section, and reworked many of the exhortations.

But Pax Christi and the Center of Concern, a liberal church think tank, went over the document carefully, preparing amendments to distribute to sympathetic bishops—which at this point included all the bishops who had backed the freeze.

The first amendment, obviously, was restoring "halt." Peace groups received some ammunition when the April 24 *Our Sunday Visitor* ran a Gallup poll showing Catholics backing an "immediate, verifiable freeze on the testing, production and deployment of nuclear weapons" between the United States and the Soviet Union by a three-to-one margin. Catholics favored a freeze by 70–23 percent, compared to 67–22 for Protestants and 70–21 for the general population.

The figure for Catholics was statistically no different than a 72–20 favorable rating for the freeze the previous November. A differently worded question used in April and May that didn't use the word "freeze" found Catholics favoring by 82–13 percent a U.S.-Soviet agreement "not to build new nuclear weapons in the future."

Other amendments proposed by the peace groups included restoring the stronger second-draft language on no-first-use, strengthening language which had been softened and made less urgent, dropping the comparative justice section, sharpening the criticism of deterrence, and softening language which seemed to blame the arms race solely on the Russians.

But the bishops didn't need much encouragement; more than five hundred amendments poured in, the most for any pastoral letter, including the National Catechetical Directory. And the vast majority of amendments called for strengthening the document.

One stack of forty amendments came from O'Connor, who told Hehir he was submitting them "like any other bishop." Some of O'Connor's amendments also turned up word for word in submissions from Hannan and Auxiliary Bishop Patrick Ahern of New York.

When the Bernardin committee first met to review the amendments, Gumbleton asked if it wasn't "irregular" for a committee member to submit amendments; Bernardin said it was highly unusual but not irregular.

Although he didn't show it, Bernardin was angry, because he had heard that while in Rome with the rest of the bishops from New York and the Military Ordinariate, O'Connor had discussed the pastoral with the pope and Casaroli. But O'Connor said he had done so only at their request. O'Connor said that while meeting with a larger group, the pope had asked about the pastoral and that he told him that while it could be helped by some amendments, it was a good document that wouldn't embarrass the Holy See.

But O'Connor's amendments didn't fare well within the committee. Because of the bulk of amendments, there was little discussion. Bernardin called for a straight up-or-down vote on each amendment, and the committee quickly knocked down weakening amendments and supported strengthening ones. "I've been defending 'curb' for three weeks now," Bernardin said, "and I don't know about you, but I'm ready to go back to 'halt.' "

So were Reilly and Fulcher. The vote to restore "halt" was four to one, but the committee added a footnote emphasizing that the bishops weren't identifying with any particular political movement. The amendment was designed to show that the bishops weren't simply following a political movement; *Time* magazine later called the amendment "wishy-washy." The committee had switched from "halt" to "curb" and claimed that it wasn't disowning the freeze; now, in going back to "halt," it seemed to be doing just that. But at least "halt" was still there.

The committee met a total of three times to discuss the amendments. Between the second and third meetings, Hehir worked in his rectory to chart the four groups into which the amendments had been divided, putting the amendments aside at one point to deal with a troubled parishioner who would only talk to him and again for a 5 A.M. sick call.

As the bishops began gathering in Chicago on Sunday, May 1, they saw a flattering piece in the New York *Times*. George Kennan, the nation's premier expert on the Soviet Union, had praised the pastoral lavishly in an op-ed piece; he had talked at length with Hehir in preparing it.

It was cold and raining in Chicago as the bishops were greeted by small groups of demonstrators, both pro and con—peace groups holding candles and critics holding signs like the one that said "Moscow's Smiling."

The first flavor of the meeting came on Sunday evening when Roach walked into a hall and found himself surrounded by about twenty reporters. In an impromptu press conference, he repeated the line that the pastoral didn't endorse the freeze per se. One reporter said that if the bishops went back to "halt," the media would report it as support for the freeze—would that be accurate reporting? "That's right," Roach replied. "That's totally right."

Later that evening, the bishops held an optional, informal, closed-door briefing with members of the committee to ask general questions about the process. It lasted only an hour and, except for O'Connor's volunteered explanation of why he opposed "halt," not much developed. Bernardin used the occasion mostly to fill in the bishops on the January Vatican meeting and his own discussions with the pope.

When the Sunday meeting ended, Hoye and Hehir briefed the press on the complicated process that had been adopted. The bishops would deal with amendments in five groups. The first, major policy issues, would begin with "curb-halt." The chair (Roach) would recognize an amendment, Bernardin would explain the committee's position in half a minute, the mover would speak for two minutes, and a maximum of four people—two pro and two con—would speak to the amendment.

A second group of "substantive amendments" would be handled the same way; a third group of less substantive amendments would be handled with the mover, one pro and one con speaker each speaking for a minute; a fourth group of noncontroversial amendments the committee had accepted would be approved en bloc with unanimous consent; and a fifth group of amendments received through 6 P.M. Monday would be handled like Group III.

Hoye had devised the procedure. In developing the strategy of dealing with the most significant issues first, Bernardin followed the advice offered in a letter by Bishop McManus, who had shepherded through the National Catechetical Directory and a pastoral letter on education while chairman of the USCC education committee. In discussing the tight procedure, Hoye said, "The time for making speeches is over."

Roach began Monday morning by summarizing the process and calling for "self-discipline"; he said the words "I withdraw" would be very welcome and urged giving the committee the benefit of every doubt. But the planned fifteen minutes for discussing procedure dragged on to an hour. A testy Ahern, vicar for Staten Island, challenged the process and argued that, despite Roach's claim, there hadn't been "ample time" for debate.

The bishops paid particular attention to the précis, which Cardinal Cooke called "something even I can understand." Roach said the committee would have ten days to revise the précis in light of amendments; Bishop Bernard Law of Springfield-Cape Girardeau, Missouri, successfully moved that the bishops vote on the précis in writing.

The bishops also approved an amendment offered by Ray Lucker, who asked that Roach announce how many people had asked to speak on each side of an amendment to avoid having the process create the impression that the bishops were evenly split on an issue. Lucker had discussed the idea with several other bishops the night before and they'd agreed it would be helpful. After the first round of amendments, it seemed that Gumbleton was the only one who had followed through, asking to speak on a number of amendments; often his only comment was, "I have nothing to add to what Bishop So-and-so has said."

When the procedural matters were completed, Roach called on Bernardin to give the committee report; he received a standing ovation.

Bernardin made it quite clear where much of the impetus of the American bishops had come from; quoting the pope's Hiroshima speech, Bernardin said, "No person alive today had more powerfully called the church to respond to the challenge of peace than Pope John Paul II."

Bernardin noted general areas of change in the third draft and cited the source—either the November bishops' meeting or the Rome meeting—for the changes. He said the deterrence section was "recast" because of the November meeting. The only sections changed because of the Reagan administration, he said, were the mention of the START and INF talks and the clarification of U.S. targeting policy.

"The basic thrust of the document," Bernardin said, "is to set the voice of the bishops of the United States against the technological dynamic of the nuclear arms race. The letter calls for stopping the race, reversing its direction, eliminating the most dangerous weapons systems and emphasizing the need for decisive political action to move world politics away from a fascination with means of destruction and towards a world order in which war will be consigned to history as a means of settling disputes."

The diluting nature of the committee process seemed most obvious when the draft was contrasted to the kind of clarity with which Bernardin spoke about the document, often in words written for him by Hehir—in the reply to Henry Hyde, the NCEA speech, this speech and, later, in his short responses to weakening amendments.

At a press conference after the Monday morning session, Bernardin was asked about Roach's comments on the freeze; he talked about people's "interpretation" of the document. But one reporter asked the question in a way that produced the right answer. How, he asked, did the pastoral's "basic thrust" described by Bernardin differ from the freeze principles?

It didn't, and Bernardin finally said so. "First, there is no single freeze resolution, there are several of them, and we didn't want to be identified with a particular one."

The first item in the afternoon session was "curb-halt," or "hurb-calt," as some committee members now referred to it. The way the major amendments were handled illustrates the use of power within the bishops' conference. First, both the "peace bishops" and the handful of hawks had clearly planned some moves ahead of time. But while there may have been some quiet arm-twisting, that wasn't the main approach; the key is in the level of respect for the person speaking for an amendment.

There are three major groups whose composition varies somewhat from issue to issue. Rank is usually not a measure of influence; for example, Cardinal Medeiros of Boston and Cardinal Timothy Manning of Los Angeles are usually silent at bishops' meetings and don't shape the discussions.

The first group, in ascending order, consists of some of the most vocal, but not necessarily influential, bishops—for example, pacifist Michael Kenny of Juneau on one side and Edward O'Rourke of Peoria on the other. The second group consists of those who have earned their colleagues' respect through past performance or by establishing intellectual or spiritual credentials; some hold prestigious positions, but others don't. This group includes an archbishop like Rembert Weakland of Milwaukee, a bishop of a small diocese like McManus or Mahony, or auxiliary bishops like Gumbleton or Frank Stafford of Baltimore before he was appointed to Memphis.

The third group consists of the heavyweights—people whose stature and respect are both high. On the pastoral, aside from the obvious in Roach and Bernardin, this group included Krol, Quinn, Hickey and Malone, whom his colleagues had regarded in a way that Rome had not by twice electing him conference vice-president.

So while Roach said people who had asked to speak on an amendment would be chosen at random, it strains credulity to think that is always the way it happened. It was no coincidence, for example, that of the eleven bishops who had asked to speak for the change back to "halt," Malone was the one picked to move the amendment. Having Malone do it was as close as Roach could get to doing it himself without jumping over the podium. Malone also offered a reminder of the Collegeville experience, which had contributed to the bishops' sense of themselves.

Originally, Hickey was scheduled to speak on "curb-halt"; he asked an aide, John Carr, to write up some talking points. But Hehir told Carr he needed Hickey to talk on another amendment and argue that it wasn't consequentialism. ("What's consequentialism?" Carr asked. "Never mind," Hehir said.) Then Malone, who knew Carr from his days as a USCC staffer, asked him to write up some notes on "curb-halt"; Carr gave him the notes he had made for Hickey. Then, as the bishops prayed before the opening of the afternoon session, Hehir told Carr Hickey would speak on "curb-halt" after all. "If he does," Carr said, "he and Malone are going to say the same thing. You've got until the end of the 'Hail Mary' to pull one of them off."

Malone, not Hickey, spoke on "curb-halt." Interestingly enough, Carr thought it was risky for Malone to link the amendment directly to the freeze—another example of the way in which the "church bureaucrats" that conservatives charged were manipulating the bishops on the issue were constantly more cautious than the bishops, often playing catch-up.

Malone went right to the point. He noted that symbolically, "halt" had been seen as support for the freeze and "curb" as opposition. "The content and symbolism of 'halt' sets the tone for the rest of the document," he said, making it crystal clear that "halt" supports the freeze and "curb" doesn't.

Bernardin, in noting that the committee supported the amendment, said it had tried various ways to express a "central moral imperative" while maintaining the bishops' own identity but, in view of the public response, now supported "halt."

O'Connor spoke against the amendment. He said using political specifics would detract from the pastoral and, using an argument advanced by some conservative critics, said the bishops who had signed the Pax Christi freeze resolution hadn't seen three pages of detailed explanation. A freeze, he said, would block testing of "smaller, safer and more reliable" nuclear weapons.

Next to speak was Krol, who argued that "halt" was more accurate, because the church's ultimate goal wasn't reduction of nuclear weapons, a "curb," but elimination, a "halt."

The only other bishop to ask to speak against the amendment was Anthony Bevilacqua, a Brooklyn auxiliary, who argued that a freeze could block negotiations for reductions in nuclear arms. Bishop Mahony, an example of a "second-group bishop," spoke for the amendment.

Archbishop Edmund Szoka of Detroit offered a substitute of "cease"; he said he could accept either "halt" or "curb," but picking one or the other would enable one side to claim victory and create the impression of division among the bishops. Walter Sullivan said he could live with "cease," but Gumbleton said the discussion was similar to the one within the committee that had led to "curb." Citing the political implications of moving away from "halt," he said the bishops should "go back to 'halt' once and for all."

Hannan tried to amend the section to include the phrase "except as needed for deterrence," but Roach ruled him out of order, saying he should submit the proposed change as an amendment under Group V.

Roach called for a standing vote, and the support for the amendment was overwhelming; there was no official count, but reporters' estimates of those opposing the change ranged from ten to twenty-five and the margin was easily ten to one.

The size of the vote surprised everyone, but the Reagan administration, which had alternately frightened, angered and insulted the bishops, could claim a great deal of the credit; its blessing of the third draft and "curb" made it clear that, for the Administration, anything other than support for the freeze would be interpreted as a blanket endorsement of Reagan policies.

The next group of amendments focused on no-first-use; the first one came from John Quinn, who had gone through the document trying to close every possible loophole on use of nuclear weapons. By now Quinn personally held an absolutist position—use of nuclear weapons could never be justified—and while the bishops couldn't agree, they clearly agreed with Quinn that the third draft had been "nuanced" far more than necessary on first-use.

Quinn argued that the language which "abhors" the initiation of nuclear war was too weak and didn't fully preclude first use. He wanted to go back to the second-draft language: "We do not perceive any situation in which the deliberate initiation of nuclear warfare, on however restricted a scale, can be morally justified. If that's what we mean," he said, striking a chord he would repeat throughout the afternoon, "we ought to say it."

Bernardin said the committee was sympathetic to the amendment, but had not supported it because it thought the stronger language would open the bishops to the charge of consequentialism. Aside from that, he said, he had no problem. ("What's consequentialism?" asked a bishop sitting near Fulcher.)

The fact that Quinn, as the new head of the bishops' Doctrine Committee, wasn't worried about consequentialism was significant; so was the fact that Hickey, the committee's past chairman, backed Quinn, saying, "I don't see the problem of consequentialism."

Hannan heatedly opposed the amendment, reading from a letter written the previous fall by the president of the West German bishops' conference. But the West Germans didn't carry much weight—the amendment carried with only a handful of opponents. Hannan lost dozens of amendments over the two-day meeting, but somehow the noes always seemed just a little louder when he quoted the German bishops. The Americans resented the German bishops' privileged relationship with the state, and more than one noted that if the Americans had tried to influence a German bishops' letter, they would have been ignored.

The next relevant amendment after Quinn's was one he had sponsored along with several other bishops—restoring the second draft's statement that "non-nuclear attacks by another state must be resisted by other than nuclear means." Victor Balke of Crookston, Minnesota, offered the amendment as a "clear statement of moral principle." Bernardin replied that the committee's initial nonsupport for the amendment was based on retaining the language amended by Quinn; now that that had been changed, he said, Balke's language fit in well. The amendment passed overwhelmingly.

In rapid succession the bishops backed two other strengthening amendments and rejected a weakening amendment from O'Connor.

The next amendment, from Ahern, would have changed a reference to "us," referring to the bishops, to "those of us who listened to the testimony." It was the first of several similar amendments he had offered. Bernardin said he didn't think it was a good idea to separate the bishops from the committee and that the amendment "would fracture the whole process." The amendment failed resoundingly.

Next came another Quinn amendment, strengthening weaker third-draft language to conclude it would be "morally unjustifiable to initiate nuclear war in any form." Bernardin again said the committee had originally opposed the amendment, but it now fit in well. The steamroller continued; the amendment passed.

The next amendment, Number 15, came from Ahern. "I waive fifteen," he said. "I waive seventeen, I waive thirty-five, I waive forty, I waive forty-two—I feel like I'm waving good-bye."

Amendment 16 was another Quinn offering, changing a statement that initiation of nuclear war would be "an unjustifiable moral risk" to say "we judge resort to nuclear weapons to counter a conventional attack to be morally unjustifiable." It passed overwhelmingly.

Next, a Bevilacqua amendment to change language to say "we are gravely concerned" about the risk of using nuclear weapons to counter a conventional attack was overwhelmingly defeated after Bernardin called it "too weak." Cooke withdrew a similarly weakening amendment because it wouldn't pass and tried to attach a footnote explaining that this was an application of a principle; Roach said he would have to bring it up as a new amendment under Group V, where it later passed. Cooke's pleasant, self-deprecating manner in public contrasted sharply with the hawkish, sternly worded comments he sent to the committee.

An Ahern amendment to talk about "moving toward" a no-first-use pledge was rejected after Bernardin said that while the bishops could back moving toward implementation of a pledge, the pledge must come immediately.

Amendment 21 was another Quinn amendment, strengthening language to say "we seek to reinforce the barriers against any use of nuclear weapons." It passed.

Quinn lost on one amendment that Bernardin said was really no different from the committee language. He lost on another that would have said that any nuclear attack would cause disproportionate damage; but an amendment offered by Bishop Howard Hubbard of Albany passed, saying, "A nuclear response to either conventional or nuclear attack can cause destruction which goes far beyond 'legitimate defense.' Such use of nuclear weapons would not be justified."

Hannan offered several amendments which were overwhelmingly defeated. He angrily accused the pastoral of having "a grievous insufficiency of adequate respect for human rights"; Bernardin replied that he disagreed with Hannan's evaluation of the treatment of human rights.

After a Quinn amendment strengthening language to say there was "no moral justification" for risking nuclear war passed overwhelmingly, Hannan tried to strike the language, arguing that the risk was worth it to protect human rights. Bernardin said the pastoral's thrust was opposition to nuclear war and he wouldn't want to say anything that would appear to endorse it.

A key issue arose when Quinn offered his amendment to restore quotes from the 1976 pastoral and the Krol testimony to the text. "If we are modifying it or changing the content," he said, "we should explain it or restore it."

Bernardin said the 1976 pastoral—which had called the threat to use strategic nuclear weapons morally wrong—had been ambiguous about the relationship between threat and intent and that the Krol testimony, with its reference to accepting deterrence as a "lesser evil," had been criticized as consequentialism—not, Bernardin said, that he meant to accuse Krol of consequentialism.

O'Rourke argued against including the two items in the text, saying they reflected an attitude toward a targeting policy of Mutual Assured Destruction but not present targeting policies.

Hickey backed Quinn, saying the bishops shouldn't be afraid to put into the text something they cited in a footnote. But he offered a compromise—dropping the "lesser evil" quote, adding that that didn't mean he didn't agree with it. Bernardin asked time for the committee to consider the proposal overnight.

Frank Murphy offered an amendment to substitute a long analysis of deterrence as a "sinful situation" for a paragraph interpreting John Paul's statement on deterrence. The draft statement described the dilemma as balancing the costs and risks of the arms race against the need to protect the independence and freedom of nations and peoples; it concluded that "a balance of forces, preventing either side from achieving superiority, can be seen as a means of safeguarding both dimensions."

Bernardin was firm. "We do not want this section removed. It is based on Cardinal Casaroli's personal interpretation of the Holy Father's statement on deterrence. It is a very delicate matter and we would not want to see this amendment stick." It didn't.

While the bishops wanted to move their 1976 pastoral and the Krol testimony from a footnote into the text, they wanted to do just the opposite with quotes from Weinberger and Clark explaining U.S. targeting policy. In moving the amendment, Mahony noted that the only other sources quoted in the text were popes, the Vatican Council and other church documents. He also said that, given the history of "curb-halt," keeping the quotes in so lofty a position might create the wrong impression. Clark and Weinberger were quickly consigned to a footnote.

As the afternoon went on, the sophisticated pattern of the bishops' voting became clear—they approved virtually everything that strengthened the document, while consistently stopping short of saying that there was no conceivable situation in which the use of nuclear weapons could be morally justified. They rejected efforts which would have either given the document a more pacifist tone or given any suggestion of support for using nuclear weapons.

Hannan, the first chaplain to land in Normandy, became increasingly incensed and abusive, taking his anger out on Bernardin. At one point, looking at Bernardin with the proverbial daggers in his eyes, he yelled at him, "We should never have entered World War II, we should have let the Nazis rule the world, that's what you're saying!"

O'Connor offered an amendment to drop all of the specific policy recommendations—the "halt," and so on—citing his wrestling with his "conscience." He said that despite his long contact with the military, he didn't feel "competent" to make policy recommendations.

Bernardin argued that having supported a "strictly conditioned moral acceptance" of deterrence, "there must be some specific applications if we are going to indicate what we mean."

Again, on a question of some sensitivity in Rome, the use of specific policy recommendations in a pastoral letter, the Doctrine Committee chairmen, Hickey and Quinn, led the way. Hickey called the amendment "a major threat to the document" that would make it "an empty shell." He said the section reflected careful consideration of the Rome meeting. If the section were deleted, Quinn said, "it would make deterrence something of a blank check."

Cooke went to the microphone to defend the amendment, but he was ruled out of order because he hadn't previously registered to speak. Cooke never did quite master the parliamentary procedure. One of the interesting aspects of the debate was that while it is usually the conservatives who use parliamentary procedure to their advantage, this time they handled it badly, while the liberals used it well. O'Connor's amendment failed, with only a handful of votes in support.

The one amendment whose defeat was something of a surprise was Quinn's effort to get the reference to the MX moved from a footnote back into the text. The vote was reasonably close, but losing didn't seem to make that much difference. Bernardin indicated that there was considerable controversy over the MX and said the committee felt if it listed the MX in the text, it would have had to list a number of other systems as well. The situation ended far short of support for the MX.

After failing to strip the specific recommendations as a unit, Hannan went after them one at a time. By now, even O'Connor was withdrawing amendments he had written, but Hannan continued to battle on. He exploded over the pastoral's call for the removal of nuclear weapons from areas where they were likely to be overrun in the early stages of battle, forcing "rapid and uncontrollable decisions on their use." Then he yelled, "I don't think you know what you're talking about, not having been in war. . . . You don't have the faintest idea what you're taking about."

Roach, as he often did after a Hannan tantrum, moved directly to call for a vote. But Bernardin, feeling a need to respond on a technical level, called on Hehir to comment. Hehir deferred to a surprised Bruce Russett; he didn't have a detailed response ready, but he was able to describe the procedure as "maintaining a firebreak" and to counter that General Bernard Rogers, chief military officer in NATO, supported the concept.

When the day's session ended, Quinn expressed surprise about how well things had gone for him, and Hannan expressed surprise about how badly they had gone for him. He didn't have many allies; asked if he thought O'Connor had balanced off Gumbleton on the committee, he said, "No—he's a Navy man. He never saw combat on land."

There was one irony in Hannan's repeated references to combat; Quinn and Hickey had experienced combat of a sort when they were exposed to gunfire and panicked crowds in the rioting that broke out at the funeral of the murdered Archbishop Oscar Romero of San Salvador.

By Monday's end, the bishops' position was strong and clear. McManus' strategy appeared more brilliant than ever; it had gotten "curb-halt" up front in a weather-vane vote. By the time the bishops had voted on Quinn's first amendment, the direction and fate of the document were sealed.

But that didn't mean that Tuesday would be dull. The day began with another Malone amendment—one calling for deletion of the new section on "comparative justice" in the just-war section. The committee wanted to keep the section. But it offered a substitute amendment with three changes that the bishops accepted. First, it moved a paragraph on U.S. and Soviet values to the section on superpower relationships. Second, it added a footnote listing five sources for including the category. Third, it inserted this paragraph:

The category of Comparative Justice is designed to emphasize the presumption against war which stands at the beginning of just-war teaching. In a world of sovereign states recognizing neither a common moral authority nor a central political authority, comparative justice stresses that no state should act on the basis that it has "absolute justice" on its side. Every party to a conflict should acknowledge the limits of its "just cause" and the consequent requirement to use only limited means in pursuit of its objectives. Far from legitimizing a crusade mentality, comparative justice is designed to relativize absolute claims and to restrain the use of force even in a "justified" conflict.

The new language represented a 180-degree turn from the "crusading mentality" tone of O'Connor's original language.

Next, in a series of votes, Hannan, O'Connor, Cooke and several others succeeded in replacing the draft's claim that the Vatican Council had "endorsed" conscientious objection with language merely repeating the council's support for laws recognizing conscientious objection. But the bishops also accepted a few other changes expressing more sympathy for conscientious objection and nonviolence, including an amendment from Law which concluded that the just war and nonviolence "diverge on some specific conclusions, but they share a common presumption against the use of force as a means of settling disputes."

The bishops then moved to the Group II, "substantive" amendments. Hannan lost on an amendment to say nuclear weapons threatened the "welfare" of the planet instead of its "existence" after Bernardin said the committee had taken the line from the pope's Hiroshima talk.

Stafford offered an amendment which would have moved a long quote from the "The Church in the Modern World" into a footnote. The passage emphasized that the document should be interpreted with the changeable nature of the subjects at hand in mind. Bernardin said the quote was important to Rome; it stayed in.

Frank Murphy succeeded in striking patronizing language (O'Connor's) on nonviolence which said no one may "simply assume" that COs are "mere pawns of conspirational forces, or guilty of cowardice."

Bernardin cited Rome again in successfully opposing a Stafford amendment to strike the paragraph emphasizing that pacifism is an option for individuals, not governments.

Hannan then offered an innocuous amendment that said, "It is presumed that all sane people prefer peace, never want to initiate war and accept even the most justifiable defensive war only as a sad necessity."

Bernardin, who had earlier told the committee he wanted to give Hannan an amendment, said that while the committee hadn't supported the amendment, it didn't feel so strongly about it. "I know this is way out of line," Roach interjected, "but Archbishop Hannan's a great guy, let's give him this one." The bishops laughed and passed the amendment. The next time a Hannan amendment came up, he said, "I'll give you this one" and withdrew it.

As the morning moved on, Cardinal John Carberry, the retired archbishop of St. Louis and a veteran leader of church conservatives, noted that Bernardin mentioned when the committee was split on an amendment but never said what the split was. "Generally," Bernardin replied, "it was four to one. It depended on the issue who the one was."

A few minutes later, Maurice Dingman of Des Moines asked that the bishops announce plans to issue another pastoral letter in two years evaluating the state of progress toward disarmament. "We were unanimous on this one," Bernardin said, adding the committee felt that issue should be discussed at another time—after the present committee had been dissolved.

O'Connor won a Pyrrhic victory on an amendment concerning the Comprehensive Test Ban Treaty. Again citing his wrestling with his conscience, he offered more general language, saying he still didn't know what the Comprehensive Test Ban Treaty was.

Bernardin summarized the committee's support for resumption of the treaty negotiations that had been dropped by the Reagan administration. Law offered a compromise amendment describing "a" (lower case) comprehensive test ban treaty. The style was changed, but there was no challenge to the committee's criticism of the Administration.

The procedure almost came unglued on Amendment 68, offered by John Quinn: "Nevertheless, there must be no misunderstanding of our opposition on moral grounds to any use of nuclear weapons."

Those close to the committee thought Bernardin would cite Rome in opposing the amendment. Instead, he merely said it would upset the pastoral's delicate argument. But after Mahony argued that the document already called for a definitive no to nuclear war, the amendment passed, placing, reporters saw immediately, the bishops firmly in the camp of nuclear pacifism—and at odds with Rome.

Michael Sheehan, newly named bishop of Lubbock, Texas, who knew Bernardin well from the days when he worked for him at the

USCC, watched him during the vote: "Bernardin blinked. And then he blinked again. And he said, 'It passed?' "

The bishops disposed of several more amendments as Bernardin looked for a way to reopen Number 68. It came on Amendment 73, another Quinn offering ruling out any moral use of nuclear weapons. Stafford argued that it broke the flow of the argument; Oscar Lipscomb of Mobile questioned the authority of the statement and asked for a suspension of the rules to reconsider 68. But Bernardin explained that the statement's level of authority wasn't a problem, so Lipscomb, who had asked for a reconsideration for the wrong reason, withdrew his request.

But Stafford asked for reconsideration of 68 and the motion passed. Roach ruled that the bishops had to deal with 73 first; they defeated it. Bernardin opposed 68 "very, very strongly," supporting the document's expression of "profound skepticism" about the possible moral use of nuclear weapons and saying "a note of ambiguity must remain" to avoid undermining the rest of the argument. The bishops quickly and overwhelmingly reversed themselves, defeating 68.

Things then settled back into routine, with the bishops rejecting most amendments that hadn't been supported by the committee. They approved a committee response to an amendment offered by retired Bishop Charles Buswell of Pueblo, Colorado, which changed a description of some Soviet actions from "monstrous" to "reprehensible."

Over the committee's objections, the bishops passed a Cooke amendment replacing a sentence that said "no single issue transcends" the need to avoid nuclear war with one that said "the need to prevent nuclear war is absolutely crucial." Cooke called the committee language "a little too much rhetoric." While some expected Cooke, as head of the Pro-Life Activities Committee, to argue that abortion was the single most important issue, that was only one of the possible candidates he cited; the others included world hunger, the need to avoid any form of war and the need to establish a world order."

There was a particularly interesting discussion of a McManus amendment to the section in which the bishops pledged themselves and called their people to fast and abstinence each Friday linked to acts of charity. McManus added language explaining this meant a call to eat less food and to abstain from eating meat on a voluntary basis as a "return to a traditional practice of penance once well observed in the U.S. church." He argued that the added wording was needed to explain the practice to many American Catholics who didn't remember the old tradition.

The whole issue of Friday penance represented a merging of the old and the new. A number of liberal bishops, including Hickey, who were unhappy with the coercive nature of the old tradition often complained that the American bishops had made a mistake by letting the practice disappear. It offered, they said, a helpful sign of identity for Catholics. The peace pastoral gave the bishops an opportunity to restore the practice in a voluntary, meaningful way.

The bishops approved another amendment on penance when Oscar Lipscomb of Mobile asked a change in the sentence calling for creating a climate making it possible for the nation to "experience profound sorrow over the atomic bombing in 1945." Lipscomb's language said, "After the passage of nearly four decades and a concomitant growth in our understanding of the ever growing horror of nuclear war, we must shape the climate of opinion . . ." Without that context, he said, the reference was anachronistic and unrealistic.

In the middle of the day Tuesday, Quinn offered a noncontroversial amendment asking specific references to deacons in the pastoral advice section. Quinn's proposal involved two amendments; the committee made a counteroffer and there was some discussion. The move became a tar baby—there was agreement on where everyone wanted to go, but the parliamentary procedure became confused and for a minute it seemed the issue would never be resolved.

But what was striking about the incident is that it was the first of its kind. During the two-day meeting, there were a few instances in which bishops shouted out "What are we voting on?" or even "What did we vote on?" but all in all, there was remarkably little confusion given the complicated procedure and the amount of interest in the topic.

The last item in Group II was an amendment from Frank Murphy and Walter Sullivan which the committee responded to by dropping language originally written by O'Connor claiming that some pacifists seem to support "wars of liberation" while denying governments the right to fight against revolutionaries.

The amendment passed, completing the de-O'Connorification of the pastoral letter. To be sure, O'Connor's influence was reflected in various ways throughout the document. But on every major issue on which the committee, by agreeing to his demands, had moved beyond the bishops' mandate, O'Connor had been solidly repudiated: on "curb-halt," on his desire to see more limited nuclear weapons, on his weasel wording, on his weakening of no-first-use language, on his desire to drop all the specifics, on comparative justice, on the Comprehensive Test Ban Treaty, and on generally nasty, inappropriate language.

As it turned out, O'Connor received a consolation prize; as he moved to the microphone to address an amendment, Archbishop Laghi stopped him to tell him he had just been named bishop of Scranton. Some church observers saw the appointment as a reward for O'Connor's efforts; some saw it as an effort to remove him from the limelight of his national military position; some said it had nothing to do with the pastoral—Scranton is one of the most conservative dioceses in the country, and conservative bishops are becoming few and far between.

When the bishops returned from lunch on Tuesday, they returned to the question of the 1976 pastoral and the Krol testimony. Bernardin offered a compromise. First, he said, the committee would prefer to stay with the third draft's quick summary of the '76 pastoral. He said the pastoral's discussion hadn't been "fully developed" and was now subject to misunderstanding.

Second, Bernardin said that because the Krol testimony was "historically" important, part of it should be quoted in the text. But he wanted to leave out the "lesser evil" paragraph to avoid misunderstanding.

Hickey accepted the compromise and the bishops approved it, effectively disowning the words of their own earlier pastoral, whose condemnation of the element of threat in deterrence was now apparently at odds with the pope's judgment that deterrence was "morally acceptable." There was no small irony in the fact that the bishops had, in fact, weakened their criticism of deterrence while escalating their opposition to nuclear war.

Hickey was a key factor again a few minutes later in discussing two of his amendments which had been misplaced and were now on an "errata" sheet. Hickey had typed all of his amendments together, not one each on the special sheets distributed by the conference, and they had been misplaced.

Hickey described his first amendment as a "middle ground" between Quinn's Amendment 68 and the committee's "skepticism." His amendment said, "We therefore express our view that the first imperative is to prevent any use of nuclear weapons and our hope that leaders will resist the notion that nuclear conflict can be limited, contained, or won in any traditional sense."

Bernardin supported the amendment and it passed easily. But Hickey ran into complications on his next amendment, a proposed page-long conclusion to the pastoral. Hickey said pedagogical theory held that "first you tell them what you're going to teach them, then you teach them, then you tell them what you taught them."

He offered what he called a clear and quotable passage which first asked, "Why do we address these questions?" and said, ". . . We are the first generation since Genesis with the power to virtually destroy God's creation. We cannot remain silent in the face of such danger . . . We are simply trying to live up to the call of Jesus to be peacemakers in our time and situation."

Asking "What are we saying?" Hickey said, ". . . we are saying that good ends (defending one's country, protecting freedoms, etc.) cannot justify immoral means (the use of weapons which kill indiscriminately and threaten whole societies). We fear that our world and nation are headed in the wrong direction. More weapons with greater destructive potential are produced every day. More and more nations are seeking to become nuclear powers. In our quest for more and more security, we fear we are actually becoming less and less secure.

"In the words of our Holy Father, we need 'a moral about-face.' The whole world must summon its moral courage and technical means to say 'no' to nuclear conflict; 'no' to weapons of mass destruction; 'no' to an arms race which robs the poor and the vulnerable; and 'no' to the moral danger of a nuclear age which places before humankind indefensible choices of constant terror or surrender.

"Peacemaking is not an optional commitment. It is a requirement of our faith. We are called to be peacemakers, not by some movement of the moment, but by our Lord Jesus. The content and context of our peacemaking is set, not by some political agenda or ideological program, but by the teaching of His Church."

Bernardin said the committee would like to use Hickey's conclusion in the précis but not in the full document. Hickey said that was a good back-up position, but said, "I would like to test the body on this."

Bernardin said the committee had supported another proposed conclusion that had not yet come up. Roach asked if the conclusions were contradictory; when Bernardin said they weren't, Roach called for a vote, and the bishops overwhelmingly accepted Hickey's amendment.

Another important amendment approved from the errata sheet came from Joseph Fiorenza of San Angelo, Texas. Fiorenza, who had raised questions about the pastoral's authority in November, added some balance to the conservatives' emphasis on the nonbinding nature of much of the document. His amendment, revised slightly by the committee, said, ". . . the moral judgments that we make in specific cases, while not binding in conscience, are to be given serious attention and consideration by Catholics as they determine whether their moral judgments are consistent with the Gospel."

Group III contained the other conclusion Bernardin had mentioned. It was offered by Ahern and was a lengthy call for creation of the kind of world organization envisioned by Popes John XXIII and Paul VI.

"There *is* a substitute for war," the amendment said. "There is negotiation, under the supervision of a global body realistically fashioned to do its job. It must be given the equipment to keep constant surveillance on the entire earth. Present technology makes this possible. It must have the authority, freely conferred upon it by all the nations, to investigate what seems to be preparations for war by any one of them. It must be empowered by all the nations to enforce its commands on every nation."

The committee originally opposed the amendment. But Bernardin said, "Because of the merit and the presenter, we reversed ourselves"; Ahern had earlier said at a press conference that despite his concern with the document's authority, he supported it strongly.

The bishops moved quickly through Groups III and IV and moved on to Group V, new amendments. Hannan, who argued several times that calling deterrence morally acceptable meant you could use nuclear weapons, again began escalating his attacks on the pastoral. He offered his amendment to add "except where necessary for deterrence" to the "halt" section. Bernardin said, "That would gut the concept of the halt." Hickey said it would "create a loophole big enough to drive through about any addition to the arms race that might be brought forward." To no one's surprise, Hannan's amendment was overwhelmingly defeated.

Hannan then attacked the pastoral's statement urging that it be used as a teaching document. Shouting, he cited Cardinal Ratzinger's comments on the limited authority of national conferences and accused Bernardin of disobeying Rome's desires. Finally, exasperated in defending his belief that the pastoral was, in fact, in line with Rome, Bernardin yelled back, "I was at the meeting."

Then, for a few moments, the bishops seemed to enter a time warp. The occasion was amendments offered by Cooke, Carberry and Bishop Jerome Hastrich of Gallup, New Mexico, calling for devotion to Our Lady of Fátima. In the alleged apparition in the early twentieth century, Mary had said praying the rosary was the true way to peace that would lead to the conversion of Russia. Cooke's amendment said "the guidance she provided on the occasion of her appearance at Fátima offers the true road to peace with justice." Part of the amendments' context was that those honoring Our Lady of Fátima had widely criticized the peace pastoral.

Bernardin offered a committee response, which would have said, ". . . we encourage devotion to Our Lady of Fátima as a great many of our people have urged." Carberry, perhaps best known for his unusual devotion to Mary and his successful efforts to delay acceptance of communion in the hand for several years, didn't like the last phrase. "It would be better to come from the top down, rather than the bottom up."

In short order, there were two votes on amendments to the amendment. Both failed; the voice votes were close and standing votes were required. Those opposing the amendment seemed to stand long enough to be counted, but not long enough to be recognized; it isn't easy for a bishop to vote against Mary in any form. For a minute, it looked like the first written vote of the meeting would come not on some point of nuclear policy but on Our Lady of Fátima.

Then Archbishop Frank Hurley offered an amendment to the amendment dropping references to Fátima and calling for devotion to "Our Lady of Peace." He noted that a large number of Hispanics in his diocese show devotion to Our Lady of Guadalupe, and said the bishops shouldn't be "partisan" in their devotion to Mary. Hurley heads the Archdiocese of Anchorage, and the influx of Hispanics into Alaska is a development everyone else had apparently missed.

Cooke replied that "that isn't in line with what we're trying to put over—I mean, put through."

By now, the press corps was in stitches and the bishops themselves seemed about to burst. Then McManus, a long-time ally of Hurley, took the floor. (Hurley's brother Mark, chairman of the USCC Committee for Social Development and World Peace, didn't attend the meeting, citing a local emergency.) In a "now, listen" tone, McManus backed Hurley's amendment, adding, "We know that some of those devoted to Our Lady of Fátima reject the sum and substance of this letter, we know who's sending those petitions coming to us—"

He was interrupted by an explosive round of applause from the bishops, who then approved Hurley's amendment in short order.

The day's last fireworks came on Hannan's unsuccessful amendment to include the Schotte memo as an appendix. "We were explicitly told that this document was not to be used in this way," Bernardin said. "They were very explicit about that," Roach added.

The final amendment to be discussed came from Archbishop William Borders of Baltimore, who wanted to shorten the document by reducing most of the papal quotes to footnotes. Not surprisingly, it didn't get very far.

When all of the amendments had been dealt with, the bishops devoted only a few minutes to discussing whether or not to approve the document. The only bishop to speak against it was Austin Vaughan, a New York auxiliary known for his conservative theology. He praised the document as a consciousness raiser on war and peace, but he said there were too many theological inconsistencies in it.

The bishops then discussed the précis and Szoka's proposal that the bishops also issue a condensed version of the pastoral. The idea failed, and the discussion ended when Auxiliary Bishop John McCarthy of Houston said that after all the work done already, it would be "a disaster" to ask the committee to produce a shortened version.

Conference staff distributed written ballots during these discussions. Before announcing the result, Roach called on Bishop Ernest Unterkoefler of Charleston, South Carolina, who was going to offer a resolution thanking Americans for their support. Roach talked of "deep gratitude to the millions of people who have supported us in prayer." The bishops were enthusiastic in their thanks, as Unterkoefler said they wanted to tell "the Catholic people and all those people of good will that we sensed their support."

Unterkoefler also praised Roach's leadership "bringing us to a new prophetic stance as bishops in the United States."

The tribute to Roach was clearly called for; while he wasn't involved in the drafting process, he was the guiding force behind it from his selection of the committee to the November bishops' meeting, the Vatican meeting, his reaction to the third draft, and his chairing of the Chicago meeting.

The tribute to Roach also highlighted the role past bishops' conference presidents had played in the process—Krol, Bernardin and Quinn. The only other post-Vatican II conference president, Cardinal Dearden, was now retired and hadn't played a visible role in this pastoral; but his influence was felt—he had, after all, named Gumbleton an auxiliary bishop, brought Bernardin to the conference as general secretary, and spoken out strongly on peace in his own right. The string seemed likely to continue; with Roach's term ending in November, Malone, Hickey or both seemed likely to succeed him at some point.

After Unterkoefler's remarks, Bernardin thanked the committee and staff and the bishops gave them all a standing ovation.

Then Roach read the vote results. With 288 active bishops, the pastoral needed 192 votes, two thirds, to pass. There were 238 votes for the pastoral and only 9 against. It was the most positive votes for any bishops' pastoral or document and about the average number of negative votes.

Before the meeting, Bernardin, the best head counter in the conference, had privately predicted 85–90 percent of the bishops would back the pastoral; the actual tally was 96 percent, more than anyone had dared predict. What happened?

A number of factors came together. One was the worsening state of arms control negotiations and the Reagan administration's continued hawkishness. Another was leadership. Some observers believe only Bernardin could have put that kind of consensus together. That view may reflect a little too much hero worship. But Bernardin did provide an important leadership by process. At the same time, there were other leaders. If the body of bishops gave the pastoral letter its spirit and the Bernardin committee gave it its intellect, Quinn and Hickey gave it its heart and Roach gave it its backbone.

By contrast, the best that critics could offer was O'Connor's whining, Hannan's ranting and Cooke's bumbling. O'Connor and Hannan made it particularly easy for the other bishops to draw the line between those who wanted to use nuclear weapons and those who didn't.

The pastoral also reflected the bishops' maturing understanding of their role as bishops—including their responsibility to teach and their responsibility to be prophetic. They felt a real need to address what they say as the major issue facing the world and to do so in a way that their people and their country could understand.

Gumbleton sees the bishops' movement on the nuclear question as a "conversion." When he and a few other bishops caucused about a discussion of nuclear war in November 1980, none of them could have predicted this outcome.

Finally, there is another factor which the bishops themselves take seriously. Bishop Pierre DuMaine of San Jose raised it jokingly during a coffee break, but he wasn't merely being flip. "We shouldn't be surprised at the direction things are taking here," he said. "After all, the Holy Spirit was a dove."

⋄ ⋄ ⋄

Some postscripts:

—The day after the bishops voted on the pastoral, the long-delayed House freeze resolution vote took place. After critics attached an amendment setting an indefinite time limit for pursuing a freeze, it passed 278–149. According to Albert J. Menendez, research director for Americans United for Separation of Church and State, Catholic Democrats backed the freeze 82–4, Catholic Republicans opposed it 23–15. Seventy-eight percent of Catholics, 82 percent of Jews and 57 percent of Protestants supported the freeze.

—The same day as the freeze vote, Soviet Premier Andropov made an apparent concession, saying his country would agree to discuss the number of nuclear warheads, not the number of missiles, in talks about arms in Europe. The same week, Reagan, in exchange for congressional support for the MX, expressed support for the concept of a "build-down" in which two old missiles would be retired for each new one deployed.

—Archbishop Weakland, chairman of the committee which was to produce a first draft of a pastoral letter on capitalism by November 1983, said he thought the organized conservative effort to influence the nuclear pastoral had sensitized the bishops to the power of money.

—Archbishop Quinn caused a stir when, citing the Nuremberg principle that obeying orders is no excuse for committing a war crime, he said no Catholic could morally obey an order to fire a nuclear weapon. Quinn again went further than most bishops. But he received support from former CIA director William Colby, a Catholic, who told a forum in Washington, "If a young lieutenant takes his company into a village and shoots people, he's a war criminal. But if a young lieutenant pushes a button and destroys a city, is he doing his duty?"

—Bishop O'Connor said too much attention had been paid to the fact that the bishops changed a few words in Chicago. Michael Novak and a State Department spokesman, who had hailed the change from "halt" to "curb" as a major victory, argued that the change back to "halt" wasn't significant.

—A survey in the Diocese of Richmond, where the military represents a major segment of the Catholic population, found 40 percent of those surveyed agreeing with the pastoral, 30 percent disagreeing and 30 percent not sure; it was a far more positive showing than diocesan officials had expected.

—The National Council of Churches' Governing Board passed a resolution which, while making some theological distinctions, praised the bishops' courage and strongly supported the pastoral, asking their member denominations and local churches to study it.

—And, in a forum at Trinity College in Washington, Cardinal Krol offered this response to critics who charged the bishops had no business talking about nuclear weapons: "We can't yield to the Marxist-Leninist view that all religious activity be confined to the sacristy."

—Shortly before the Chicago meeting, Roach created a follow-up committee to help dioceses implement the pastoral. No political balancing act here—he named Fulcher to chair it with Kenneth Untener of Saginaw and Kenneth Povish of Lansing, two activists.

—And a word of blessing came from the Vatican when Cardinal Ratzinger told *Der Spiegel* on May 9 that he understood the subtleties of the U.S. bishops' position that a no-first-use policy couldn't be implemented immediately. But, he said, "Indeed, I believe that the Americans are right in saying that the so-called first use of nuclear weapons is not, as regards morality, justifiable."

AFTERWORD:
A REVOLUTION OF POSITIVE
AMBIGUITY

In the closing minutes of the bishops' discussion of their pastoral letter on nuclear war, Auxiliary Bishop Austin Vaughan of New York said he couldn't support the document because it was "a pastoral and theological minefield."

Auxiliary Bishop James Lyke of Cleveland countered that he was sure that many bishops had felt that way after Vatican II.

Both men were right. The letter is a pastoral and theological minefield; most of the bishops who voted for it understand that and accept it. The Vatican II analogy is apt. In terms of both its impact on internal church affairs and the church's relationship to the world, "The Challenge of Peace" is the most significant event in the American Catholic Church, and perhaps in the international church, since the Second Vatican Council.

Both the process and the product itself qualify as revolutionary. The emphasis on the different levels of church teaching—ranging, as one bishop noted, from binding universal principles to "it would be nice . . ."—was a major, visible acknowledgment of a reality previously familiar primarily to theologians.

A related development, largely due to the insistence of Rome, is the unprecedented, almost dramatic, emphasis on the role of individual conscience and the right to dissent on matters of contingent, prudential judgment.

If people may legitimately disagree over whether or not it is moral to start a nuclear war and still remain Catholics in good standing, the mind boggles at the implications for less cosmic issues like contraception, sterilization, abortion, divorce. The church will, no doubt, try to draw a line between issues like those and issues of war and peace; but many American Catholics, including many bishops, won't accept that. A conscience, once awakened, doesn't easily go back to sleep.

The public nature of the process surrounding the pastoral will not be repeated on every issue the bishops address, but it will remain the standard by which everything else will be compared. The bishops involved far more Catholics and, for that matter, non-Catholics at the grass-roots level than ever before; they were encouraged and enlightened by that participation and will look for it again in the future.

The public process, which saw the document effectively going through four drafts and considerable revision, some of it contradictory, has also impressed upon American Catholics the human dimension of the church and the men who lead it. The "development of doctrine" seen in the process and in the bishops' reversal of positions taken in the past must inevitably encourage a more questioning attitude toward that leadership.

The American bishops also made a significant contribution to the developing role of the national bishops' conference. Local bishops can have an impact—the Latin American bishops gave the church the "preferential option for the poor"; the American bishops gave it a preferential option for peace. Despite the Vatican's efforts to emphasize the limits of national bishops' conferences' authority, that authority is now, thanks to the Americans, greater than ever; the American bishops may well have unilaterally pulled off Vatican III.

The whole process surrounding the pastoral represents a revolution of positive ambiguity; the most important single comment during the pastoral's development was Archbishop Roach's remark that "ambiguity has been a legitimate, treasured part of the whole moral tradition of the church."

When Roach made that comment at a press conference, Hehir blanched; he had expected him to talk about "ambiguity" in the context of deterrence. The "centimeter of ambiguity" about the possible use of nuclear weapons that Hehir talked about did seem necessary to leave an aura of credibility and legitimacy around deterrence.

In both policy and theology, clarity seemed to create new problems. For example, Bishop DuMaine—chairman of the USCC Communication Committee and far from a hawk—was searching for clarity when he offered an amendment trying to set rules for the use of nuclear weapons in response to nuclear attack.

But the amendment failed, because the bishops seemed to sense that such efforts end up becoming loopholes. Archbishop Oscar Lipscomb of Mobile put it succinctly at a press conference during the Chicago meeting: "This pastoral letter is against all nuclear wars—don't get lost asking if you can have a little, itty-bitty nuclear war."

The refusal to discuss possible legitimate uses of nuclear weapons may be seen as irresponsible; it can also be seen as a very responsible way to shift the discussion away from ways to use nuclear weapons to ways to avoid using them.

But Roach was both candid and insightful in acknowledging the role of ambiguity in moral decision making. From the first draft on, the bishops' seat-of-the-pants judgment was clear—the world had to move out of the present arms race, but, because unilateral disarmament posed grave risks to freedom and peace, it would take time to change, time in which dramatic efforts to end the arms race must be made. The problem was finding a way to translate that into the terms of Catholic moral theology.

Ultimately, it couldn't be done without raising the hackles of the most orthodox within the church. The third draft and the final document all but abandoned any rationale for the "strictly conditioned moral acceptance" of deterrence; in taking the pope's evaluation as a starting point, the bishops virtually argued the point from authority, concentrating on explaining what the position meant, rather than how it was developed.

But that still didn't clear the bishops of the charge that in accepting deterrence even conditionally they were not somehow indicating acceptance of evil or the intent to accept it. That argument exists in reality, if not in print. There is no other way to reconcile John Paul's judgment on deterrence with all of the devastating criticisms he, other popes, the Vatican Council and other church leaders have expressed about the arms race.

The bishops' "centimeter of ambiguity" on this point carries considerable risk from their point of view; but it is the inevitable result of the church's own teaching and a recognition that people, let alone nations, are seldom presented with antiseptic moral choices.

The pastoral's impact on the church can perhaps be seen best in the response to a now standard question: given the fact that so many American Catholics have ignored *Humanae Vitae*, why should anyone expect them to pay any more attention to "The Challenge of Peace?"

The answer is simple. In "The Challenge of Peace," the bishops responded to an urgent need among their people; they produced their document after significant consultation with and respect for them in a way that previous church leaders have not.

The American bishops risked a good deal of claimed, formal authority in this process; but in so doing, they greatly increased the strength of their informal, earned authority. The American bishops are closer to their people than they have ever been.

The pastoral's impact within the church parallels its impact on American society. The bishops both fed and were fed by the growing antinuclear movement in the United States. They firmly established the moral dimension of the debate over nuclear policies.

One of the background papers the bishops received in preparation for their ten-day retreat at Collegeville in June 1982 was an article by Rev. Richard Neuhaus, a neoconservative critic. Neuhaus noted what others have also pointed out—the decline of the liberal Protestant churches which set the U.S. moral agenda for much of its history. Those churches show no signs of regaining their lost influence, Neuhaus said, and other groups are contending for that role, most notably the Christian right and the less conservative evangelical movement.

The American Catholic Church is composed of increasingly affluent and powerful members; it has a highly visible hierarchical and international structure with a popular leader in Pope John Paul II; it has the added aura of mystery provided by a celibate clergy. *"The Thornbirds* didn't hurt the pastoral," one observer noted.

The Catholic Church will never set the public agenda on issues perceived as "parochial"—abortion and aid to church schools. But with the peace pastoral and all that led up to it, the Catholic Church, once described as a "despised and scorned minority," has clearly assumed the role of the major religious shaper of national morality on issues of justice and peace.

But while the pastoral has been rightly called "prophetic," it's still amazing how mainstream its policy recommendations are; they would appear far more moderate in a different political climate.

The bishops' support for nuclear "sufficiency" to maintain a deterrent is hardly pacifist; their opposition to destabilizing new nuclear weapons systems and to weapons and policies that blur the distinction between conventional and nuclear war is only rational; their call for the freeze concept is supported by a majority in the House of Representatives, many former government officials, and 70 percent of the American people; their support for a Comprehensive Test Ban Treaty and a no-first-use pledge are also mainstream, and they acknowledge that a no-first-use pledge can't be implemented overnight; their call for deep reductions in U.S.-Soviet nuclear stockpiles reflects the stated goal of present U.S. proposals.

The bishops' major contribution may be that they have made the previously unthinkable unthinkable once again. For decades, the world lived with nuclear weapons, fearing them, but assuming that they would never be used. Since 1981, the combination of new technological possibilities and Administration rhetoric convinced millions of people that the use of nuclear weapons was not only possible but inevitable. The bishops dared to say that we could survive and remain free without using nuclear weapons.

The bishops bring to mind the words of the Russian poet Yevtushenko:

. . . our descendents will burn with bitter shame
to remember, when punishing vile acts,
that most peculiar
                    time,
                              when
plain honesty
          was labeled 'courage,' . . .

APPENDIX

The Pastoral Letter on War and Peace

THE CHALLENGE OF PEACE: GOD'S PROMISE AND OUR RESPONSE

Contents

Summary

The Second Vatican Council opened its evaluation of modern warfare with the statement: "The whole human race faces a moment of supreme crisis in its advance toward maturity." We agree with the council's assessment; the crisis of the moment is embodied in the threat which nuclear weapons pose for the world and much that we hold dear in the world. We have seen and felt the effects of the crisis of the nuclear age in the lives of people we serve. Nuclear weaponry has drastically changed the nature of warfare, and the arms race poses a threat to human life and human civilization which is without precedent.

We write this letter from the perspective of Catholic faith. Faith does not insulate us from the daily challenges of life but intensifies our desire to address them precisely in light of the gospel which has come to us in the person of the risen Christ. Through the resources of faith and reason we desire in this letter to provide hope for people in our day and direction toward a world freed of the nuclear threat.

As Catholic bishops we write this letter as an exercise of our teaching ministry. The Catholic tradition on war and peace is a long and complex one; it stretches from the Sermon on the Mount to the statements of Pope John Paul II. We wish to explore and explain the resources of the moral-religious teaching and to apply it to specific questions of our day. In doing this we realize, and we want readers of this letter to recognize, that not all statements in this letter have the same moral authority. At times we state universally binding moral principles found in the teaching of the Church; at other times the pastoral letter makes specific applications, observations and recommendations which allow for diversity of opinion on the part of those who assess the factual data of situations differently. However, we expect Catholics to give our moral judgments serious consideration when they are forming their own views on specific problems.

The experience of preparing this letter has manifested to us the range of strongly held opinion in the Catholic community on questions of fact and judgment concerning issues of war and peace. We urge mutual respect among individuals and groups in the Church as this letter is analyzed and discussed. Obviously, as bishops, we believe that such differences should be expressed within the framework of Catholic moral teaching. We need in the Church not only conviction and commitment but also civility and charity.

While this letter is addressed principally to the Catholic community, we want it to make a contribution to the wider public debate in our country on the dangers and dilemmas of the nuclear age. Our contribution will not be primarily technical or political, but we are convinced that there is no satisfactory answer to the human problems of the nuclear age which fails to consider the moral and religious dimensions of the questions we face.

Although we speak in our own name, as Catholic bishops of the Church in the United States, we have been conscious in the preparation of this letter of the consequences our teaching will have not only for the United States but for other nations as well. One important expression of this awareness has been the consultation we have had, by correspondence and in an important meeting held at the Vatican (January 18–19, 1983), with representatives of European bishops' conferences. This consultation with bishops of other countries, and, of course, with the Holy See, has been very helpful to us.

Catholic teaching has always understood peace in positive terms. In the words of Pope John Paul II: "Peace is not just the absence of war. . . . Like a cathedral, peace must be constructed patiently and with unshakable faith." (Coventry, England, 1982) Peace is the fruit of order. Order in human society must be shaped on the basis of respect for the transcendence of God and the unique dignity of each person, understood in terms of freedom, justice, truth and love. To avoid war in our day we must be intent on building peace in an increasingly interdependent world. In Part III of this letter we set forth a positive vision of peace and the demands such a vision makes on diplomacy, national policy, and personal choices.

While pursuing peace incessantly, it is also necessary to limit the use of force in a world comprised of nation states, faced with common problems but devoid of an adequate international political authority. Keeping the peace in the nuclear age is a moral and political imperative. In Parts I and II of this letter we set forth both the principles of

Catholic teaching on war and a series of judgments, based on these principles, about concrete policies. In making these judgments we speak as moral teachers, not as technical experts.

I. Some Principles, Norms and Premises of Catholic Teaching

A. On War

1. Catholic teaching begins in every case with a presumption against war and for peaceful settlement of disputes. In exceptional cases, determined by the moral principles of the just-war tradition, some uses of force are permitted.

2. Every nation has a right and duty to defend itself against unjust aggression.

3. Offensive war of any kind is not morally justifiable.

4. It is never permitted to direct nuclear or conventional weapons to "the indiscriminate destruction of whole cities or vast areas with their populations. . . ." *(Pastoral Constitution,* #80.) The intentional killing of innocent civilians or non-combatants is always wrong.

5. Even defensive response to unjust attack can cause destruction which violates the principle of proportionality, going far beyond the limits of legitimate defense. This judgment is particularly important when assessing planned use of nuclear weapons. No defensive strategy, nuclear or conventional, which exceeds the limits of proportionality is morally permissible.

B. On Deterrence

1. "In current conditions 'deterrence' based on balance, certainly not as an end in itself but as a step on the way toward a progressive disarmament, may still be judged morally acceptable. Nonetheless, in order to ensure peace, it is indispensable not to be satisfied with this minimum which is always susceptible to the real danger of explosion." (Pope John Paul II, "Message to U.N. Special Session on Disarmament," #8, June 1982.)

2. No *use* of nuclear weapons which would violate the principles of discrimination or proportionality may be *intended* in a strategy of deterrence. The moral demands of Catholic teaching require resolute willingness not to intend or to do moral evil even to save our own lives or the lives of those we love.

3. Deterrence is not an adequate strategy as a long-term basis for peace; it is a transitional strategy justifiable only in conjunction with resolute determination to pursue arms control and disarmament. We are convinced that "the fundamental principle on which our present peace depends must be replaced by another, which declares that the true and solid peace of nations consists not

in equality of arms but in mutual trust alone." (Pope John XXIII, *Peace on Earth,* #113.)

C. The Arms Race and Disarmament

1. The arms race is one of the greatest curses on the human race; it is to be condemned as a danger, an act of aggression against the poor, and a folly which does not provide the security it promises. (Cf: *Pastoral Constitution,* #81, *Statement of the Holy See to the United Nations,* 1976.)

2. Negotiations must be pursued in every reasonable form possible; they should be governed by the "demand that the arms race should cease; that the stockpiles which exist in various countries should be reduced equally and simultaneously by the parties concerned; that nuclear weapons should be banned; and that a general agreement should eventually be reached about progressive disarmament and an effective method of control." (Pope John XXIII, *Peace on Earth,* #112.)

D. On Personal Conscience

1. *Military Service:* "All those who enter the military service in loyalty to their country should look upon themselves as the custodians of the security and freedom of their fellow countrymen; and when they carry out their duty properly, they are contributing to the maintenance of peace." *(Pastoral Constitution,* #79.)

2. *Conscientious Objection:* "Moreover, it seems just that laws should make humane provision for the case of conscientious objectors who refuse to carry arms, provided they accept some other form of community service." *(Pastoral Constitution,* #79.)

3. *Non-violence:* "In this same spirit we cannot but express our admiration for all who forego the use of violence to vindicate their rights and resort to other means of defense which are available to weaker parties, provided it can be done without harm to the rights and duties of others and of the community." *(Pastoral Constitution,* #78.)

4. *Citizens and Conscience:* "Once again we deem it opportune to remind our children of their duty to take an active part in public life, and to contribute towards the attainment of the common good of the entire human family as well as to that of their own political community. . . . In other words, it is necessary that human beings, in the intimacy of their own consciences, should so live and act in their temporal lives as to create a synthesis between scientific, technical and professional elements on the one hand, and spiritual values on the other." (Pope John XXIII, *Peace on Earth,* #146, 150.)

II. Moral Principles and Policy Choices

As bishops in the United States, assessing the concrete circumstances of our society, we have made a number of observations and recommendations in the process of applying moral principles to specific policy choices.

A. On The Use of Nuclear Weapons

1. *Counter Population Use:* Under no circumstances may nuclear weapons or other instruments of mass slaughter be used for the purpose of destroying population centers or other predominantly civilian targets. Retaliatory action which would indiscriminately and disproportionately take many wholly innocent lives, lives of people who are in no way responsible for reckless actions of their government, must also be condemned.

2. *The Initiation of Nuclear War:* We do not perceive any situation in which the deliberate initiation of nuclear war, on however restricted a scale, can be morally justified. Non-nuclear attacks by another state must be resisted by other than nuclear means. Therefore, a serious moral obligation exists to develop non-nuclear defensive strategies as rapidly as possible. In this letter we urge NATO to move rapidly toward the adoption of a "no-first-use" policy, but we recognize this will take time to implement and will require the development of an adequate alternative defense posture.

3. *Limited Nuclear War:* Our examination of the various arguments on this question makes us highly skeptical about the real meaning of "limited." One of the criteria of the just-war teaching is that there must be a reasonable hope of success in bringing about justice and peace. We must ask whether such a reasonable hope can exist once nuclear weapons have been exchanged. The burden of proof remains on those who assert that meaningful limitation is possible. In our view the first imperative is to prevent any use of nuclear weapons and we hope that leaders will resist the notion that nuclear conflict can be limited, contained or won in any traditional sense.

B. On Deterrence

In concert with the evaluation provided by Pope John Paul II, we have arrived at a strictly conditional moral acceptance of deterrence. In this letter we have outlined criteria and recommendations which indicate the meaning of conditional acceptance of deterrence policy. We cannot consider such a policy adequate as a long-term basis for peace.

C. On Promoting Peace

1. We support immediate, bilateral verifiable agreements to halt the testing, production and deployment of new nuclear weapons systems. This recommendation is not to be identified with any specific political initiative.

2. We support efforts to achieve deep cuts in the arsenals of both superpow-

ers; efforts should concentrate first on systems which threaten the retaliatory forces of either major power.

3. We support early and successful conclusion of negotiations of a comprehensive test ban treaty.

4. We urge new efforts to prevent the spread of nuclear weapons in the world, and to control the conventional arms race, particularly the conventional arms trade.

5. We support, in an increasingly interdependent world, political and economic policies designed to protect human dignity and to promote the human rights of every person, especially the least among us. In this regard, we call for the establishment of some form of global authority adequate to the needs of the international common good.

This letter includes many judgments from the perspective of ethics, politics and strategy needed to speak concretely and correctly to the "moment of supreme crisis" identified by Vatican II. We stress again that readers should be aware, as we have been, of the distinction between our statement of moral principles and of official Church teaching and our application of these to concrete issues. We urge that special care be taken not to use passages out of context; neither should brief portions of this document be cited to support positions it does not intend to convey or which are not truly in accord with the spirit of its teaching.

In concluding this summary we respond to two key questions often asked about this pastoral letter:

Why do we address these matters fraught with such complexity, controversy and passion? We speak as pastors, not politicians. We are teachers, not technicians. We cannot avoid our responsibility to lift up the moral dimensions of the choices before our world and nation. The nuclear age is an era of moral as well as physical danger. We are the first generation since Genesis with the power to threaten the created order. We cannot remain silent in the face of such danger. Why do we address these issues? We are simply trying to live up to the call of Jesus to be peacemakers in our own time and situation.

What are we saying? Fundamentally, we are saying that the decisions about nuclear weapons are among the most pressing moral questions of our age. While these decisions have obvious military and political aspects, they involve fundamental moral choices. In simple terms, we are saying that good ends (defending one's country, protecting freedom, etc.) cannot justify immoral means (the use of weapons which kill indiscriminately and threaten whole societies). We fear that our world and nation are headed in the wrong direction. More weapons with greater destructive potential are produced every day. More and more nations are seeking to become nuclear powers. In our quest for more and more security we fear we are actually becoming less and less secure.

In the words of our Holy Father, we need a "moral about-face." The whole world must summon the moral courage and technical means to say no to nuclear conflict; no to weapons of mass destruction; no to an arms race which robs the poor and the vulnerable; and no to the moral danger of a nuclear age which places before humankind indefensible choices of constant terror or surrender. Peacemaking is not an optional commitment. It is a requirement of our faith. We are called to be peacemakers, not by some movement of the moment, but by our Lord Jesus. The content and context of our peacemaking is set not by some political agenda or ideological program, but by the teaching of his Church.

Ultimately, this letter is intended as an expression of Christian faith, affirming the confidence we have that the risen Lord remains with us precisely in moments of crisis. It is our belief in his presence and power among us which sustain us in confronting the awesome challenge of the nuclear age. We speak from faith to provide hope for all who recognize the challenge and are working to confront it with the resources of faith and reason.

To approach the nuclear issue in faith is to recognize our absolute need for prayer: we urge and invite all to unceasing prayer for peace with justice for all people. In a spirit of prayerful hope we present this message of peace.

Introduction

1. "The whole human race faces a moment of supreme crisis in its advance toward maturity." Thus the Second Vatican Council opened its treatment of modern warfare.[1] Since the council, the dynamic of the nuclear arms race has intensified. Apprehension about nuclear war is almost tangible and visible today. As Pope John Paul II said in his message to the United Nations concerning disarmament: "Currently, the fear and preoccupation of so many groups in various parts of the world reveals that people are more frightened about what would happen if irresponsible parties unleash some nuclear war."[2]

2. As bishops and pastors ministering in one of the major nuclear nations, we have encountered this terror in the minds and hearts of our people—indeed, we share it. We write this letter because we agree that the world is at a moment of crisis, the effects of which are evident in people's lives. It is not our intent to play on fears, however, but to speak words of hope and encouragement in time of fear. Faith does not insulate us from the challenges of life; rather, it intensifies our desire to help solve them precisely in light of the good news which has come to us in the person of Jesus, the Lord of history. From the resources of our faith we wish to provide hope and strength to all who seek a world free of the nuclear threat. Hope sustains one's capacity to live with danger without being overwhelmed by it; hope is the will to struggle against obstacles even when they appear insuperable. Ultimately our hope rests in the God who gave us life, sustains the world by his power, and has called us to revere the lives of every person and all peoples.

3. The crisis of which we speak arises from this fact: nuclear war threatens the existence of our planet; this is a more menacing threat than any the world has known. It is neither tolerable nor necessary that human beings live under this threat. But removing it will require a major effort of intelligence, courage, and faith. As Pope John Paul II said at Hiroshima: "From now on it is only through a conscious choice and through a deliberate policy that humanity can survive."[3]

4. As Americans, citizens of the nation which was first to produce atomic weapons, which has been the only one to use them and which today is one of the handful of nations capable of decisively influencing the course of the nuclear age, we have grave human, moral and political responsibilities to see that a "conscious choice" is made to save humanity. This letter is therefore both an invitation and a challenge to Catholics in the United States to join with others in shaping the conscious choices and deliberate policies required in this "moment of supreme crisis."

I. Peace in the Modern World: Religious Perspectives and Principles

5. The global threat of nuclear war is a central concern of the universal Church, as the words and deeds of recent popes and the Second Vatican Council vividly demonstrate. In this pastoral letter we speak as bishops of the universal Church, heirs of the religious and moral teaching on modern warfare of the last four decades. We also speak as bishops of the Church in the United States, who have both the obligation and the opportunity to share and interpret the moral and religious wisdom of the Catholic tradition by applying it to the problems of war and peace today.

6. The nuclear threat transcends religious, cultural, and national boundaries. To confront its danger requires all the resources reason and faith can muster. This letter is a contribution to a wider common effort, meant to call Catholics and all members of our political community to dialogue and specific decisions about this awesome question.

7. The Catholic tradition on war and peace is a long and complex one, reaching from the Sermon on the Mount to the statements of Pope John Paul II. Its development cannot be sketched in a straight line and it seldom gives a simple answer to complex questions. It speaks through many voices and has produced multiple forms of religious witness. As we locate ourselves in this tradition, seeking to draw from it and to develop it, the document which provides profound inspiration and guidance for us is the *Pastoral Constitution on the Church in the Modern World* of Vatican II, for it is based on doctrinal principles and addresses the relationship of the Church to the world with respect to the most urgent issues of our day.[4]

8. A rule of interpretation crucial for the *Pastoral Constitution* is equally important for this pastoral letter although the authority inherent in these two documents is quite distinct. Both documents use principles of Catholic moral teaching and apply them to specific contemporary issues. The bishops at Vatican II opened the *Pastoral Constitution* with the following guideline on how to relate principles to concrete issues:

> In the first part, the Church develops her teaching on man, on the world which is the enveloping context of man's existence, and on man's relations to his fellow men. In Part II, the Church gives closer consideration to various aspects of modern life and human society; special considera-

tion is given to those questions and problems which, in this general area, seem to have a greater urgency in our day. As a result, in Part II the subject matter which is viewed in the light of doctrinal principles is made up of diverse elements. Some elements have a permanent value; others, only a transitory one. Consequently, the constitution must be interpreted according to the general norms of theological interpretation. Interpreters must bear in mind—especially in Part II—the changeable circumstances which the subject matter, by its very nature, involves.[5]

9. In this pastoral letter, too, we address many concrete questions concerning the arms race, contemporary warfare, weapons systems, and negotiating strategies. We do not intend that our treatment of each of these issues carry the same moral authority as our statement of universal moral principles and formal Church teaching. Indeed, we stress here at the beginning that not every statement in this letter has the same moral authority. At times we reassert universally binding moral principles (e.g., non-combatant immunity and proportionality). At still other times we reaffirm statements of recent popes and the teaching of Vatican II. Again, at other times we apply moral principles to specific cases.

10. When making applications of these principles we realize—and we wish readers to recognize—that prudential judgments are involved based on specific circumstances which can change or which can be interpreted differently by people of good will (e.g., the treatment of "no-first-use"). However, the moral judgments that we make in specific cases, while not binding in conscience, are to be given serious attention and consideration by Catholics as they determine whether their moral judgments are consistent with the Gospel.

11. We shall do our best to indicate, stylistically and substantively, whenever we make such applications. We believe such specific judgments are an important part of this letter, but they should be interpreted in light of another passage from the *Pastoral Constitution:*

> Often enough the Christian view of things will itself suggest some specific solution in certain circumstances. Yet it happens rather frequently, and legitimately so, that with equal sincerity some of the faithful will disagree with others on a given matter. Even against the intention of their proponents, however, solutions proposed on one side or another may be easily confused by many people with the Gospel message. Hence it is necessary for people to remember that no one is allowed in the aforementioned situations to appropriate the Church's authority for his opinion. They should always try to enlighten one another through honest discussion, preserving mutual charity and caring above all for the common good.[6]

12. This passage acknowledges that, on some complex social questions, the Church expects a certain diversity of views even though all hold the same

universal moral principles. The experience of preparing this pastoral letter has shown us the range of strongly held opinion in the Catholic community on questions of war and peace. Obviously, as bishops we believe that such differences should be expressed within the framework of Catholic moral teaching. We urge mutual respect among different groups in the Church as they analyze this letter and the issues it addresses. Not only conviction and commitment are needed in the Church, but also civility and charity.

13. The *Pastoral Constitution* calls us to bring the light of the gospel to bear upon "the signs of the times." Three signs of the times have particularly influenced the writing of this letter. The first, to quote Pope John Paul II at the United Nations, is that "the world wants peace, the world needs peace."[7] The second is the judgment of Vatican II about the arms race: "The arms race is one of the greatest curses on the human race and the harm it inflicts upon the poor is more than can be endured."[8] The third is the way in which the unique dangers and dynamics of the nuclear arms race present qualitatively new problems which must be addressed by fresh applications of traditional moral principles. In light of these three characteristics, we wish to examine Catholic teaching on peace and war.

14. The Catholic social tradition, as exemplified in the *Pastoral Constitution* and recent papal teachings, is a mix of biblical, theological, and philosophical elements which are brought to bear upon the concrete problems of the day. The biblical vision of the world, created and sustained by God, scarred by sin, redeemed in Christ and destined for the kingdom, is at the heart of our religious heritage. This vision requires elaboration, explanation, and application in each age; the important task of theology is to penetrate ever more adequately the nature of the biblical vision of peace and relate it to a world not yet at peace. Consequently, the teaching about peace examines both how to construct a more peaceful world and how to assess the phenomenon of war.

15. At the center of the Church's teaching on peace and at the center of all Catholic social teaching are the transcendence of God and the dignity of the human person. The human person is the clearest reflection of God's presence in the world; all of the Church's work in pursuit of both justice and peace is designed to protect and promote the dignity of every person. For each person not only reflects God, but is the expression of God's creative work and the meaning of Christ's redemptive ministry. Christians approach the problem of war and peace with fear and reverence. God is the Lord of life, and so each human life is sacred; modern warfare threatens the obliteration of human life on a previously unimaginable scale. The sense of awe and "fear of the Lord" which former generations felt in approaching these issues weighs upon us with new urgency. In the words of the *Pastoral Constitution:*

Men of this generation should realize that they will have to render an account of their warlike behavior; the destiny of generations to come depends largely on the decisions they make today.[9]

16. Catholic teaching on peace and war has had two purposes: to help Catholics form their consciences and to contribute to the public policy debate about the morality of war. These two purposes have led Catholic teaching to address two distinct but overlapping audiences. The first is the Catholic faithful, formed by the premises of the gospel and the principles of Catholic moral teaching. The second is the wider civil community, a more pluralistic audience, in which our brothers and sisters with whom we share the name Christian, Jews, Moslems, other religious communities, and all people of good will also make up our polity. Since Catholic teaching has traditionally sought to address both audiences, we intend to speak to both in this letter, recognizing that Catholics are also members of the wider political community.

17. The conviction, rooted in Catholic ecclesiology, that both the community of the faithful and the civil community should be addressed on peace and war has produced two complementary but distinct styles of teaching. The religious community shares a specific perspective of faith and can be called to live out its implications. The wider civil community, although it does not share the same vision of faith, is equally bound by certain key moral principles. For all men and women find in the depth of their consciences a law written on the human heart by God.[10] From this law reason draws moral norms. These norms do not exhaust the gospel vision, but they speak to critical questions affecting the welfare of the human community, the role of states in international relations, and the limits of acceptable action by individuals and nations on issues of war and peace.

18. Examples of these two styles can be found in recent Catholic teaching. At times the emphasis is upon the problems and requirements for a just public policy (e.g., Pope John Paul II at the U.N. Special Session 1982); at other times the emphasis is on the specific role Christians should play (e.g., Pope John Paul II at Coventry, England, 1982). The same difference of emphasis and orientation can be found in Pope John XXIII's *Peace on Earth* and Vatican II's *Pastoral Constitution.*

19. As bishops we believe that the nature of Catholic moral teaching, the principles of Catholic ecclesiology, and the demands of our pastoral ministry require that this letter speak both to Catholics in a specific way and to the wider political community regarding public policy. Neither audience and neither mode of address can be neglected when the issue has the cosmic dimensions of the nuclear arms race.

20. We propose, therefore, to discuss both the religious vision of peace among peoples and nations and the problems associated with realizing this vision in a world of sovereign states, devoid of any central authority and divided by ideology, geography, and competing claims. We believe the religious vision has an objective basis and is capable of progressive realization. Christ is our peace, for he has "made us both one, and has broken down the dividing wall of hostility . . . that he might create in himself one new man in place of the two, so making peace, and might reconcile us both to God" (Eph. 2:14–16). We also know that this peace will be achieved fully only in the kingdom of God. The realization of the kingdom, therefore, is a continuing work, progressively accomplished, precariously maintained, and needing constant effort to preserve the peace achieved and expand its scope in personal and political life.

21. Building peace within and among nations is the work of many individuals and institutions; it is the fruit of ideas and decisions taken in the political, cultural, economic, social, military, and legal sectors of life. We believe that the Church, as a community of faith and social institution, has a proper, necessary, and distinctive part to play in the pursuit of peace.

22. The distinctive contribution of the Church flows from her religious nature and ministry. The Church is called to be, in a unique way, the instrument of the kingdom of God in history. Since peace is one of the signs of that kingdom present in the world, the Church fulfills part of her essential mission by making the peace of the kingdom more visible in our time.

23. Because peace, like the kingdom of God itself, is both a divine gift and a human work, the Church should continually pray for the gift and share in the work. We are called to be a Church at the service of peace, precisely because peace is one manifestation of God's word and work in our midst. Recognition of the Church's responsibility to join with others in the work of peace is a major force behind the call today to develop a theology of peace. Much of the history of Catholic theology on war and peace has focused on limiting the resort to force in human affairs; this task is still necessary, and is reflected later in this pastoral letter, but it is not a sufficient response to Vatican II's challenge "to undertake a completely fresh reappraisal of war."[11]

24. A fresh reappraisal which includes a developed theology of peace will require contributions from several sectors of the Church's life: biblical studies, systematic and moral theology, ecclesiology, and the experience and insights of members of the Church who have struggled in various ways to make and keep the peace in this often violent age. This pastoral letter is more an invitation to continue the new appraisal of war and peace than a final synthesis of the results of such an appraisal. We have some sense of the characteristics of a theology of peace, but not a systematic statement of their relationships.

25. A theology of peace should ground the task of peacemaking solidly in the biblical vision of the kingdom of God, then place it centrally in the ministry of the Church. It should specify the obstacles in the way of peace, as

these are understood theologically and in the social and political sciences. It should both identify the specific contributions a community of faith can make to the work of peace and relate these to the wider work of peace pursued by other groups and institutions in society. Finally, a theology of peace must include a message of hope. The vision of hope must be available to all, but one source of its content should be found in a Church at the service of peace.

26. We offer now a first step toward a message of peace and hope. It consists of a sketch of the biblical conception of peace; a theological understanding of how peace can be pursued in a world marked by sin; a moral assessment of key issues facing us in the pursuit of peace today; and an assessment of the political and personal tasks required of all people of good will in this most crucial period of history.

A. Peace and the Kingdom

27. For us as believers, the sacred scriptures provide the foundation for confronting war and peace today. Any use of scripture in this area is conditioned by three factors. *First,* the term "peace" has been understood in different ways at various times and in various contexts. For example, peace can refer to an individual's sense of well-being or security, or it can mean the cessation of armed hostility, producing an atmosphere in which nations can relate to each other and settle conflicts without resorting to the use of arms. For men and women of faith, peace will imply a right relationship with God, which entails forgiveness, reconciliation, and union. Finally, the scriptures point to eschatological peace, a final, full realization of God's salvation when all creation will be made whole. Among these various meanings, the last two predominate in the scriptures and provide direction to the first two.

28. *Second,* the scriptures as we have them today were written over a long period of time and reflect many varied historical situations, all different from our own. Our understanding of them is both complicated and enhanced by these differences, but not in any way obscured or diminished by them. *Third,* since the scriptures speak primarily of God's intervention in history, they contain no specific treatise on war and peace. Peace and war must always be seen in light of God's intervention in human affairs and our response to that intervention. Both are elements within the ongoing revelation of God's will for creation.

29. Acknowledging this complexity, we will recognize in the scriptures a unique source of revelation, a word of God which is addressed to us as surely as it has been to all preceding generations. We call upon the spirit of God who speaks in that word and in our hearts to aid us in our listening. The sacred texts have much to say to us about the ways in which God calls us to live in union with and in fidelity to the divine will. They provide us with direction for

our lives and hold out to us an object of hope, a final promise, which guides and directs our actions here and now.

1. The Old Testament
30. War and peace are significant and highly complex elements within the multilayered accounts of the creation and development of God's people in the Old Testament.

a. War
31. Violence and war are very much present in the history of the people of God, particularly from the Exodus period to the monarchy. God is often seen as the one who leads the Hebrews in battle, protects them from their enemies, makes them victorious over other armies (see, for example, Deut. 1:30; 20:4; Jos. 2:24; Jgs. 3:28). The metaphor of warrior carried multifaceted connotations for a people who knew themselves to be smaller and weaker than the nations which surrounded them. It also enabled them to express their conviction about God's involvement in their lives and his desire for their growth and development. This metaphor provided the people with a sense of security; they had a God who would protect them even in the face of overwhelming obstacles. It was also a call to faith and to trust; the mighty God was to be obeyed and followed. No one can deny the presence of such images in the Old Testament nor their powerful influence upon the articulation of this people's understanding of the involvement of God in their history. The warrior God was highly significant during long periods of Israel's understanding of its faith. But this image was not the only image, and it was gradually transformed, particularly after the experience of the exile, when God was no longer identified with military victory and might. Other images and other understandings of God's activity became predominant in expressing the faith of God's people.

b. Peace
32. Several points must be taken into account in considering the image of peace in the Old Testament. First, all notions of peace must be understood in light of Israel's relation to God. Peace is always seen as gift from God and as fruit of God's saving activity. Secondly, the individual's personal peace is not greatly stressed. The well-being and freedom from fear which result from God's love are viewed primarily as they pertain to the community and its unity and harmony. Furthermore, this unity and harmony extend to all of creation; true peace implied a restoration of the right order not just among peoples, but within all of creation. Third, while the images of war and the warrior God become less dominant as a more profound and complex understanding of God is presented in the texts, the images of peace and the demands

upon the people for covenantal fidelity to true peace grow more urgent and more developed.

c. Peace and Fidelity to the Covenant

33. If Israel obeyed God's laws, God would dwell among them. "I will walk among you and will be your God and you shall be my people" (Lv. 26:12). God would strengthen the people against those who opposed them and would give peace in the land. The description of life in these circumstances witnesses to unity among peoples and creation, to freedom from fear and to security (Lv. 26:3–16). The right relationship between the people and God was grounded in and expressed by a covenantal union. The covenant bound the people to God in fidelity and obedience; God was also committed in the covenant, to be present with the people, to save them, to lead them to freedom. Peace is a special characteristic of this covenant; when the prophet Ezekiel looked to the establishment of the new, truer covenant, he declared that God would establish an everlasting covenant of peace with the people (Ez. 37:26).

34. Living in covenantal fidelity with God had ramifications in the lives of the people. It was part of fidelity to care for the needy and helpless; a society living with fidelity was one marked by justice and integrity. Furthermore, covenantal fidelity demanded that Israel put its trust in God alone and look only to him for its security. When Israel tended to forget the obligations of the covenant, prophets arose to remind the people and call them to return to God. True peace is an image which they stressed.

35. Ezekiel, who promised a covenant of peace, condemned in no uncertain terms the false prophets who said there was peace in the land while idolatry and injustice continued (Ez. 13:16). Jeremiah followed in this tradition and berated those who "healed the wounds of the people lightly" and proclaimed peace while injustice and infidelity prevailed (Jer. 6:14; 8:10–12). Jeremiah and Isaiah both condemned the leaders when, against true security, they depended upon their own strength or alliances with other nations rather than trusting in God (Is. 7:1–9; 30:1–4; Jer. 37:10). The lament of Isaiah 48:18 makes clear the connection between justice, fidelity to God's law, and peace; he cries out: "O that you had hearkened to my commandments! Then your peace would have been like a river, and your righteousness like the waves of the sea."

d. Hope for Eschatological Peace

36. Experience made it clear to the people of God that the covenant of peace and the fullness of salvation had not been realized in their midst. War and enmity were still present, injustices thrived, sin still manifested itself. These same experiences also convinced the people of God's fidelity to a covenant which they often neglected. Because of this fidelity, God's promise of a final salvation involving all peoples and all creation and of an ultimate

reign of peace became an integral part of the hope of the Old Testament. In the midst of their failures and sin, God's people strove for greater fidelity to him and closer relationship with him; they did so because, believing in the future they had been promised, they directed their lives and energies toward an eschatological vision for which they longed. Peace is an integral component of that vision.

37. The final age, the Messianic time, is described as one in which the "Spirit is poured on us from on high." In this age, creation will be made whole, "justice will dwell in the wilderness," the effect of righteousness will be peace, and the people will "abide in a peaceful habitation and in secure dwellings and in quiet resting places" (Is. 32:15–20). There will be no need for instruments of war (Is. 2:4; Mi. 4:3),[12] God will speak directly to the people and "righteousness and peace will embrace each other" (Ps. 85:10–11). A messiah will appear, a servant of God upon whom God has placed his spirit and who will faithfully bring forth justice to the nations: "He will not cry or lift up his voice, or make it heard in the street; a bruised reed he will not break and a dimly burning wick he will not quench; he will faithfully bring forth justice" (Is. 42:2–3).

38. The Old Testament provides us with the history of a people who portrayed their God as one who intervened in their lives, who protected them and led them to freedom, often as a mighty leader in battle. They also appear as a people who longed constantly for peace. Such peace was always seen as a result of God's gift which came about in fidelity to the covenantal union. Furthermore, in the midst of their unfulfilled longing, God's people clung tenaciously to hope in the promise of an eschatological time when, in the fullness of salvation, peace and justice would embrace and all creation would be secure from harm. The people looked for a messiah, one whose coming would signal the beginning of that time. In their waiting, they heard the prophets call them to love according to the covenantal vision, to repent, and to be ready for God's reign.

2. New Testament

39. As Christians we believe that Jesus is the messiah or Christ so long awaited. God's servant (Mt. 12:18–21), prophet and more than prophet (Jn. 4:19–26), the one in whom the fullness of God was pleased to dwell, through whom all things in heaven and on earth were reconciled to God, Jesus made peace by the blood of the cross (Col. 1:19–20). While the characteristics of the *shalom* of the Old Testament (gift from God, inclusive of all creation, grounded in salvation and covenantal fidelity, inextricably bound up with justice) are present in the New Testament traditions, all discussion of war and peace in the New Testament must be seen within the context of the unique revelation of God that is Jesus Christ and of the reign of God which Jesus proclaimed and inaugurated.

a. War

40. There is no notion of a warrior God who will lead the people in an historical victory over its enemies in the New Testament. The only war spoken of is found in apocalyptic images of the final moments, especially as they are depicted in the Book of Revelation. Here war stands as image of the eschatological struggle between God and Satan. It is a war in which the Lamb is victorious (Rv. 17:14).

41. Military images appear in terms of the preparedness which one must have for the coming trials (Lk. 14:31; 22:35–38). Swords appear in the New Testament as an image of division (Mt. 12:34; Heb. 4:12); they are present at the arrest of Jesus, and he rejects their use (Lk. 22:51 and parallel texts); weapons are transformed in Ephesians, when the Christians are urged to put on the whole armor of God which includes the breastplate of righteousness, the helmet of salvation, the sword of the Spirit, "having shod your feet in the equipment of the gospel of peace" (Eph. 6:10–17; cf. I Thes. 5:8–9). Soldiers, too, are present in the New Testament. They are at the crucifixion of Jesus, of course, but they are also recipients of the baptism of John, and one centurion receives the healing of his servant (Mt. 8:5–13 and parallel texts; cf. Jn. 4:46–53).

42. Jesus challenged everyone to recognize in him the presence of the reign of God and to give themselves over to that reign. Such a radical change of allegiance was difficult for many to accept and families found themselves divided, as if by a sword. Hence, the gospels tell us that Jesus said he came not to bring peace but rather the sword (Mt. 10:34). The peace which Jesus did not bring was the false peace which the prophets had warned against. The sword which he did bring was that of the division caused by the word of God which, like a two-edged sword, "pierces to the division of soul and spirit, of joints and marrow, and discerns the thoughts and intentions of the heart" (Heb. 4:12).

43. All are invited into the reign of God. Faith in Jesus and trust in God's mercy are the criteria. Living in accord with the demands of the kingdom rather than those of one's specific profession is decisive.[13]

b. Jesus and Reign of God

44. Jesus proclaimed the reign of God in his words and made it present in his actions. His words begin with a call to conversion and a proclamation of the arrival of the kingdom. "The time is fulfilled, and the kingdom of God is at hand; repent, and believe in the gospel" (Mk. 1:15, Mt. 4:17). The call to conversion was at the same time an invitation to enter God's reign. Jesus went beyond the prophets' cries for conversion when he declared that, in him, the

reign of God had begun and was in fact among the people (Lk. 17:20–21; 12:32).

45. His words, especially as they are preserved for us in the Sermon on the Mount, describe a new reality in which God's power is manifested and the longing of the people is fulfilled. In God's reign the poor are given the kingdom, the mourners are comforted, the meek inherit the earth, those hungry for righteousness are satisfied, the merciful know mercy, the pure see God, the persecuted know the kingdom, and peacemakers are called the children of God (Mt. 5:3–10).

46. Jesus' words also depict for us the conduct of one who lives under God's reign. His words call for a new way of life which fulfills and goes beyond the law. One of the most striking characteristics of this new way is forgiveness. All who hear Jesus are repeatedly called to forgive one another, and to do so not just once, but many, many times (Mt. 6:14–15; Lk. 6:37; Mt. 18:21–22; Mk. 11:25; Lk. 11:4; 17:3–4). The forgiveness of God, which is the beginning of salvation, is manifested in communal forgiveness and mercy.

47. Jesus also described God's reign as one in which love is an active, life-giving, inclusive force. He called for a love which went beyond family ties and bonds of friendship to reach even those who were enemies (Mt. 5:44–48; Lk. 6:27–28). Such a love does not seek revenge but rather is merciful in the face of threat and opposition (Mt. 5:39–42; Lk. 6:29–31). Disciples are to love one another as Jesus has loved them (Jn. 15:12).

48. The words of Jesus would remain an impossible, abstract ideal were it not for two things: the actions of Jesus and his gift of the spirit. In his actions, Jesus showed the way of living in God's reign; he manifested the forgiveness which he called for when he accepted all who came to him, forgave their sins, healed them, released them from the demons who possessed them. In doing these things, he made the tender mercy of God present in a world which knew violence, oppression, and injustice. Jesus pointed out the injustices of his time and opposed those who laid burdens upon the people or defiled true worship. He acted aggressively and dramatically at times, as when he cleansed the temple of those who had made God's house into a "den of robbers" (Mt. 21:12–17 and parallel texts; Jn. 3:13–25).

49. Most characteristic of Jesus' actions are those in which he showed his love. As he had commanded others, his love led him even to the giving of his own life to effect redemption. Jesus' message and his actions were dangerous ones in his time, and they led to his death—a cruel and viciously inflicted death, a criminal's death (Gal. 3:13). In all of his suffering, as in all of his life and ministry, Jesus refused to defend himself with force or with violence. He endured violence and cruelty so that God's love might be fully manifest and the world might be reconciled to the One from whom it had become es-

tranged. Even at his death, Jesus cried out for forgiveness for those who were his executioners: "Father, forgive them . . ." (Lk. 23:34).

50. The resurrection of Jesus is the sign to the world that God indeed does reign, does give life in death, and that the love of God is stronger even than death (Rom. 8:36–39).

51. Only in light of this, the fullest demonstration of the power of God's reign, can Jesus' gift of peace—a peace which the world cannot give (Jn. 14:27)—be understood. Jesus gives that peace to his disciples, to those who had witnessed the helplessness of the crucifixion and the power of the resurrection (Jn. 20:19, 20, 26). The peace which he gives to them as he greets them as their risen Lord is the fullness of salvation. It is the reconciliation of the world and God (Rom. 5:1–2; Col. 1:20); the restoration of the unity and harmony of all creation which the Old Testament spoke of with such longing. Because the walls of hostility between God and humankind were broken down in the life and death of the true, perfect servant, union and well-being between God and the world were finally fully possible (Eph. 2:13–22; Gal. 3:28).

c. Jesus and the Community of Believers

52. As his first gift to his followers, the risen Jesus gave his gift of peace. This gift permeated the meetings between the risen Jesus and his followers (Jn. 20:19–29). So intense was that gift and so abiding was its power that the remembrance of that gift and the daily living of it became the hallmark of the community of faith. Simultaneously, Jesus gave his spirit to those who followed him. These two personal and communal gifts are inseparable. In the spirit of Jesus the community of believers was enabled to recognize and to proclaim the savior of the world.

53. Gifted with Jesus' own spirit, they could recognize what God had done and know in their own lives the power of the One who creates from nothing. The early Christian communities knew that this power and the reconciliation and peace which marked it were not yet fully operative in their world. They struggled with external persecution and with interior sin, as do all people. But their experience of the spirit of God and their memory of the Christ who was with them nevertheless enabled them to look forward with unshakable confidence to the time when the fullness of God's reign would make itself known in the world. At the same time, they knew that they were called to be ministers of reconciliation (2 Cor. 5:19–20), people who would make the peace which God had established visible through the love and the unity within their own communities.

54. Jesus Christ, then, is our peace, and in his death-resurrection he gives God's peace to our world. In him God has indeed reconciled the world, made it one, and has manifested definitively that his will is this reconciliation, this unity between God and all peoples, and among the peoples themselves. The way to union has been opened, the covenant of peace established. The risen Lord's gift of peace is inextricably bound to the call to follow Jesus and to continue the proclamation of God's reign. Matthew's gospel (Mt. 28:16–20; cf. Lk. 24:44–53) tells us that Jesus' last words to his disciples were a sending forth and a promise: "I shall be with you all days." In the continuing presence of Jesus, disciples of all ages find the courage to follow him. To follow Jesus Christ implies continual conversion in one's own life as one seeks to act in ways which are consonant with the justice, forgiveness, and love of God's reign. Discipleship reaches out to the ends of the earth and calls for reconciliation among all peoples so that God's purpose, "a plan for the fullness of time, to unite all things in him" (Eph. 1:10), will be fulfilled.

3. Conclusion

55. Even a brief examination of war and peace in the scriptures makes it clear that they do not provide us with detailed answers to the specifics of the questions which we face today. They do not speak specifically of nuclear war or nuclear weapons, for these were beyond the imagination of the communities in which the scriptures were formed. The sacred texts do, however, provide us with urgent direction when we look at today's concrete realities. The fullness of eschatological peace remains before us in hope and yet the gift of peace is already ours in the reconciliation effected in Jesus Christ. These two profoundly religious meanings of peace inform and influence all other meanings for Christians. Because we have been gifted with God's peace in the risen Christ, we are called to our own peace and to the making of peace in our world. As disciples and as children of God, it is our task to seek for ways in which to make the forgiveness, justice and mercy and love of God visible in a world where violence and enmity are too often the norm. When we listen to God's word, we hear again and always the call to repentance and to belief: to repentance because although we are redeemed we continue to need redemption; to belief, because although the reign of God is near, it is still seeking its fullness.

B. Kingdom and History

56. The Christian understanding of history is hopeful and confident but also sober and realistic. "Christian optimism based on the glorious cross of Christ and the outpouring of the Holy Spirit is no excuse for self-deception. For Christians, peace on earth is always a challenge because of the presence of sin in man's heart."[14] Peace must be built on the basis of justice in a world where the personal and social consequences of sin are evident.

57. Christian hope about history is rooted in our belief in God as creator and sustainer of our existence and our conviction that the kingdom of God will come in spite of sin, human weakness, and failure. It is precisely because

sin is part of history that the realization of the peace of the kingdom is never permanent or total. This is the continuing refrain from the patristic period to Pope John Paul II:

> For it was sin and hatred that were an obstacle to peace with God and with others: he destroyed them by the offering of life on the cross; he reconciled in one body those who were hostile (cf. Eph. 2:16; Rom. 12:5) . . . Although Christians put all their best energies into preventing war or stopping it, they do not deceive themselves about their ability to cause peace to triumph, nor about the effect of their efforts to this end. They therefore concern themselves with all human initiatives in favor of peace and very often take part in them. But they regard them with realism and humility. One could almost say that they relativize them in two senses: they relate them both to the self-deception of humanity and to God's saving plan.[15]

58. Christians are called to live the tension between the vision of the reign of God and its concrete realization in history. The tension is often described in terms of "already but not yet": i.e., we already live in the grace of the kingdom, but it is not yet the completed kingdom. Hence, we are a pilgrim people in a world marked by conflict and injustice. Christ's grace is at work in the world; his command of love and his call to reconciliation are not purely future ideals but call us to obedience today.

59. With Pope Paul VI and Pope John Paul II we are convinced that "peace is possible."[16] At the same time, experience convinces us that "in this world a totally and permanently peaceful human society is unfortunately a utopia, and that ideologies that hold up that prospect as easily attainable are based on hopes that cannot be realized, whatever the reason behind them."[17]

60. This recognition—that peace is possible but never assured and that its possibility must be continually protected and preserved in the face of obstacles and attacks upon it—accounts in large measure for the complexity of Catholic teaching on warfare. In the kingdom of God, peace and justice will be fully realized. Justice is always the foundation of peace. In history, efforts to pursue both peace and justice are at times in tension, and the struggle for justice may threaten certain forms of peace.

61. It is within this tension of kingdom and history that Catholic teaching has addressed the problem of war. Wars mark the fabric of human history, distort the life of nations today, and, in the form of nuclear weapons, threaten the destruction of the world as we know it and the civilization which has been patiently constructed over centuries. The causes of war are multiple and not easily identified. Christians will find in any violent situation the consequences of sin: not only sinful patterns of domination, oppression or aggression, but the conflict of values and interests which illustrate the limitations of a sinful world. The threat of nuclear war which affects the world today reflects such sinful patterns and conflicts.

62. In the "already but not yet" of Christian existence, members of the Church choose different paths to move toward the realization of the kingdom in history. As we examine both the positions open to individuals for forming their consciences on war and peace and the Catholic teaching on the obligation of the state to defend society, we draw extensively on the *Pastoral Constitution* for two reasons.

63. First, we find its treament of the nature of peace and the avoidance of war compelling, for it represents the prayerful thinking of bishops of the entire world and calls vigorously for fresh new attitudes, while faithfully reflecting traditional Church teaching. Secondly, the council fathers were familiar with more than the horrors of World Wars I and II. They saw conflicts continuing "to produce their devastating effect day by day somewhere in the world," the increasing ferocity of warfare made possible by modern scientific weapons, guerrilla warfare "drawn out by new methods of deceit and subversion," and terrorism regarded as a new way to wage war.[18] The same phenomena mark our day.

64. For similar reasons we draw heavily upon the popes of the nuclear age, from Pope Pius XII through Pope John Paul II. The teaching of popes and councils must be incarnated by each local church in a manner understandable to its culture. This allows each local church to bring its unique insights and experience to bear on the issues shaping our world. From 1966 to the present, American bishops, individually and collectively, have issued numerous statements on the issues of peace and war, ranging from the Vietnam War to conscientious objection and the use of nuclear weapons. These statements reflect not only the concerns of the hierarchy but also the voices of our people who have increasingly expressed to us their alarm over the threat of war. In this letter we wish to continue and develop the teaching on peace and war which we have previously made, and which reflects both the teaching of the universal Church and the insights and experience of the Catholic community of the United States.

65. It is significant that explicit treatment of war and peace is reserved for the final chapter of the *Pastoral Constitution*. Only after exploring the nature and destiny of the human person does the council take up the nature of peace, which it sees not as an end in itself, but as an *indispensable condition* for the task "of constructing for all men everywhere a world more genuinely human."[19] An understanding of this task is crucial to understanding the Church's view of the moral choices open to us as Christians.

C. The Moral Choices for the Kingdom

66. In one of its most frequently quoted passages, the *Pastoral Constitution* declares that it is necessary "to undertake a completely fresh reappraisal of

war."[20] The council's teaching situates this call for a "fresh reappraisal" within the context of a broad analysis of the dignity of the human person and the state of the world today. If we lose sight of this broader discussion we cannot grasp the council's wisdom. For the issue of war and peace confronts everyone with a basic question: what contributes to, and what impedes, the construction of a more genuinely human world? If we are to evaluate war with an entirely new attitude, we must be serious about approaching the human person with an entirely new attitude. The obligation for all of humanity to work toward universal respect for human rights and human dignity is a fundamental imperative of the social, economic, and political order.

67. It is clear, then, that to evaluate war with a new attitude, we must go far beyond an examination of weapons systems or military strategies. We must probe the meaning of the moral choices which are ours as Christians. In accord with the vision of Vatican II, we need to be sensitive to both the danger of war and the conditions of true freedom within which moral choices can be made.[21] Peace is the setting in which moral choice can be most effectively exercised. How can we move toward that peace which is indispensable for true human freedom? How do we define such peace?

1. The Nature of Peace

68. The Catholic tradition has always understood the meaning of peace in positive terms. Peace is both a gift of God and a human work. It must be constructed on the basis of central human values: truth, justice, freedom, and love. The *Pastoral Constitution* states the traditional conception of peace:

> Peace is not merely the absence of war. Nor can it be reduced solely to the maintenance of a balance of power between enemies. Nor is it brought about by dictatorship. Instead, it is rightly and appropriately called "an enterprise of justice" (Is. 32:7). Peace results from that harmony built into human society by its divine founder and actualized by men as they thirst after ever greater justice.[22]

69. Pope John Paul II has enhanced this positive conception of peace by relating it with new philosophical depth to the Church's teaching on human dignity and human rights. The relationship was articulated in his 1979 Address to the General Assembly of the United Nations and also in his "World Day of Peace Message 1982":

> Unconditional and effective respect for each one's unprescriptable and inalienable rights is the necessary condition in order that peace may reign in a society. Vis-a-vis these basic rights all others are in a way derivatory and secondary. In a society in which these rights are not protected, the very idea of universality is dead, as soon as a small group of individuals set up for their own exclusive advantage a principle of discrimination

whereby the rights and even the lives of others are made dependent on the whim of the stronger.[23]

70. As we have already noted, however, the protection of human rights and the preservation of peace are tasks to be accomplished in a world marked by sin and conflict of various kinds. The Church's teaching on war and peace establishes a strong presumption against war which is binding on all; it then examines when this presumption may be overridden, precisely in the name of preserving the kind of peace which protects human dignity and human rights.

2. The Presumption Against War and the Principle of Legitimate Self-Defense

71. Under the rubric, "curbing the savagery of war," the council contemplates the "melancholy state of humanity." It looks at this world as it is, not simply as we would want it to be. The view is stark: ferocious new means of warfare threatening savagery surpassing that of the past, deceit, subversion, terrorism, genocide. This last crime, in particular, is vehemently condemned as horrendous, but all activities which deliberately conflict with the all-embracing principles of universal natural law, which is permanently binding, are criminal, as are all orders commanding such action. Supreme commendation is due the courage of those who openly and fearlessly resist those who issue such commands. All individuals, especially government officials and experts, are bound to honor and improve upon agreements which are "aimed at making military activity and its consequences less inhuman" and which "better and more workably lead to restraining the frightfulness of war."[24]

72. This remains a realistic appraisal of the world today. Later in this section the council calls for us "to strain every muscle as we work for the time when all war can be completely outlawed by international consent." We are told, however, that this goal requires the establishment of some universally recognized public authority with effective power "to safeguard, on the behalf of all, security, regard for justice, and respect for rights."[25] *But what of the present?* The council is exceedingly clear, as are the popes:

> Certainly, war has not been rooted out of human affairs. As long as the danger of war remains and there is no competent and sufficiently powerful authority at the international level, governments cannot be denied the right to legitimate defense once every means of peaceful settlement has been exhausted. Therefore, government authorities and others who share public responsibility have the duty to protect the welfare of the people entrusted to their care and to conduct such grave matters soberly.
>
> But it is one thing to undertake military action for the just defense of the people, and something else again to seek the subjugation of other nations. Nor does the possession of war potential make every military or

political use of it lawful. Neither does the mere fact that war has unhappily begun mean that all is fair between the warring parties.[26]

73. The Christian has no choice but to defend peace, properly understood, against aggression. This is an inalienable obligation. It is the *how* of defending peace which offers moral options. We stress this principle again because we observe so much misunderstanding about both those who resist bearing arms and those who bear them. Great numbers from both traditions provide examples of exceptional courage, examples the world continues to need. Of the millions of men and women who have served with integrity in the armed forces, many have laid down their lives. Many others serve today throughout the world in the difficult and demanding task of helping to preserve that "peace of a sort" of which the council speaks. We see many deeply sincere individuals who, far from being indifferent or apathetic to world evils, believe strongly in conscience that they are best defending true peace by refusing to bear arms. In some cases they are motivated by their understanding of the gospel and the life and death of Jesus as forbidding all violence. In others, their motivation is simply to give personal example of Christian forbearance as a positive, constructive approach toward loving reconciliation with enemies. In still other cases, they propose or engage in "active non-violence" as programmed resistance to thwart aggression, or to render ineffective any oppression attempted by force of arms. No government, and certainly no Christian, may simply assume that such individuals are mere pawns of conspiratorial forces or guilty of cowardice.

74. Catholic teaching sees these two distinct moral responses as having a complementary relationship, in the sense that both seek to serve the common good. They differ in their perception of how the common good is to be defended most effectively, but both responses testify to the Christian conviction that peace must be pursued and rights defended within moral restraints and in the context of defining other basic human values.

75. In all of this discussion of distinct choices, of course, we are referring to options open to individuals. The council and the popes have stated clearly that governments threatened by armed, unjust aggression must defend their people. This includes defense by armed force if necessary as a last resort. We shall discuss below the conditions and limits imposed on such defense. Even when speaking of individuals, however, the council is careful to preserve the fundamental *right* of defense. Some choose not to vindicate their rights by armed force and adopt other methods of defense, but they do not lose the right of defense nor may they renounce their obligations to others. They are praised by the council, as long as the rights and duties of others or of the community itself are not injured.

76. Pope Pius XII is especially strong in his conviction about the responsibility of the Christian to resist unjust aggression:

A people threatened with an unjust aggression, or already its victim, may not remain passively indifferent, if it would think and act as befits a Christian. All the more does the solidarity of the family of nations forbid others to behave as mere spectators, in any attitude of apathetic neutrality. Who will ever measure the harm already caused in the past by such indifference to war of aggression, which is quite alien to the Christian instinct? How much more keenly has it brought any advantage in recompense? On the contrary, it has only reassured and encouraged the authors and fomentors of aggression, while it obliges the several peoples, left to themselves, to increase their armaments indefinitely . . . Among (the) goods (of humanity) some are of such importance for society, that it is perfectly lawful to defend them against unjust aggression. *Their defense is even an obligation for the nations as a whole, who have a duty not to abandon a nation that is attacked.*[27]

77. None of the above is to suggest, however, that armed force is the only defense against unjust aggression, regardless of circumstances. Well does the council require that grave matters concerning the protection of peoples be conducted *soberly.* The council fathers were well aware that in today's world, the "horror and perversity of war are immensely magnified by the multiplication of scientific weapons. For acts of war involving these weapons can inflict massive and indiscriminate destruction far exceeding the bounds of legitimate defense."[28] Hence, we are warned: "Men of our time must realize that they will have to give a somber reckoning for their deeds of war. For the course of the future will depend largely on the decisions they make today."[29] There must be serious and continuing study and efforts to develop programmed methods for both individuals and nations to defend against unjust aggression without using violence.

78. We believe work to develop non-violent means of fending off aggression and resolving conflict best reflects the call of Jesus both to love and to justice. Indeed, each increase in the potential destructiveness of weapons and therefore of war serves to underline the rightness of the way that Jesus mandated to his followers. But, on the other hand, the fact of aggression, oppression and injustice in our world also serves to legitimate the resort to weapons and armed force in defense of justice. We must recognize the reality of the paradox we face as Christians living in the context of the world as it presently exists; we must continue to articulate our belief that love is possible and the only real hope for all human relations, and yet accept that force, even deadly force, is sometimes justified and that nations must provide for their defense. It is the mandate of Christians, in the face of this paradox, to strive to resolve it through an even greater commitment to Christ and his message. As Pope John Paul II said:

Christians are aware that plans based on aggression, domination and the manipulation of others lurk in human hearts, and sometimes even secretly nourish human intentions, in spite of certain declarations or manifestations of a pacifist nature. For Christians know that in this world a totally and permanently peaceful human society is unfortunately a utopia, and that ideologies that hold up that prospect as easily attainable are based on hopes that cannot be realized, whatever the reason behind them. It is a question of a mistaken view of the human condition, a lack of application in considering the question as a whole; or it may be a case of evasion in order to calm fear, or in still other cases a matter of calculated self-interest. Christians are convinced, if only because they have learned from personal experience, that these deceptive hopes lead straight to the false peace of totalitarian regimes. But this realistic view in no way prevents Christians from working for peace; instead, it stirs up their ardor, for they also know that Christ's victory over deception, hate and death gives those in love with peace a more decisive motive for action than what the most generous theories about man have to offer; Christ's victory likewise gives a hope more surely based than any hope held out by the most audacious dreams.

This is why Christians, even as they strive to resist and prevent every form of warfare, have no hesitation in recalling that, in the name of an elementary requirement of justice, peoples have a right and even a duty to protect their existence and freedom by proportionate means against an unjust aggressor.[30]

79. In light of the framework of Catholic teaching on the nature of peace, the avoidance of war, and the state's right of legitimate defense, we can now spell out certain moral principles within the Catholic tradition which provide guidance for public policy and individual choice.

3. The Just-War Criteria

80. The moral theory of the "just-war" or "limited-war" doctrine begins with the presumption which binds all Christians: we should do no harm to our neighbors; how we treat our enemy is the key test of whether we love our neighbor; and the possibility of taking even one human life is a prospect we should consider in fear and trembling. How is it possible to move from these presumptions to the idea of a justifiable use of lethal force?

81. Historically and theologically the clearest answer to the question is found in St. Augustine. Augustine was impressed by the fact and the consequences of sin in history—the "not yet" dimension of the kingdom. In his view war was both the result of sin and a tragic remedy for sin in the life of political societies. War arose from disordered ambitions, but it could also be used, in some cases at least, to restrain evil and protect the innocent. The classic case which illustrated his view was the use of lethal force to prevent aggression against innocent victims. Faced with the fact of attack on the innocent, the presumption that we do no harm, even to our enemy, yielded to the command of love understood as the need to restrain an enemy who would injure the innocent.

82. The just-war argument has taken several forms in the history of Catholic theology, but this Augustinian insight is its central premise.[31] In the twentieth century, papal teaching has used the logic of Augustine and Aquinas[32] to articulate a right of self-defense for states in a decentralized international order and to state the criteria for exercising that right. The essential position was stated by Vatican II: "As long as the danger of war persists and there is no international authority with the necessary competence and power, governments cannot be denied the right of lawful self-defense, once all peace efforts have failed."[33] We have already indicated the centrality of this principle for understanding Catholic teaching about the state and its duties.

83. Just-war teaching has evolved, however, as an effort to prevent war; only if war cannot be rationally avoided does the teaching then seek to restrict and reduce its horrors. It does this by establishing a set of rigorous conditions which must be met if the decision to go to war is to be morally permissible. Such a decision, especially today, requires extraordinarily strong reasons for overriding the presumption *in favor of peace* and *against* war. This is one significant reason why valid just-war teaching makes provision for conscientious dissent. It is presumed that all sane people prefer peace, never *want* to initiate war, and accept even the most justifiable defensive war only as a sad necessity. Only the most powerful reasons may be permitted to override such objection. In the words of Pope Pius XII:

> The Christian will for peace . . . is very careful to avoid recourse to the force of arms in the defense of rights which, however legitimate, do not offset the risk of kindling a blaze with all its spiritual and material consequences.[34]

84. The determination of *when* conditions exist which allow the resort to force in spite of the strong presumption against it is made in light of *jus ad bellum* criteria. The determination of *how* even a justified resort to force must be conducted is made in light of the *jus in bello* criteria. We shall briefly explore the meaning of both.[35]

Jus ad Bellum

85. Why and when recourse to war is permissible.

86. *a) Just Cause:* War is permissible only to confront "a real and certain danger," i.e., to protect innocent life, to preserve conditions necessary for decent human existence, and to secure basic human rights. As both Pope Pius XII and Pope John XXIII made clear, if war of retribution was ever justifiable, the risks of modern war negate such a claim today.

87. *b) Competent Authority:* In the Catholic tradition the right to use force

has always been joined to the common good; war must be declared by those with responsibility for public order, not by private groups or individuals.

88. The requirement that a decision to go to war must be made by competent authority is particularly important in a democratic society. It needs detailed treatment here since it involves a broad spectrum of related issues. Some of the bitterest divisions of society in our own nation's history, for example, have been provoked over the question of whether or not a president of the United States has acted constitutionally and legally in involving our country in a *de facto* war, even if—indeed, especially if—war was never formally declared. Equally perplexing problems of conscience can be raised for individuals expected or legally required to go to war even though our duly elected representatives in Congress have, in fact, voted for war.

89. The criterion of competent authority is of further importance in a day when revolutionary war has become commonplace. Historically, the just-war tradition has been open to a "just revolution" position, recognizing that an oppressive government may lose its claim to legitimacy. Insufficient analytical attention has been given to the moral issues of revolutionary warfare. The mere possession of sufficient weaponry, for example, does not legitimize the initiation of war by "insurgents" against an established government, any more than the government's systematic oppression of its people can be carried out under the doctrine of "national security."

90. While the legitimacy of revolution in some circumstances cannot be denied, just-war teachings must be applied as rigorously to revolutionary-counterrevolutionary conflicts as to others. The issue of who constitutes competent authority and how such authority is exercised is essential.

91. When we consider in this letter the issues of conscientious objection (C.O.) and selective conscientious objection (S.C.O.), the issue of competent authority will arise again.

92. c) Comparative Justice: Questions concerning the *means* of waging war today, particularly in view of the destructive potential of weapons, have tended to override questions concerning the comparative justice of the positions of respective adversaries or enemies. In essence: which side is sufficiently "right" in a dispute, and are the values at stake critical enough to override the presumption against war? The question in its most basic form is this: do the rights and values involved justify killing? For whatever the means used, war, by definition, involves violence, destruction, suffering, and death.

93. The category of comparative justice is designed to emphasize the presumption against war which stands at the beginning of just-war teaching. In a world of sovereign states recognizing neither a common moral authority nor a central political authority, comparative justice stresses that no state should act on the basis that it has "absolute justice" on its side. Every party to a conflict should acknowledge the limits of its "just cause" and the consequent requirement to use *only* limited means in pursuit of its objectives. Far from legitimizing a crusade mentality, comparative justice is designed to relativize absolute claims and to restrain the use of force even in a "justified" conflict.[36]

94. Given techniques of propaganda and the ease with which nations and individuals either assume or delude themselves into believing that God or right is clearly on their side, the test of comparative justice may be extremely difficult to apply. Clearly, however, this is not the case in every instance of war. Blatant aggression from without and subversion from within are often enough readily identifiable by all reasonably fair-minded people.

95. *d) Right Intention:* Right intention is related to just cause—war can be legitimately intended only for the reasons set forth above as a just cause. During the conflict, right intention means pursuit of peace and reconciliation, including avoiding unnecessarily destructive acts or imposing unreasonable conditions (e.g., unconditional surrender).

96. *e) Last Resort:* For resort to war to be justified, all peaceful alternatives must have been exhausted. There are formidable problems in this requirement. No international organization currently in existence has exercised sufficient internationally recognized authority to be able either to mediate effectively in most cases or to prevent conflict by the intervention of United Nations or other peacekeeping forces. Furthermore, there is a tendency for nations or peoples which perceive conflict between or among other nations as advantageous to themselves to attempt to prevent a peaceful settlement rather than advance it.

97. We regret the apparent unwillingness of some to see in the United Nations organization the potential for world order which exists and to encourage its development. Pope Paul VI called the United Nations the last hope for peace. The loss of this hope cannot be allowed to happen. Pope John Paul II is again instructive on this point:

> I wish above all to repeat my confidence in you, the leaders and members of the International Organizations, and in you, the international officials! In the course of the last ten years, your organizations have too often been the object of attempts at manipulation on the part of nations wishing to exploit such bodies. However it remains true that the present multiplicity of violent clashes, divisions and blocks on which bilateral relations founder, offer the great International Organizations the opportunity to engage upon the qualitative change in their activities, even to reform on certain points their own structures in order to take into account new realities and to enjoy effective power.[37]

98. *f) Probability of Success:* This is a difficult criterion to apply, but its purpose is to prevent irrational resort to force or hopeless resistance when the outcome of either will clearly be disproportionate or futile. The determination

includes a recognition that at times defense of key values, even against great odds, may be a "proportionate" witness.

99. g) Proportionality: In terms of the *jus ad bellum* criteria, proportionality means that the damage to be inflicted and the costs incurred by war must be proportionate to the good expected by taking up arms. Nor should judgments concerning proportionality be limited to the temporal order without regard to a spiritual dimension in terms of "damage," "cost," and "the good expected." In today's interdependent world even a local conflict can affect people everywhere; this is particularly the case when the nuclear powers are involved. Hence a nation cannot justly go to war today without considering the effect of its action on others and on the international community.

100. This principle of proportionality applies throughout the conduct of the war as well as to the decision to begin warfare. During the Vietnam war our bishops' conference ultimately concluded that the conflict had reached such a level of devastation to the adversary and damage to our own society that continuing it could not be justified.[38]

Jus in Bello

101. Even when the stringent conditions which justify resort to war are met, the conduct of war (i.e., strategy, tactics, and individual actions) remains subject to continuous scrutiny in light of two principles which have special significance today precisely because of the destructive capability of modern technological warfare. These principles are proportionality and discrimination. In discussing them here, we shall apply them to the question of *jus ad bellum* as well as *jus in bello;* for today it becomes increasingly difficult to make a decision to use any kind of armed force, however limited initially in intention and in the destructive power of the weapons employed, without facing at least the possibility of escalation to broader, or even total, war and to the use of weapons of horrendous destructive potential. This is especially the case when adversaries are "superpowers," as the council clearly envisioned:

> Indeed, if the kind of weapons now stocked in the arsenals of the great powers were to be employed to the fullest, the result would be the almost complete reciprocal slaughter of one side by the other, not to speak of the widespread devastation that would follow in the world and the deadly aftereffects resulting from the use of such weapons.[39]

102. It should not be thought, of course, that massive slaughter and destruction would result only from the extensive use of nuclear weapons. We recall with horror the carpet and incendiary bombings of World War II, the deaths of hundreds of thousands in various regions of the world through "conventional" arms, the unspeakable use of gas and other forms of chemical warfare, the destruction of homes and of crops, the utter suffering war has wrought during the centuries before and the decades since the use of the "atom bomb." Nevertheless, every honest person must recognize that, especially given the proliferation of modern scientific weapons, we now face possibilities which are appalling to contemplate. Today, as never before, we must ask not merely what *will* happen, but what *may* happen, especially if major powers embark on war. Pope John Paul II has repeatedly pleaded that world leaders confront this reality:

> [I]n view of the difference between classical warfare and nuclear or bacteriological war—a difference so to speak of nature—and in view of the scandal of the arms race seen against the background of the needs of the Third World, this right [of defense], which is very real in principle, only underlines the urgency of world society to equip itself with effective means of negotiation. In this way the nuclear terror that haunts our time can encourage us to enrich our common heritage with a very simple discovery that is within our reach, namely that war is the most barbarous and least effective way of resolving conflicts.[40]

103. The Pontifical Academy of Sciences reaffirmed the Holy Father's theme in its November 1981 "Statement on the Consequences of Nuclear War." Then, in a meeting convoked by the Pontifical Academy, representatives of national academies of science from throughout the world issued a "Declaration on the Prevention of Nuclear War" which specified the meaning of Pope John Paul II's statement that modern warfare differs by nature from previous forms of war. The scientists said:

> Throughout its history humanity has been confronted with war, but since 1945 the nature of warfare has changed so profoundly that the future of the human race, of generations yet unborn, is imperiled. . . . For the first time it is possible to cause damage on such a catastrophic scale as to wipe out a large part of civilization and to endanger its very survival. The large-scale use of such weapons could trigger major and irreversible ecological and genetic changes whose limits cannot be predicted.[41]

And earlier, with such thoughts plainly in mind, the council had made its own "the condemnation of total war already pronounced by recent popes."[42] This condemnation is demanded by the principles of proportionality and discrimination. Response to aggression must not exceed the nature of the aggression. To destroy civilization as we know it by waging a "total war" as today it *could* be waged would be a monstrously disproportionate response to aggression on the part of any nation.

104. Moreover, the lives of innocent persons may never be taken directly, regardless of the purpose alleged for doing so. To wage truly "total" war is by definition to take huge numbers of innocent lives. Just response to aggression must be discriminate; it must be directed against unjust aggressors, not against innocent people caught up in a war not of their making. The council therefore issued its memorable declaration:

> Any act of war aimed indiscriminately at the destruction of entire cities or of extensive areas along with their population is a crime against God and man himself. It merits unequivocal and unhesitating condemnation.[43]

105. When confronting choices among specific military options, the question asked by proportionality is: once we take into account not only the military advantages that will be achieved by using this means but also all the harms reasonably expected to follow from using it, can its use still be justified? We know, of course, that no end can justify means evil in themselves, such as the executing of hostages or the targeting of non-combatants. Nonetheless, even if the means adopted is not evil in itself, it is necessary to take into account the probable harms that will result from using it and the justice of accepting those harms. It is of utmost importance, in assessing harms and the justice of accepting them, to think about the poor and the helpless, for they are usually the ones who have the least to gain and the most to lose when war's violence touches their lives.

106. In terms of the arms race, if the *real* end in view is legitimate defense against unjust aggression, and the means to this end are not evil in themselves, we must still examine the question of proportionality concerning attendant evils. Do the exorbitant costs, the general climate of insecurity generated, the possibility of accidental detonation of highly destructive weapons, the danger of error and miscalculation that could provoke retaliation and war—do such evils or others attendant upon and indirectly deriving from the arms race make the arms race itself a disproportionate response to aggression? Pope John Paul II is very clear in his insistence that the exercise of the right and duty of a people to protect their existence and freedom is contingent on the use of proportionate means.[44]

107. Finally, another set of questions concerns the interpretation of the principle of discrimination. The principle prohibits directly intended attacks on non-combatants and non-military targets. It raises a series of questions about the term "intentional," the category of "non-combatant," and the meaning of "military."

108. These questions merit the debate occurring with increasing frequency today. We encourage such debate, for concise and definitive answers still appear to be wanting. Mobilization of forces in modern war includes not only the military, but to a significant degree the political, economic, and social sectors. It is not always easy to determine who is directly involved in a "war effort" or to what degree. Plainly, though, not even by the broadest definition can one rationally consider combatants entire classes of human beings such as schoolchildren, hospital patients, the elderly, the ill, the average industrial worker producing goods not directly related to military purposes, farmers, and many others. They may never be directly attacked.

109. Direct attacks on military targets involve similar complexities. Which targets are "military" ones and which are not? To what degree, for instance, does the use (by either revolutionaries or regular military forces) of a village or housing in a civilian-populated area invite attack? What of a munitions factory in the heart of a city? Who is directly responsible for the deaths of non-combatants should the attack be carried out? To revert to the question raised earlier, how many deaths of non-combatants are "tolerable" as a result of indirect attacks—attacks directed against combat forces and military targets, which nevertheless kill non-combatants at the same time?

110. These two principles, in all their complexity, must be applied to the range of weapons—conventional, nuclear, biological, and chemical—with which nations are armed today.

4. *The Value of Non-violence*

111. Moved by the example of Jesus' life and by his teaching, some Christians have from the earliest days of the Church committed themselves to a non-violent lifestyle.[45] Some understood the gospel of Jesus to prohibit all killing. Some affirmed the use of prayer and other spiritual methods as means of responding to enmity and hostility.

112. In the middle of the second century, St. Justin proclaimed to his pagan readers that Isaiah's prophecy about turning swords into ploughshares and spears into sickles had been fulfilled as a consequence of Christ's coming:

> And we who delighted in war, in the slaughter of one another, and in every other kind of iniquity have in every part of the world converted our weapons into implements of peace—our swords into ploughshares, our spears into farmers' tools—and we cultivate piety, justice, brotherly charity, faith and hope, which we derive from the Father through the crucified Savior . . .[46]

113. Writing in the third century, St. Cyprian of Carthage struck a similar note when he indicated that the Christians of his day did not fight against their enemies. He himself regarded their conduct as proper:

> They do not even fight against those who are attacking since it is not granted to the innocent to kill even the aggressor, but promptly to deliver up their souls and blood that, since so much malice and cruelty are rampant in the world, they may more quickly withdraw from the malicious and the cruel.[47]

114. Some of the early Christian opposition to military service was a response to the idolatrous practices which prevailed in the Roman army. Another powerful motive was the fact that army service involved preparation for fighting and killing. We see this in the case of St. Martin of Tours during the fourth century, who renounced his soldierly profession with the explanation: "Hitherto I have served you as a soldier. Allow me now to become a soldier of God . . . I am a soldier of Christ. It is not lawful for me to fight."[48]

115. In the centuries between the fourth century and our own day, the theme of Christian non-violence and Christian pacifism has echoed and re-echoed, sometimes more strongly, sometimes more faintly. One of the great non-violent figures in those centuries was St. Francis of Assisi. Besides making personal efforts on behalf of reconciliation and peace, Francis stipulated that laypersons who became members of his Third Order were not "to take up lethal weapons, or bear them about, against anybody."

116. The vision of Christian non-violence is not passive about injustice and the defense of the rights of others; it rather affirms and exemplifies what it means to resist injustice through non-violent methods.

117. In the twentieth century, prescinding from the non-Christian witness of a Mahatma Gandhi and its worldwide impact, the non-violent witness of such figures as Dorothy Day and Martin Luther King has had a profound impact upon the life of the Church in the United States. The witness of numerous Christians who had preceded them over the centuries was affirmed in a remarkable way at the Second Vatican Council.

118. Two of the passages which were included in the final version of the *Pastoral Constitution* gave particular encouragement for Catholics in all walks of life to assess their attitudes toward war and military service in the light of Christian pacifism. In paragraph 79 the council fathers called upon governments to enact laws protecting the rights of those who adopted the position of conscientious objection to all war: "Moreover, it seems right that laws make humane provisions for the case of those who for reasons of conscience refuse to bear arms, provided, however, that they accept some other form of service to the human community."[49] This was the first time a call for legal protection of conscientious objection had appeared in a document of such prominence. In addition to its own profound meaning this statement took on even more significance in the light of the praise that the council fathers had given in the preceding section "to those who renounce the use of violence and the vindication of their rights."[50] In *Human Life in Our Day* (1968) we called for legislative provision to recognize selective conscientious objectors as well.[51]

119. As Catholic bishops it is incumbent upon us to stress to our own community and to the wider society the significance of this support for a pacifist option for individuals in the teaching of Vatican II and the reaffirmation that the popes have given to nonviolent witness since the time of the council.

120. In the development of a theology of peace and the growth of the Christian pacifist position among Catholics, these words of the *Pastoral Con-*

stitution have special significance: "All these factors force us to undertake a completely fresh reappraisal of war."[52] The council fathers had reference to "the development of armaments by modern science (which) has immeasurably magnified the horrors and wickedness of war."[53] While the just-war teaching has clearly been in possession for the past 1,500 years of Catholic thought, the "new moment" in which we find ourselves sees the just-war teaching and non-violence as distinct but interdependent methods of evaluating warfare. They diverge on some specific conclusions, but they share a common presumption against the use of force as a means of settling disputes.

121. Both find their roots in the Christian theological tradition; each contributes to the full moral vision we need in pursuit of a human peace. We believe the two perspectives support and complement one another, each preserving the other from distortion. Finally, in an age of technological warfare, analysis from the viewpoint of non-violence and analysis from the viewpoint of the just-war teaching often converge and agree in their opposition to methods of warfare which are in fact indistinguishable from total warfare.

II. War and Peace in the Modern World: Problems and Principles

122. Both the just-war teaching and non-violence are confronted with a unique challenge by nuclear warfare. This must be the starting point of any further moral reflection: nuclear weapons particularly and nuclear warfare as it is planned today, raise new moral questions. No previously conceived moral position escapes the fundamental confrontation posed by contemporary nuclear strategy. Many have noted the similarity of the statements made by eminent scientists and Vatican II's observation that we are forced today "to undertake a completely fresh reappraisal of war." The task before us is not simply to repeat what we have said before; it is first to consider anew whether and how our religious-moral tradition can assess, direct, contain, and, we hope, help to eliminate the threat posed to the human family by the nuclear arsenals of the world. Pope John Paul II captured the essence of the problem during his pilgrimage to Hiroshima:

> In the past it was possible to destroy a village, a town, a region, even a country. Now it is the whole planet that has come under threat.[54]

123. The Holy Father's observation illustrates why the moral problem is also a religious question of the most profound significance. In the nuclear arsenals of the United States or the Soviet Union alone, there exists a capacity to do something no other age could imagine: we can threaten the entire planet.[55] For people of faith this means we read the Book of Genesis with a new awareness; the moral issue at stake in nuclear war involves the meaning of sin in its most graphic dimensions. Every sinful act is a confrontation of the creature and the Creator. Today the destructive potential of the nuclear powers threatens the human person, the civilization we have slowly constructed, and even the created order itself.

124. We live today, therefore, in the midst of a cosmic drama; we possess a power which should never be used, but which might be used if we do not reverse our direction. We live with nuclear weapons knowing we cannot afford to make one serious mistake. This fact dramatizes the precariousness of our position, politically, morally, and spiritually.

125. A prominent "sign of the times" today is a sharply increased awareness of the danger of the nuclear arms race. Such awareness has produced a public discussion about nuclear policy here and in other countries which is unprecedented in its scope and depth. What has been accepted for years with almost no question is now being subjected to the sharpest criticism. What previously had been defined as a safe and stable system of deterrence is today viewed with political and moral skepticism. Many forces are at work in this new evaluation, and we believe one of the crucial elements is the gospel vision of peace which guides our work in this pastoral letter. The nuclear age has been the theater of our existence for almost four decades; today it is being evaluated with a new perspective. For many the leaven of the gospel and the light of the Holy Spirit create the decisive dimension of this new perspective.

A. The New Moment

126. At the center of the new evaluation of the nuclear arms race is a recognition of two elements: the destructive potential of nuclear weapons, and the stringent choices which the nuclear age poses for both politics and morals.

127. The fateful passage into the nuclear age as a military reality began with the bombing of Nagasaki and Hiroshima, events described by Pope Paul VI as a "butchery of untold magnitude."[56] Since then, in spite of efforts at control and plans for disarmament (e.g., the Baruch Plan of 1946), the nuclear arsenals have escalated, particularly in the two superpowers. The qualitative superiority of these two states, however, should not overshadow the fact that four other countries possess nuclear capacity and a score of states are only steps away from becoming "nuclear nations."

128. This nuclear escalation has been opposed sporadically and selectively but never effectively. The race has continued in spite of carefully expressed doubts by analysts and other citizens and in the face of forcefully expressed opposition by public rallies. Today the opposition to the arms race is no longer selective or sporadic, it is widespread and sustained. The danger and destructiveness of nuclear weapons are understood and resisted with new urgency and intensity. There is in the public debate today an endorsement of the position submitted by the Holy See at the United Nations in 1976: the arms race is to be condemned as a danger, an act of aggression against the poor, and a folly which does not provide the security it promises.[57]

129. Papal teaching has consistently addressed the folly and danger of the arms race; but the new perception of it which is now held by the general public is due in large measure to the work of scientists and physicians who have described for citizens the concrete human consequences of a nuclear war.[58]

130. In a striking demonstration of his personal and pastoral concern for preventing nuclear war, Pope John Paul II commissioned a study by the Pontifical Academy of Sciences which reinforced the findings of other scientific bodies. The Holy Father had the study transmitted by personal representative to the leaders of the United States, the Soviet Union, the United

Kingdom, and France, and to the president of the General Assembly of the United Nations. One of its conclusions is especially pertinent to the public debate in the United States:

> Recent talk about winning or even surviving a nuclear war must reflect a failure to appreciate a medical reality: Any nuclear war would inevitably cause death, disease and suffering of pandemonic proportions and without the possibility of effective medical intervention. That reality leads to the same conclusion physicians have reached for life-threatening epidemics throughout history. Prevention is essential for control.[59]

131. This medical conclusion has a moral corollary. Traditionally, the Church's moral teaching sought first to prevent war and then to limit its consequences if it occurred. Today the possibilities for placing political and moral limits on nuclear war are so minimal that the moral task, like the medical, is prevention: as a people, we must refuse to legitimate the idea of nuclear war. Such a refusal will require not only new ideas and new vision, but what the gospel calls conversion of the heart.

132. To say "no" to nuclear war is both a necessary and a complex task. We are moral teachers in a tradition which has always been prepared to relate moral principles to concrete problems. Particularly in this letter we could not be content with simply restating general moral principles or repeating well-known requirements about the ethics of war. We have had to examine, with the assistance of a broad spectrum of advisors of varying persuasions, the nature of existing and proposed weapons systems, the doctrines which govern their use, and the consequences of using them. We have consulted people who engage their lives in protest against the existing nuclear strategy of the United States, and we have consulted others who have held or do hold responsibility for this strategy. It has been a sobering and perplexing experience. In light of the evidence which witnesses presented and in light of our study, reflection, and consultation, we must reject nuclear war. But we feel obliged to relate our judgment to the specific elements which comprise the nuclear problem.

133. Though certain that the dangerous and delicate nuclear relationship the superpowers now maintain should not exist, we understand how it came to exist. In a world of sovereign states devoid of central authority and possessing the knowledge to produce nuclear weapons, many choices were made, some clearly objectionable, others well-intended with mixed results, which brought the world to its present dangerous situation.

134. We see with increasing clarity the political folly of a system which threatens mutual suicide, the psychological damage this does to ordinary people, especially the young, the economic distortion of priorities—billions readily spent for destructive instruments while pitched battles are waged daily in our legislatures over much smaller amounts for the homeless, the hungry, and the helpless here and abroad. But it is much less clear how we translate a "no" to nuclear war into the personal and public choices which can move us in a new direction, toward a national policy and an international system which more adequately reflect the values and vision of the kingdom of God.

135. These tensions in our assessment of the politics and strategy of the nuclear age reflect the conflicting elements of the nuclear dilemma and the balance of terror which it has produced. We have said earlier in this letter that the fact of war reflects the existence of sin in the world. The nuclear threat and the danger it poses to human life and civilization exemplify in a qualitatively new way the perennial struggle of the political community to contain the use of force, particularly among states.

136. Precisely because of the destructive nature of nuclear weapons, strategies have been developed which previous generations would have found unintelligible. Today military preparations are undertaken on a vast and sophisticated scale, but the declared purpose is not to use the weapons produced. Threats are made which would be suicidal to implement. The key to security is no longer only military secrets, for in some instances security may best be served by informing one's adversary publicly what weapons one has and what plans exist for their use. The presumption of the nation-state system, that sovereignty implies an ability to protect a nation's territory and population, is precisely the presumption denied by the nuclear capacities of both superpowers. In a sense each is at the mercy of the other's perception of what strategy is "rational," what kind of damage is "unacceptable," how "convincing" one side's threat is to the other.

137. The political paradox of deterrence has also strained our moral conception. May a nation threaten what it may never do? May it possess what it may never use? Who is involved in the threat each superpower makes: government officials? or military personnel? or the citizenry in whose defense the threat is made?

138. In brief, the danger of the situation is clear; but how to prevent the use of nuclear weapons, how to assess deterrence, and how to delineate moral responsibility in the nuclear age are less clearly seen or stated. Reflecting the complexity of the nuclear problem, our arguments in this pastoral must be detailed and nuanced; but our "no" to nuclear war must, in the end, be definitive and decisive.

B. Religious Leadership and the Public Debate

139. Because prevention of nuclear war appears, from several perspectives, to be not only the surest but only way to limit its destructive potential, we see our role as moral teachers precisely in terms of helping to form public opinion with a clear determination to resist resort to nuclear war as an instrument of national policy. If "prevention is the only cure," then there are diverse tasks to be performed in preventing what should never occur. As bishops we see a specific task defined for us in Pope John Paul II's "World Day of Peace Message 1982":

> Peace cannot be built by the power of rulers alone. Peace can be firmly constructed only if it corresponds to the resolute determination of all people of good will. Rulers must be supported and enlightened by a public opinion that encourages them or, where necessary, expresses disapproval.[60]

140. The pope's appeal to form public opinion is not an abstract task. Especially in a democracy, public opinion can passively acquiesce in policies and strategies or it can, through a series of measures, indicate the limits beyond which a government should not proceed. The "new moment" which exists in the public debate about nuclear weapons provides a creative opportunity and a moral imperative to examine the relationship between public opinion and public policy. We believe it is necessary, for the sake of prevention, to build a barrier against the concept of nuclear war as a viable strategy for defense. There should be a clear public resistance to the rhetoric of "winnable" nuclear wars, or unrealistic expectations of "surviving" nuclear exchanges, and strategies of "protracted nuclear war." We oppose such rhetoric.

141. We seek to encourage a public attitude which sets stringent limits on the kind of actions our own government and other governments will take on nuclear policy. We believe religious leaders have a task in concert with public officials, analysts, private organizations, and the media to set the limits beyond which our military policy should not move in word or action. Charting a moral course in a complex public policy debate involves several steps. We will address four questions, offering our reflections on them as an invitation to a public moral dialogue:

1) the use of nuclear weapons;
2) the policy of deterrence in principle and in practice;
3) specific steps to reduce the danger of war;
4) long-term measures of policy and diplomacy.

C. The Use of Nuclear Weapons

142. Establishing moral guidelines in the nuclear debate means addressing first the question of the use of nuclear weapons. That question has several dimensions.

143. It is clear that those in the Church who interpret the gospel teaching as forbidding all use of violence would oppose any use of nuclear weapons under any conditions. In a sense the existence of these weapons simply confirms and reinforces one of the initial insights of the non-violent position, namely, that Christians should not use lethal force since the hope of using it selectively and restrictively is so often an illusion. Nuclear weapons seem to prove this point in a way heretofore unknown.

144. For the tradition which acknowledges some legitimate use of force, some important elements of contemporary nuclear strategies move beyond the limits of moral justification. A justifiable use of force must be both discriminatory and proportionate. Certain aspects of both U.S. and Soviet strategies fail both tests as we shall discuss below. The technical literature and the personal testimony of public officials who have been closely associated with U.S. nuclear strategy have both convinced us of the overwhelming probability that major nuclear exchange would have no limits.[61]

145. On the more complicated issue of "limited" nuclear war, we are aware of the extensive literature and discussion which this topic has generated.[62] As a general statement, it seems to us that public officials would be unable to refute the following conclusion of the study made by the Pontifical Academy of Sciences:

> Even a nuclear attack directed only at military facilities would be devastating to the country as a whole. This is because military facilities are widespread rather than concentrated at only a few points. Thus, many nuclear weapons would be exploded.
>
> Furthermore, the spread of radiation due to the natural winds and atmospheric mixing would kill vast numbers of people and contaminate large areas. The medical facilities of any nation would be inadequate to care for the survivors. An objective examination of the medical situation that would follow a nuclear war leads to but one conclusion: prevention is our only recourse.[63]

Moral Principles and Policy Choices

146. In light of these perspectives we address three questions more explicitly: (1) counter-population warfare; (2) initiation of nuclear war; and (3) limited nuclear war.

1. Counter-Population Warfare

147. Under no circumstances may nuclear weapons or other instruments of mass slaughter be used for the purpose of destroying population centers or other predominantly civilian targets. Popes have repeatedly condemned "total war" which implies such use. For example, as early as 1954 Pope Pius XII condemned nuclear warfare "when it entirely escapes the control of man," and results in "the pure and simple annihilation of all human life within the radius of action."[64] The condemnation was repeated by the Second Vatican Council:

Any act of war aimed indiscriminately at the destruction of entire cities or of extensive areas along with their population is a crime against God and man itself. It merits unequivocal and unhesitating condemnation.[65]

148. Retaliatory action whether nuclear or conventional which would indiscriminately take many wholly innocent lives, lives of people who are in no way responsible for reckless actions of their government, must also be condemned. This condemnation, in our judgment, applies even to the retaliatory use of weapons striking enemy cities after our own have already been struck. No Christian can rightfully carry out orders or policies deliberately aimed at killing non-combatants.[66]

149. We make this judgment at the beginning of our treatment of nuclear strategy precisely because the defense of the principle of non-combatant immunity is so important for an ethic of war and because the nuclear age has posed such extreme problems for the principle. Later in this letter we shall discuss specific aspects of U.S. policy in light of this principle and in light of recent U.S. policy statements stressing the determination not to target directly or strike directly against civilian populations. Our concern about protecting the moral value of non-combatant immunity, however, requires that we make a clear reassertion of the principle our first word on this matter.

2. The Initiation of Nuclear War

150. We do not perceive any situation in which the deliberate initiation of nuclear warfare, on however restricted a scale, can be morally justified. Nonnuclear attacks by another state must be resisted by other than nuclear means. Therefore, a serious moral obligation exists to develop non-nuclear defensive strategies as rapidly as possible.

151. A serious debate is under way on this issue.[67] It is cast in political terms, but it has a significant moral dimension. Some have argued that at the very beginning of a war nuclear weapons might be used, only against military targets, perhaps in limited numbers. Indeed it has long been American and NATO policy that nuclear weapons, especially so-called tactical nuclear weapons, would likely be used if NATO forces in Europe seemed in danger of losing a conflict that until then had been restricted to conventional weapons. Large numbers of tactical nuclear weapons are now deployed in Europe by the NATO forces and about as many by the Soviet Union. Some are substantially smaller than the bomb used on Hiroshima, some are larger. Such weapons, if employed in great numbers, would totally devastate the densely populated countries of Western and Central Europe.

152. Whether under conditions of war in Europe, parts of Asia or the Middle East, or the exchange of strategic weapons directly between the United States and the Soviet Union, the difficulties of limiting the use of nuclear weapons are immense. A number of expert witnesses advise us that commanders operating under conditions of battle probably would not be able to exercise strict control; the number of weapons used would rapidly increase, the targets would be expanded beyond the military, and the level of civilian casualties would rise enormously.[68] No one can be certain that this escalation would not occur, even in the face of political efforts to keep such an exchange "limited." The chances of keeping use limited seem remote, and the consequences of escalation to mass destruction would be appalling. Former public officials have testified that it is improbable that any nuclear war could actually be kept limited. Their testimony and the consequences involved in this problem lead us to conclude that the danger of escalation is so great that it would be morally unjustifiable to initiate nuclear war in any form. The danger is rooted not only in the technology of our weapons systems but in the weakness and sinfulness of human communities. We find the moral responsibility of beginning nuclear war not justified by rational political objectives.

153. This judgment affirms that the willingness to initiate nuclear war entails a distinct, weighty moral responsibility; it involves transgressing a fragile barrier—political, psychological, and moral—which has been constructed since 1945. We express repeatedly in this letter our extreme skepticism about the prospects for controlling a nuclear exchange, however limited the first use might be. Precisely because of this skepticism, we judge resort to nuclear weapons to counter a conventional attack to be morally unjustifiable.[69] Consequently we seek to reinforce the barrier against any use of nuclear weapons. Our support of a "no-first-use" policy must be seen in this light.

154. At the same time we recognize the responsibility the United States has had and continues to have in assisting allied nations in their defense against either a conventional or a nuclear attack. Especially in the European theater, the deterrence of a *nuclear* attack may require nuclear weapons for a time, even though their possession and deployment must be subject to rigid restrictions.

155. The need to defend against a conventional attack in Europe imposes the political and moral burden of developing adequate, alternative modes of defense to present reliance on nuclear weapons. Even with the best coordinated effort—hardly likely in view of contemporary political division on this question—development of an alternative defense position will still take time.

156. In the interim, deterrence against a conventional attack relies upon two factors: the not inconsiderable conventional forces at the disposal of NATO and the recognition by a potential attacker that the outbreak of large-scale conventional war could escalate to the nuclear level through accident or miscalculation by either side. We are aware that NATO's refusal to adopt a "no-first-use" pledge is to some extent linked to the deterrent effect of this inherent ambiguity. Nonetheless, in light of the probable effects of initiating nuclear war, we urge NATO to move rapidly toward the adoption of a "no-first-use" policy, but doing so in tandem with development of an adequate alternative defense posture.

3. Limited Nuclear War

157. It would be possible to agree with our first two conclusions and still not be sure about retaliatory use of nuclear weapons in what is called a "limited exchange." The issue at stake is the *real* as opposed to the *theoretical* possibility of a "limited nuclear exchange."

158. We recognize that the policy debate on this question is inconclusive and that all participants are left with hypothetical projections about probable reactions in a nuclear exchange. While not trying to adjudicate the technical debate, we are aware of it and wish to raise a series of questions which challenge the actual meaning of "limited" in this discussion.

—Would leaders have sufficient information to know what is happening in a nuclear exchange?

—Would they be able under the conditions of stress, time pressures, and fragmentary information to make the extraordinarily precise decision needed to keep the exchange limited if this were technically possible?

—Would military commanders be able, in the midst of the destruction and confusion of a nuclear exchange, to maintain a policy of "discriminate targeting"? Can this be done in modern warfare, waged across great distances by aircraft and missiles?

—Given the accidents we know about in peacetime conditions, what assurances are there that computer errors could be avoided in the midst of a nuclear exchange?

—Would not the casualties, even in a war defined as limited by strategists, still run in the millions?

—How "limited" would be the long-term effects of radiation, famine, social fragmentation, and economic dislocation?

159. Unless these questions can be answered satisfactorily, we will continue to be highly skeptical about the real meaning of "limited." One of the criteria of the just-war tradition is a reasonable hope of success in bringing about justice and peace. We must ask whether such a reasonable hope can exist once nuclear weapons have been exchanged. The burden of proof remains on those who assert that meaningful limitation is possible.

160. A nuclear response to either conventional or nuclear attack can cause destruction which goes far beyond "legitimate defense." Such use of nuclear weapons would not be justified.

161. In the face of this frightening and highly speculative debate on a matter involving millions of human lives, we believe the most effective contribution or moral judgment is to introduce perspectives by which we can assess the empirical debate. Moral perspective should be sensitive not only to the quantitative dimensions of a question but to its psychological, human, and religious characteristics as well. The issue of limited war is not simply the size of weapons contemplated or the strategies projected. The debate should include the psychological and political significance of crossing the boundary from the conventional to the nuclear arena in any form. To cross this divide is to enter a world where we have no experience of control, much testimony against its possibility, and therefore no moral justification for submitting the human community to this risk.[70] We therefore express our view that the first imperative is to prevent any use of nuclear weapons and our hope that leaders will resist the notion that nuclear conflict can be limited, contained, or won in any traditional sense.

D. Deterrence in Principle and Practice

162. The moral challenge posed by nuclear weapons is not exhausted by an analysis of their possible uses. Much of the political and moral debate of the nuclear age has concerned the strategy of deterrence. Deterrence is at the heart of the U.S.-Soviet relationship, currently the most dangerous dimension of the nuclear arms race.

1. The Concept and Development of Deterrence Policy

163. The concept of deterrence existed in military strategy long before the nuclear age, but it has taken on a new meaning and significance since 1945. Essentially, deterrence means "dissuasion of a potential adversary from initiating an attack or conflict, often by the threat of unacceptable retaliatory damage."[71] In the nuclear age, deterrence has become the centerpiece of both U.S. and Soviet policy. Both superpowers have for many years now been able to promise a retaliatory response which can inflict "unacceptable damage." A situation of stable deterrence depends on the ability of each side to deploy its retaliatory forces in ways that are not vulnerable to an attack (i.e., protected against a "first strike"); preserving stability requires a willingness by both sides to refrain from deploying weapons which appear to have a first-strike capability.

164. This general definition of deterrence does not explain either the elements of a deterrence strategy or the evolution of deterrence policy since 1945. A detailed description of either of these subjects would require an extensive essay, using materials which can be found in abundance in the technical literature on the subject of deterrence.[72] Particularly significant is the relationship between "declaratory policy" (the public explanation of our strategic intentions and capabilities) and "action policy" (the actual planning and targeting policies to be followed in a nuclear attack).

165. The evolution of deterrence strategy has passed through several stages of declaratory policy. Using the U.S. case as an example, there is a significant difference between "massive retaliation" and "flexible response," and between "mutual assured destruction" and "countervailing strategy." It is also possible to distinguish between "counterforce" and "countervalue" targeting policies; and to contrast a posture of "minimum deterrence" with "extended deterrence." These terms are well known in the technical debate on nuclear policy; they are less well known and sometimes loosely used in the wider public debate. It is important to recognize that there has been substantial continuity in U.S. action policy in spite of real changes in declaratory policy.[73]

166. The recognition of these different elements in the deterrent and the evolution of policy means that moral assessment of deterrence requires a series of distinct judgments. They include: an analysis of the *factual character* of the deterrent (e.g., what is involved in targeting doctrine); analysis of the *historical development* of the policy (e.g., whether changes have occurred which are significant for moral analysis of the policy): the relationship of deterrence policy and other aspects of *U.S.-Soviet affairs;* and determination of the key *moral questions* involved in deterrence policy.

2. The Moral Assessment of Deterrence

167. The distinctively new dimensions of nuclear deterrence were recognized by policymakers and strategists only after much reflection. Similarly, the moral challenge posed by nuclear deterrence was grasped only after careful deliberation. The moral and political paradox posed by deterrence was concisely stated by Vatican II:

> Undoubtedly, armaments are not amassed merely for use in wartime. Since the defensive strength of any nation is thought to depend on its capacity for immediate retaliation, the stockpiling of arms which grows from year to year serves, in a way hitherto unthought of, as a deterrent to potential attackers. Many people look upon this as the most effective way known at the present time for maintaining some sort of peace among nations. Whatever one may think of this form of deterrent, people are convinced that the arms race, which quite a few countries have entered, is no infallible way of maintaining real peace and that the resulting so-called balance of power is no sure genuine path to achieving it. Rather than eliminate the causes of war, the arms race serves only to aggravate the position. As long as extravagant sums of money are poured into the development of new weapons, it is impossible to devote adequate aid in tackling the misery which prevails at the present day in the world. Instead of eradicating international conflict once and for all, the contagion is spreading to other parts of the world. New approaches, based on reformed attitudes, will have to be chosen in order to remove this stumbling block, to free the earth from its pressing anxieties, and give back to the world a genuine peace.[74]

168. Without making a specific moral judgment on deterrence, the council clearly designated the elements of the arms race: the tension between "peace of a sort" preserved by deterrence and "genuine peace" required for a stable international life; the contradiction between what is spent for destructive capacity and what is needed for constructive development.

169. In the post-conciliar assessment of war and peace, and specifically of deterrence, different parties to the political-moral debate within the Church and in civil society have focused on one aspect or another of the problem. For some, the fact that nuclear weapons have not been used since 1945 means that deterrence has worked, and this fact satisfies the demands of both the political and the moral order. Others contest this assessment by highlighting the risk of failure involved in continued reliance on deterrence and pointing out how politically and morally catastrophic even a single failure would be. Still others note that the absence of nuclear war is not necessarily proof that the policy of deterrence has prevented it. Indeed, some would find in the policy of deterrence the driving force in the superpower arms race. Still other observers, many of them Catholic moralists, have stressed that deterrence may not morally include the intention of deliberately attacking civilian populations or non-combatants.

170. The statements of the NCCB/USCC over the past several years have both reflected and contributed to the wider moral debate on deterrence. In the NCCB pastoral letter, *To Live In Christ Jesus* (1976), we focused on the moral limits of declaratory policy while calling for stronger measures of arms control.[75] In 1979 John Cardinal Krol, speaking for the USCC in support of SALT II ratification, brought into focus the other element of the deterrence problem: the actual use of nuclear weapons may have been prevented (a moral good), but the risk of failure and the physical harm and moral evil resulting from possible nuclear war remained. "This explains," Cardinal Krol stated, "the Catholic dissatisfaction with nuclear deterrence and the urgency of the Catholic demand that the nuclear arms race be reversed. It is of the utmost importance that negotiations proceed to meaningful and continuing reductions in nuclear stockpiles, and eventually to the phasing out altogether of nuclear deterrence and the threat of mutual-assured destruction."[76]

171. These two texts, along with the conciliar statement, have influenced much of Catholic opinion expressed recently on the nuclear question.

172. In June 1982, Pope John Paul II provided new impetus and insight to the moral analysis with his statement to the United Nations Second Special Session on Disarmament. The pope first situated the problem of deterrence within the context of world politics. No power, he observes, will admit to wishing to start a war, but each distrusts others and considers it necessary to mount a strong defense against attack. He then discusses the notion of deterrence:

Many even think that such preparations constitute the way—even the only way—to safeguard peace in some fashion or at least to impede to the utmost in an efficacious way the outbreak of wars, especially major conflicts which might lead to the ultimate holocaust of humanity and the destruction of the civilization that man has constructed so laboriously over the centuries.

In this approach one can see the "philosophy of peace" which was proclaimed in the ancient Roman principle: *Si vis pacem, para bellum.* Put in modern terms, this "philosophy" has the label of "deterrence" and one can find it in various guises of the search for a "balance of forces" which sometimes has been called, and not without reason, the "balance of terror."[77]

173. Having offered this analysis of the general concept of deterrence, the Holy Father introduces his considerations on disarmament, especially, but not only, nuclear disarmament. Pope John Paul II makes this statement about the morality of deterrence:

In current conditions "deterrence" based on balance, certainly not as an end in itself but as a step on the way toward a progressive disarmament, may still be judged morally acceptable. Nonetheless in order to ensure peace, it is indispensable not to be satisfied with this minimum which is always susceptible to the real danger of explosion.[78]

174. In Pope John Paul II's assessment we perceive two dimensions of the contemporary dilemma of deterrence. One dimension is the danger of nuclear war, with its human and moral costs. The possession of nuclear weapons, the continuing quantitative growth of the arms race, and the danger of nuclear proliferation all point to the grave danger of basing "peace of a sort" on deterrence. The other dimension is the independence and freedom of nations and entire peoples, including the need to protect smaller nations from threats to their independence and integrity. Deterrence reflects the radical distrust which marks international politics, a condition identified as a major problem by Pope John XXIII in *Peace on Earth* and reaffirmed by Pope Paul VI and Pope John Paul II. Thus a balance of forces, preventing either side from achieving superiority, can be seen as a means of safeguarding both dimensions.

175. The moral duty today is to prevent nuclear war from ever occurring *and* to protect and preserve those key values of justice, freedom and independence which are necessary for personal dignity and national integrity. In reference to these issues, Pope John Paul II judges that deterrence may still be judged morally acceptable, "certainly not as an end in itself but as a step on the way toward a progressive disarmament."

176. On more than one occasion the Holy Father has demonstrated his awareness of the fragility and complexity of the deterrence relationship among nations. Speaking to UNESCO in June 1980, he said:

> Up to the present, we are told that nuclear arms are a force of dissuasion which have prevented the eruption of a major war. And that is probably true. Still, we must ask if it will always be this way.[79]

In a more recent and more specific assessment Pope John Paul II told an international meeting of scientists on August 23, 1982:

> You can more easily ascertain that the logic of nuclear deterrence cannot be considered a final goal or an appropriate and secure means for safeguarding international peace.[80]

177. Relating Pope John Paul's general statements to the specific policies of the U.S. deterrent requires both judgments of fact and an application of moral principles. In preparing this letter we have tried, through a number of sources, to determine as precisely as possible the factual character of U.S. deterrence strategy. Two questions have particularly concerned us: (1) the targeting doctrine and strategic plans for the use of the deterrent, particularly their impact on civilian casualties; and (2) the relationship of deterrence strategy and nuclear war-fighting capability to the likelihood that war will in fact be prevented.

Moral Principles and Policy Choices

178. Targeting doctrine raises significant moral questions because it is a significant determinant of what would occur if nuclear weapons were ever to be used. Although we acknowledge the need for deterrent, not all forms of deterrence are morally acceptable. There are moral limits to deterrence policy as well as to policy regarding use. Specifically, it is not morally acceptable to intend to kill the innocent as part of a strategy of deterring nuclear war. The question of whether U.S. policy involves an intention to strike civilian centers (directly targeting civilian populations) has been one of our factual concerns.

179. This complex question has always produced a variety of responses, official and unofficial in character. The NCCB Committee has received a series of statements of clarification of policy from U.S. government officials.[81] Essentially these statements declare that it is not U.S. strategic policy to target the Soviet civilian population as such or to use nuclear weapons deliberately for the purpose of destroying population centers. These statements respond, in principle at least, to one moral criterion for assessing deterrence policy: the immunity of non-combatants from direct attack either by conventional or nuclear weapons.

180. These statements do not address or resolve another very troublesome moral problem, namely, that an attack on military targets or militarily significant industrial targets could involve "indirect" (i.e., unintended) but massive civilian casualties. We are advised, for example, that the United States strategic nuclear targeting plan (SIOP—Single Integrated Operational Plan) has identified 60 "military" targets within the city of Moscow alone, and that 40,000 "military" targets for nuclear weapons have been identified in the whole of the Soviet Union.[82] It is important to recognize that Soviet policy is subject to the same moral judgment; attacks on several "industrial targets" or politically significant targets in the United States could produce massive civilian casualties. The number of civilians who would necessarily be killed by such strikes is horrendous.[83] This problem is unavoidable because of the way modern military facilities and production centers are so thoroughly interspersed with civilian living and working areas. It is aggravated if one side deliberately positions military targets in the midst of a civilian population. In our consultations, administration officials readily admitted that, while they hoped any nuclear exchange could be kept limited, they were prepared to retaliate in a massive way if necessary. They also agreed that once any substantial numbers of weapons were used, the civilian casualty levels would quickly become truly catastrophic, and that even with attacks limited to "military" targets, the number of deaths in a substantial exchange would be almost indistinguishable from what might occur if civilian centers had been deliberately and directly struck. These possibilities pose a different moral question and are to be judged by a different moral criterion: the principle of proportionality.

181. While any judgment of proportionality is always open to differing evaluations, there are actions which can be decisively judged to be disproportionate. A narrow adherence exclusively to the principle of non-combatant immunity as a criterion for policy is an inadequate moral posture for it ignores some evil and unacceptable consequences. Hence, we cannot be satisfied that the assertion of an intention not to strike civilians directly, or even the most honest effort to implement that intention, by itself constitutes a "moral policy" for the use of nuclear weapons.

182. The location of industrial or militarily significant economic targets within heavily populated areas or in those areas affected by radioactive fallout could well involve such massive civilian casualties that, in our judgment, such a strike would be deemed morally disproportionate, even though not intentionally indiscriminate.

183. The problem is not simply one of producing highly accurate weapons that might minimize civilian casualties in any single explosion, but one of increasing the likelihood of escalation at a level where many, even "discriminating," weapons would cumulatively kill very large numbers of civilians. Those civilian deaths would occur both immediately and from the long-term effects of social and economic devastation.

184. A second issue of concern to us is the relationship of deterrence doctrine to war-fighting strategies. We are aware of the argument that war-fighting capabilities enhance the credibility of the deterrent, particularly the strategy of extended deterrence. But the development of such capabilities raises other strategic and moral questions. The relationship of war-fighting capabilities and targeting doctrine exemplifies the difficult choices in this area of policy. Targeting civilian populations would violate the principle of discrimination—one of the central moral principles of a Christian ethic of war. But "counterforce targeting," while preferable from the perspective of protecting civilians, is often joined with a declaratory policy which conveys the notion that nuclear war is subject to precise rational and moral limits. We have already expressed our severe doubts about such a concept. Furthermore, a purely counterforce strategy may seem to threaten the viability of other nations' retaliatory forces, making deterrence unstable in a crisis and war more likely.

185. While we welcome any effort to protect civilian populations, we do not want to legitimize or encourage moves which extend deterrence beyond the specific objective of preventing the use of nuclear weapons or other actions which could lead directly to a nuclear exchange.

186. These considerations of concrete elements of nuclear deterrence policy, made in light of John Paul II's evaluation, but applying it through our own prudential judgments, lead us to a strictly conditioned moral acceptance of nuclear deterrence. We cannot consider it adequate as a long-term basis for peace.

187. This strictly conditioned judgment yields *criteria* for morally assessing the elements of deterrence strategy. Clearly, these criteria demonstrate that we cannot approve of every weapons system, strategic doctrine, or policy initiative advanced in the name of strengthening deterrence. On the contrary, these criteria require continual public scrutiny of what our government proposes to do with the deterrent.

188. On the basis of these criteria we wish now to make some specific evaluations:

1) If nuclear deterrence exists only to prevent the *use* of nuclear weapons by others, then proposals to go beyond this to planning for prolonged periods of repeated nuclear strikes and counter-strikes, or "prevailing" in nuclear war, are not acceptable. They encourage notions that nuclear war can be engaged in with tolerable human and moral consequences. Rather, we must continually say "no" to the idea of nuclear war.

2) If nuclear deterrence is our goal, "sufficiency" to deter is an adequate strategy; the quest for nuclear superiority must be rejected.

3) Nuclear deterrence should be used as a step on the way toward progressive disarmament. Each proposed addition to our strategic system or change

in strategic doctrine must be assessed precisely in light of whether it will render steps toward "progressive disarmament" more or less likely.

189. Moreover, these criteria provide us with the means to make some judgments and recommendations about the present direction of U.S. strategic policy. Progress toward a world freed of dependence on nuclear deterrence must be carefully carried out. But it must not be delayed. There is an urgent moral and political responsibility to use the "peace of a sort" we have as a framework to move toward authentic peace through nuclear arms control, reductions, and disarmament. Of primary importance in this process is the need to prevent the development and deployment of destabilizing weapons systems on either side; a second requirement is to insure that the more sophisticated command and control systems do not become mere hair triggers for automatic launch on warning; a third is the need to prevent the proliferation of nuclear weapons in the international system.

190. In light of these general judgments *we oppose* some specific proposals in respect to our present deterrence posture:

1) The addition of weapons which are likely to be vulnerable to attack, yet also possess a "prompt hard-target kill" capability that threatens to make the other side's retaliatory forces vulnerable. Such weapons may seem to be useful primarily in a first strike;[84] we resist such weapons for this reason and we oppose Soviet deployment of such weapons which generate fear of a first strike against U.S. forces.

2) The willingness to foster strategic planning which seeks a nuclear war-fighting capability that goes beyond the limited function of deterrence outlined in this letter.

3) Proposals which have the effect of lowering the nuclear threshold and blurring the difference between nuclear and conventional weapons.

191. In support of the concept of "sufficiency" as an adequate deterrent, and in light of the present size and composition of both the U.S. and Soviet strategic arsenals, *we recommend:*

1) Support for immediate, bilateral, verifiable agreements to halt the testing, production, and deployment of new nuclear weapons systems.[85]

2) Support for negotiated bilateral deep cuts in the arsenals of both superpowers, particularly those weapons systems which have destabilizing characteristics; U.S. proposals like those for START (Strategic Arms Reduction Talks) and INF (Intermediate-range Nuclear Forces) negotiations in Geneva are said to be designed to achieve deep cuts;[86] our hope is that they will be pursued in a manner which will realize these goals.

3) Support for early and successful conclusion of negotiations of a comprehensive test ban treaty.

4) Removal by all parties of short-range nuclear weapons which multiply dangers disproportionate to their deterrent value.

5) Removal by all parties of nuclear weapons from areas where they are likely to be overrun in the early stages of war, thus forcing rapid and uncontrollable decisions on their use.

6) Strengthening of command and control over nuclear weapons to prevent inadvertent and unauthorized use.

192. These judgments are meant to exemplify how a lack of unequivocal condemnation of deterrence is meant only to be an attempt to acknowledge the role attributed to deterrence, but not to support its extension beyond the limited purpose discussed above. Some have urged us to condemn all aspects of nuclear deterrence. This urging has been based on a variety of reasons, but has emphasized particularly the high and terrible risks that either deliberate use or accidental detonation of nuclear weapons could quickly escalate to something utterly disproportionate to any acceptable moral purpose. That determination requires highly technical judgments about hypothetical events. Although reasons exist which move some to condemn reliance on nuclear weapons for deterrence, we have not reached this conclusion for the reasons outlined in this letter.

193. Nevertheless, there must be no misunderstanding of our profound skepticism about the moral acceptability of any use of nuclear weapons. It is obvious that the use of any weapons which violate the principle of discrimination merits unequivocal condemnation. We are told that some weapons are designed for purely "counterforce" use against military forces and targets. The moral issue, however, is not resolved by the design of weapons or the planned intention for use; there are also consequences which must be assessed. It would be a perverted political policy or moral casuistry which tried to justify using a weapon which "indirectly" or "unintentionally" killed a million innocent people because they happened to live near a "militarily significant target."

194. Even the "indirect effects" of initiating nuclear war are sufficient to make it an unjustifiable moral risk in any form. It is not sufficient, for example, to contend that "our" side has plans for "limited" or "discriminate" use. Modern warfare is not readily contained by good intentions or technological designs. The psychological climate of the world is such that mention of the term "nuclear" generates uneasiness. Many contend that the use of one tactical nuclear weapon could produce panic, with completely unpredictable consequences. It is precisely this mix of political, psychological, and technological uncertainty which has moved us in this letter to reinforce with moral prohibitions and prescriptions the prevailing political barrier against resort to nuclear weapons. Our support for enhanced command and control facilities, for major reductions in strategic and tactical nuclear forces, and for a "no-first-use" policy (as set forth in this letter) is meant to be seen as a complement to our desire to draw a moral line against nuclear war.

195. Any claim by any government that it is pursuing a morally acceptable policy of deterrence must be scrutinized with the greatest care. We are prepared and eager to participate in our country in the ongoing public debate on moral grounds.

196. The need to rethink the deterrence policy of our nation, to make the revisions necessary to reduce the possibility of nuclear war, and to move toward a more stable system of national and international security will demand a substantial intellectual, political, and moral effort. It also will require, we believe, the willingness to open ourselves to the providential care, power and word of God, which call us to recognize our common humanity and the bonds of mutual responsibility which exist in the international community in spite of political differences and nuclear arsenals.

197. Indeed, we do acknowledge that there are many strong voices within our own episcopal ranks and within the wider Catholic community in the United States which challenge the strategy of deterrence as an adequate response to the arms race today. They highlight the historical evidence that deterrence has not, in fact, set in motion substantial processes of disarmament.

198. Moreover, these voices rightly raise the concern that even the conditional acceptance of nuclear deterrence as laid out in a letter such as this might be inappropriately used by some to reinforce the policy of arms buildup. In its stead, they call us to raise a prophetic challenge to the community of faith—a challenge which goes beyond nuclear deterrence, toward more resolute steps to actual bilateral disarmament and peacemaking. We recognize the intellectual ground on which the argument is built and the religious sensibility which gives it its strong force.

199. The dangers of the nuclear age and the enormous difficulties we face in moving toward a more adequate system of global security, stability and justice require steps beyond our present conceptions of security and defense policy. In the following section we propose a series of steps aimed at a more adequate policy for preserving peace in a nuclear world.

III. The Promotion of Peace: Proposals and Policies

200. In a world which is not yet the fulfillment of God's kingdom, a world where both personal actions and social forces manifest the continuing influence of sin and disorder among us, consistent attention must be paid to preventing and limiting the violence of war. But this task, addressed extensively in the previous section of this letter, does not exhaust Catholic teaching on war and peace. A complementary theme, reflected in the Scriptures and the theology of the Church and significantly developed by papal teaching in this century, is the building of peace as the way to prevent war. This traditional theme was vividly reasserted by Pope John Paul in his homily at Coventry Cathedral:

> Peace is not just the absence of war. It involves mutual respect and confidence between peoples and nations. It involves collaboration and binding agreements. Like a cathedral, peace must be constructed patiently and with unshakable faith.[87]

201. This positive conception of peacemaking profoundly influences many people in our time. At the beginning of this letter we affirmed the need for a more fully developed theology of peace. The basis of such a theology is found in the papal teaching of this century. In this section of our pastoral we wish to illustrate how the positive vision of peace contained in Catholic teaching provides direction for policy and personal choices.

A. Specific Steps to Reduce the Danger of War

202. The dangers of modern war are specific and visible; our teaching must be equally specific about the needs of peace. Effective arms control leading to mutual disarmament, ratification of pending treaties,[88] development of nonviolent alternatives, are but some of the recommendations we would place before the Catholic community and all men and women of good will. These should be part of a foreign policy which recognizes and respects the claims of citizens of every nation to the same inalienable rights we treasure, and seeks to ensure an international security based on the awareness that the Creator has provided this world and all its resources for the sustenance and benefit of the entire human family. The truth that the globe is inhabited by a single family in which all have the same basic needs and all have a right to the goods of the earth is a fundamental principle of Catholic teaching which we believe to be of increasing importance today. In an interdependent world all need to affirm their common nature and destiny; such a perspective should inform our policy vision and negotiating posture in pursuit of peace today.

1. Accelerated Work for Arms Control, Reduction, and Disarmament

203. Despite serious efforts, starting with the Baruch plans and continuing through SALT I and SALT II, the results have been far too limited and partial to be commensurate with the risks of nuclear war. Yet efforts for negotiated control and reduction of arms must continue. In his 1982 address to the United Nations, Pope John Paul II left no doubt about the importance of these efforts:

> Today once again before you all I reaffirm my confidence in the power of true negotiations to arrive at just and equitable solutions.[89]

204. In this same spirit, we urge negotiations to halt the testing, production, and deployment of new nuclear weapons systems. Not only should steps be taken to end development and deployment, but the numbers of existing weapons must be reduced in a manner which lessens the danger of war.

205. Arms control and disarmament must be a process of verifiable agreements especially between two superpowers. While we do not advocate a policy of unilateral disarmament, we believe the urgent need for control of the arms race requires a willingness for each side to take some first steps. The United States has already taken a number of important independent initiatives to reduce some of the gravest dangers and to encourage a constructive Soviet response; additional initiatives are encouraged. By independent initiatives we mean carefully chosen limited steps which the United States could take for a defined period of time, seeking to elicit a comparable step from the Soviet Union. If an appropriate response is not forthcoming, the United States would no longer be bound by steps taken. Our country has previously taken calculated risks in favor of freedom and of human values; these have included independent steps taken to reduce some of the gravest dangers of nuclear war.[90] Certain risks are required today to help free the world from bondage to nuclear deterrence and the risk of nuclear war. Both sides, for example, have an interest in avoiding deployment of destabilizing weapons systems.

206. There is some history of successful independent initiatives which have beneficially influenced the arms race without a formal public agreement. In 1963 President Kennedy announced that the United States would unilaterally forgo further nuclear testing; the next month Soviet Premier Nikita Khrushchev proposed a limited test ban which eventually became the basis of the U.S.-Soviet partial test ban treaty. Subsequently, both superpowers removed abut 10,000 troops from Central Europe and each announced a cut in production of nuclear material for weapons.

207. a) Negotiation on arms control agreements in isolation, without persistent and parallel efforts to reduce the political tensions which motivate the buildup of armaments, will not suffice. The United States should therefore have a continuing policy of maximum political engagement with governments of potential adversaries, providing for repeated, systematic discussion and negotiation of areas of friction. This policy should be carried out by a system of periodic, carefully prepared meetings at several levels of government, including summit meetings at regular intervals. Such channels of discussion are too important to be regarded by either of the major powers as a concession or an event made dependent on daily shifts in international developments.

208. b) The Nuclear Non-Proliferation Treaty of 1968 (NPT) acknowledged that the spread of nuclear weapons to hitherto non-nuclear states (horizontal proliferation) could hardly be prevented in the long run in the absence of serious efforts by the nuclear states to control and reduce their own nuclear arsenals (vertical proliferation). Article VI of the NPT pledged the superpowers to serious efforts to control and to reduce their own nuclear arsenals; unfortunately, this promise has not been kept. Moreover, the multinational controls envisaged in the treaty seem to have been gradually relaxed by the states exporting fissionable materials for the production of energy. If these tendencies are not constrained, the treaty may eventually lose its symbolic and practical effectiveness. For this reason the United States should, in concert with other nuclear-exporting states, seriously reexamine its policies and programs and make clear its determination to uphold the spirit as well as the letter of the treaty.

2. Continued Insistence on Efforts to Minimize the Risk of Any War

209. While it is right and proper that priority be given to reducing and ultimately eliminating the likelihood of nuclear war, this does not of itself remove the threat of other forms of warfare. Indeed, negotiated reduction in nuclear weapons available to the superpowers could conceivably increase the danger of non-nuclear wars.

210. a) Because of this we strongly support negotiations aimed at reducing and limiting conventional forces and at building confidence between possible adversaries, especially in regions of potential military confrontations. We urge that prohibitions outlawing the production and use of chemical and biological weapons be reaffirmed and observed. Arms control negotiations must take account of the possibility that conventional conflict could trigger the nuclear confrontation the world must avoid.

211. b) Unfortunately, as is the case with nuclear proliferation, we are witnessing a relaxation of restraints in the international commerce in conventional arms. Sales of increasingly sophisticated military aircraft, missiles, tanks, anti-tank weapons, anti-personnel bombs, and other systems by the major supplying countries (especially the Soviet Union, the United States, France, and Great Britain) have reached unprecedented levels.

212. Pope John Paul II took specific note of the problem in his U.N. address:

> The production and sale of conventional weapons throughout the world is a truly alarming and evidently growing phenomenon. . . . Moreover the traffic in these weapons seems to be developing at an increasing rate and seems to be directed most of all toward developing countries.[91]

213. It is a tragic fact that U.S. arms sales policies in the last decade have contributed significantly to the trend the Holy Father deplores. We call for a reversal of this course. The United States should renew earlier efforts to develop multilateral controls on arms exports, and should in this case also be willing to take carefully chosen independent initiatives to restrain the arms trade. Such steps would be particularly appropriate where the receiving government faces charges of gross and systematic human rights violations.[92]

214. c) Nations must accept a limited view of those interests justifying military force. True self-defense may include the protection of weaker states, but does not include seizing the possessions of others, or the domination of other states or peoples. We should remember the caution of Pope John Paul II: "In alleging the threat of a potential enemy, is it really not rather the intention to keep for itself a means of threat, in order to get the upper hand with the aid of one's own arsenal of destruction?"[93] Central to a moral theory of force is the principle that it must be a last resort taken only when *all* other means of redress have been exhausted. Equally important in the age of modern warfare is the recognition that the justifiable reasons for using force have been restricted to instances of self-defense or defense of others under attack.

3. The Relationship of Nuclear and Conventional Defenses

215. The strong position we have taken against the use of nuclear weapons, and particularly the stand against the initiation of nuclear war in any form, calls for further clarification of our view of the requirements for conventional defense.

216. Nuclear threats have often come to take the place of efforts to deter or defend against non-nuclear attack with weapons that are themselves non-nuclear, particularly in the NATO-Warsaw Pact confrontation. Many analysts conclude that, in the absence of nuclear deterrent threats, more troops and conventional (non-nuclear) weapons would be required to protect our allies. Rejection of some forms of nuclear deterrence could therefore conceivably require a willingness to pay higher costs to develop conventional forces. Leaders and peoples of other nations might also have to accept higher costs for their own defense, particularly in Western Europe, if the threat to use nuclear weapons first were withdrawn. We cannot judge the strength of these arguments in particular cases. It may well be that some strengthening of conventional defense would be a proportionate price to pay, if this will reduce the possibility of a nuclear war. We acknowledge this reluctantly, aware as we are of the vast amount of scarce resources expended annually on instruments of defense in a world filled with other urgent, unmet human needs.

217. It is not for us to settle the technical debate about policy and budgets. From the perspective of a developing theology of peace, however, we feel obliged to contribute a moral dimension to the discussion. We hope that a significant reduction in numbers of conventional arms and weaponry would go hand in hand with diminishing reliance on nuclear deterrence. The history of recent wars (even so-called "minor" or "limited" wars) has shown that conventional war can also become indiscriminate in conduct and disproportionate to any valid purpose. We do not want in any way to give encouragement to a notion of "making the world safe for conventional war," which introduces its own horrors.

218. Hence, we believe that any program directed at reducing reliance on nuclear weapons is not likely to succeed unless it includes measures to reduce tensions, and to work for the balanced reduction of conventional forces. We believe that important possibilities exist which, if energetically pursued, would ensure against building up conventional forces as a concomitant of reductions in nuclear weapons. Examples are to be found in the ongoing negotiations for mutual balanced force reductions, the prospects for which are certainly not dim and would be enhanced by agreements on strategic weapons, and in the confidence-building measures still envisaged under the Helsinki agreement and review conference.

219. We must re-emphasize with all our being, nonetheless, that it is not only nuclear war that must be prevented, but war itself. Therefore, with Pope John Paul II we declare:

> Today, the scale and the horror of modern warfare—whether nuclear or not—makes it totally unacceptable as a means of settling differences between nations. War should belong to the tragic past, to history; it should find no place on humanity's agenda for the future.[94]

Reason and experience tell us that a continuing upward spiral, even in conventional arms, coupled with an unbridled increase in armed forces, instead of securing true peace will almost certainly be provocative of war.

4. Civil Defense

220. Attention must be given to existing programs for civil defense against nuclear attack, including blast and fallout shelters and relocation plans. It is unclear in the public mind whether these are intended to offer significant protection against at least some forms of nuclear attack or are being put into place to enhance the credibility of the strategic deterrent forces by demonstrating an ability to survive attack. This confusion has led to public skepticism and even ridicule of the program and casts doubt on the credibility of the government. An independent commission of scientists, engineers, and weapons experts is needed to examine if these or any other plans offer a realistic prospect of survival for the nation's population or its cherished values, which a nuclear war would presumably be fought to preserve.

5. *Efforts to Develop Non-violent Means of Conflict Resolution*

221. We affirm a nation's right to defend itself, its citizens, and its values. Security is the right of all, but that right, like everything else, must be subject to divine law and the limits defined by that law. We must find means of defending peoples that do not depend upon the threat of annihilation. Immoral means can never be justified by the end sought; no objective, however worthy of good in itself, can justify sinful acts or policies. Though our primary concern through this statement is war and the nuclear threat, these principles apply as well to all forms of violence, including insurgency, counter-insurgency, "destabilization," and the like.

222. a) The Second Vatican Council praised "those who renounce the use of violence in the vindication of their rights and who resort to methods of defense which are otherwise available to weaker parties, provided that this can be done without injury to the rights and duties of others or of the community itself."[95] To make such renunciation effective and still defend what must be defended, the arts of diplomacy, negotiation, and compromise must be developed and fully exercised. Non-violent means of resistance to evil deserve much more study and consideration than they have thus far received. There have been significant instances in which people have successfully resisted oppression without recourse to arms.[96] Non-violence is not the way of the weak, the cowardly, or the impatient. Such movements have seldom gained headlines, even though they have left their mark on history. The heroic Danes who would not turn Jews over to the Nazis and the Norwegians who would not teach Nazi propaganda in schools serve as inspiring examples in the history of non-violence.

223. Non-violent resistance, like war, can take many forms depending upon the demands of a given situation. There is, for instance, organized popular defense instituted by government as part of its contingency planning. Citizens would be trained in the techniques of peaceable non-compliance and non-cooperation as a means of hindering an invading force or non-democratic government from imposing its will. Effective non-violent resistance requires the united will of a people and may demand as much patience and sacrifice from those who practice it as is now demanded by war and preparation for war. It may not always succeed. Nevertheless, before the possibility is dismissed as impractical or unrealistic, we urge that it be measured against the almost certain effects of a major war.

224. b) Non-violent resistance offers a common ground of agreement for those individuals who choose the option of Christian pacifism even to the point of accepting the need to die rather than to kill, and those who choose the option of lethal force allowed by the theology of just war. Non-violent resistance makes clear that both are able to be committed to the same objective: defense of their country.

225. c) Popular defense would go beyond conflict resolution and compromise to a basic synthesis of beliefs and values. In its practice, the objective is not only to avoid causing harm or injury to another creature, but, more positively, to seek the good of the other. Blunting the aggression of an adversary or oppressor would not be enough. The goal is winning the other over, making the adversary a friend.

226. It is useful to point out that these principles are thoroughly compatible with—and to some extent derived from—Christian teachings and must be part of any Christian theology of peace. Spiritual writers have helped trace the theory of non-violence to its roots in scripture and tradition and have illustrated its practice and success in their studies of the church fathers and the age of martyrs. Christ's own teachings and example provide a model way of life incorporating the truth, and a refusal to return evil for evil.

227. Non-violent popular defense does not insure that lives would not be lost. Nevertheless, once we recognize that the almost certain consequences of existing policies and strategies of war carry with them a very real threat to the future existence of humankind itself, practical reason as well as spiritual faith demand that it be given serious consideration as an alternative course of action.

228. d) Once again we declare that the only true defense for the world's population is the rejection of nuclear war and the conventional wars which could escalate into nuclear war. With Pope John Paul II, we call upon educational and research institutes to take a lead in conducting peace studies: "Scientific studies on war, its nature, causes, means, objectives and risks have much to teach us on the conditions for peace . . ."[97] To achieve this end, we urge that funds equivalent to a designated percentage (even one-tenth of one percent) of current budgetary allotments for military purposes be set aside to support such peace research.

229. In 1981, the Commission on Proposals for the National Academy of Peace and Conflict Resolution recommended the establishment of the U. S. Academy of Peace, a recommendation nearly as old as this country's constitution. The commission found that "peace is a legitimate field of learning that encompasses rigorous, interdisciplinary research, education, and training directed toward peacemaking expertise."[98] We endorse the commission's recommendation and urge all citizens to support training in conflict resolution, non-violent resistance, and programs devoted to service to peace and education for peace. Such an academy would not only provide a center for peace studies and activities, but also be a tangible evidence of our nation's sincerity in its often professed commitment to international peace and the abolition of war. We urge universities, particularly Catholic universities, in our country to develop programs for rigorous, interdisciplinary research, education and training directed toward peacemaking expertise.

230. We, too, must be prepared to do our part to achieve these ends. We encourage churches and educational institutions, from primary schools to colleges and institutes of higher learning, to undertake similar programs at their own initiative. Every effort must be made to understand and evaluate the arms race, to encourage truly transnational perspectives on disarmament, and to explore new forms of international cooperation and exchange. No greater challenge or higher priority can be imagined than the development and perfection of a theology of peace suited to a civilization poised on the brink of self-destruction. It is our prayerful hope that this document will prove to be a starting point and inspiration for that endeavor.

6. The Role of Conscience

231. A dominant characteristic of the Second Vatican Council's evaluation of modern warfare was the stress it placed on the requirement for proper formation of conscience. Moral principles are effective restraints on power only when policies reflect them and individuals practice them. The relationship of the authority of the state and the conscience of the individual on matters of war and peace takes a new urgency in the face of the destructive nature of modern war.

232. a) In this connection we reiterate the position we took in 1980. Catholic teaching does not question the right in principle of a government to require military service of its citizens provided the government shows it is necessary. A citizen may not casually disregard his country's conscientious decision to call its citizens to acts of "legitimate defense." Moreover, the role of Christian citizens in the armed forces is a service to the common good and an exercise of the virtue of patriotism, so long as they fulfill this role within defined moral norms.[99]

233. b) At the same time, no state may demand blind obedience. Our 1980 statement urged the government to present convincing reasons for draft registration, and opposed reinstitution of conscription itself except in the case of a national defense emergency. Moreover, it reiterated our support for conscientious objection in general and for selective conscientious objection to participation in a particular war, either because of the ends being pursued or the means being used. We called selective conscientious objection a moral conclusion which can be validly derived from the classical teaching of just-war principles. We continue to insist upon respect for and legislative protection of the rights of both classes of conscientious objectors. We also approve requiring alternative service to the community—not related to military needs —by such persons.

B. Shaping a Peaceful World

234. Preventing nuclear war is a moral imperative; but the avoidance of war, nuclear or conventional, is not a sufficient conception of international relations today. Nor does it exhaust the content of Catholic teaching. Both the political needs and the moral challenge of our time require a positive conception of peace, based on a vision of a first world order. Pope Paul VI summarized classical Catholic teaching in his encyclical, *The Development of Peoples:* "Peace cannot be limited to a mere absence of war, the result of an ever precarious balance of forces. No, peace is something built up day after day, in the pursuit of an order intended by God, which implies a more perfect form of justice among men and women."[100]

1. World Order in Catholic Teaching

235. This positive conception of peace sees it as the fruit of order; order, in turn, is shaped by the values of justice, truth, freedom and love. The basis of this teaching is found in sacred scripture, St. Augustine and St. Thomas. It has found contemporary expression and development in papal teaching of this century. The popes of the nuclear age, from Pius XII through John Paul II have affirmed pursuit of international order as the way to banish the scourge of war from human affairs.[101]

236. The fundamental premise of world order in Catholic teaching is a theological truth: the unity of the human family—rooted in common creation, destined for the kingdom, and united by moral bonds of rights and duties. This basic truth about the unity of the human family pervades the entire teaching on war and peace: for the pacifist position it is one of the reasons why life cannot be taken, while for the just-war position, even in a justified conflict bonds of responsibility remain in spite of the conflict.

237. Catholic teaching recognizes that in modern history, at least since the Peace of Westphalia (1648) the international community has been governed by nation-states. Catholic moral theology, as expressed for example in chapters 2 and 3 of *Peace on Earth,* accords a real but relative moral value to sovereign states. The value is real because of the functions states fulfill as sources of order and authority in the political community; it is relative because boundaries of the sovereign state do not dissolve the deeper relationships of responsibility existing in the human community. Just as within nations the moral fabric of society is described in Catholic teaching in terms of reciprocal rights and duties—between individuals, and then between the individual and the state—so in the international community *Peace on Earth* defines the rights and duties which exist among states.[102]

238. In the past twenty years Catholic teaching has become increasingly specific about the content of these international rights and duties. In 1963, *Peace on Earth* sketched the political and legal order among states. In 1966, *The Development of Peoples* elaborated on order of economic rights and duties. In 1979, Pope John Paul II articulated the human rights basis of international relations in his "Address to the United Nations General Assembly."

239. These documents and others which build upon them outlined a moral order of international relations, i.e., how the international community *should* be organized. At the same time this teaching has been sensitive to the actual pattern of relations prevailing among states. While not ignoring present geopolitical realities, one of the primary functions of Catholic teaching on world order has been to point the way toward a more integrated international system.

240. In analyzing this path toward world order, the category increasingly used in Catholic moral teaching (and, more recently, in the social sciences also) is the interdependence of the world today. The theological principle of unity has always affirmed a human interdependence; but today this bond is complemented by the growing political and economic interdependence of the world, manifested in a whole range of international issues.[103]

241. An important element missing from world order today is a properly constituted political authority with the capacity to shape our material interdependence in the direction of moral interdependence. Pope John XXIII stated the case in the following way:

> Today the universal common good poses problems of world-wide dimensions, which cannot be adequately tackled or solved except by the efforts of public authority endowed with a wideness of powers, structure and means of the same proportions: that is, of public authority which is in a position to operate in an effective manner on a world-wide basis. The moral order itself, therefore, demands that such a form of public authority be established.[104]

242. Just as the nation-state was a step in the evolution of government at a time when expanding trade and new weapons technologies made the feudal system inadequate to manage conflicts and provide security, so we are now entering an era of new, global interdependencies requiring global systems of governance to manage the resulting conflicts and ensure our common security. Major global problems—such as worldwide inflation, trade and payments deficits, competition over scarce resources, hunger, widespread unemployment, global environmental dangers, the growing power of transnational corporations, and the threat of international financial collapse, as well as the danger of world war resulting from these growing tensions—cannot be remedied by a single nation-state approach. They shall require the concerted effort of the whole world community. As we shall indicate below, the United Nations should be particularly considered in this effort.

243. In the nuclear age, it is in the regulation of interstate conflicts and ultimately the replacement of military by negotiated solutions that the supreme importance and necessity of a moral as well as a political concept of the international common good can be grasped. The absence of adequate structures for addressing these issues places even greater responsibility on the policies of individual states. By a mix of political vision and moral wisdom, states are called to interpret the national interest in light of the larger global interest.

244. We are living in a global age with problems and conflicts on a global scale. Either we shall learn to resolve these problems together, or we shall destroy one another. Mutual security and survival require a new vision of the world as one interdependent planet. We have rights and duties not only within our diverse national communities but within the larger world community.

2. The Superpowers in a Disordered World

245. No relationship more dramatically demonstrates the fragile nature of order in international affairs today than that of the United States and the Soviet Union. These two sovereign states have avoided open war, nuclear or conventional, but they are divided by philosophy, ideology and competing ambitions. Their competition is global in scope and involves everything from comparing nuclear arsenals to printed propaganda. Both have been criticized in international meetings because of their policies in the nuclear arms race.[105]

246. In our 1980 pastoral letter on Marxism, we sought to portray the significant differences between Christian teaching and Marxism; at the same time we addressed the need for states with different political systems to live together in an interdependent world:

> The Church recognizes the depth and dimensions of the ideological differences that divide the human race, but the urgent practical need for cooperative efforts in the human interest overrules these differences. Hence Catholic teaching seeks to avoid exacerbating the ideological opposition and to focus upon the problems requiring common efforts across the ideological divide: keeping the peace and empowering the poor.[106]

247. We believe this passage reflects the teaching of *Peace on Earth*, the continuing call for dialogue of Pope Paul VI and the 1979 address of Pope John Paul II at the United Nations. We continue to stress this theme even while we recognize the difficulty of realizing its objectives.

248. The difficulties are particularly severe on the issue of the arms race. For most Americans, the danger of war is commonly defined primarily in terms of the threat of Soviet military expansionism and the consequent need to deter or defend against a Soviet military threat. Many assume that the existence of this threat is permanent and that nothing can be done about it except to build and maintain overwhelming or at least countervailing military power.[107]

249. The fact of a Soviet threat, as well as the existence of a Soviet imperial drive for hegemony, at least in regions of major strategic interest, cannot be denied. The history of the Cold War has produced varying interpretations of which side caused which conflict, but whatever the details of history illustrate, the plain fact is that the memories of Soviet policies in Eastern Europe and recent events in Afghanistan and Poland have left their mark in the American political debate. Many peoples are forcibly kept under communist domination despite their manifest wishes to be free. Soviet power is very great. Whether the Soviet Union's pursuit of military might is motivated primarily by defensive or aggressive aims might be debated, but the effect is nevertheless to leave profoundly insecure those who must live in the shadow of that might.

250. Americans need have no illusions about the Soviet system of repression and the lack of respect in that system for human rights, or about Soviet covert operations and pro-revolutionary activities. To be sure, our own system is not without flaws. Our government has sometimes supported repressive governments in the name of preserving freedom, has carried out repugnant covert operations of its own, and remains imperfect in its domestic record of ensuring equal rights for all. At the same time, there is a difference. NATO is an alliance of democratic countries which have freely chosen their association; the Warsaw Pact is not.

251. To pretend that as a nation we have lived up to all our own ideals would be patently dishonest. To pretend that all evils in the world have been or are now being perpetrated by dictatorial regimes would be both dishonest and absurd. But having said this, and admitting our own faults, it is imperative that we confront reality. The facts simply do not support the invidious comparisons made at times, even in our own society, between our way of life, in which most basic human rights are at least recognized even if they are not always adequately supported, and those totalitarian and tyrannical regimes in which such rights are either denied or systematically suppressed. Insofar as this is true, however, it makes the promotion of human rights in our foreign policy, as well as our domestic policy, all the more important. It is the acid test of our commitment to our democratic values. In this light, any attempts to justify, for reasons of state, support for regimes that continue to violate human rights is all the more morally reprehensible in its hypocrisy.

252. A glory of the United States is the range of political freedoms its system permits us. We, as bishops, as Catholics, as citizens, exercise those freedoms in writing this letter, with its share of criticisms of our government. We have true freedom of religion, freedom of speech, and access to a free press. We could not exercise the same freedoms in contemporary Eastern Europe or in the Soviet Union. Free people must always pay a proportionate price and run some risks—responsibly—to preserve their freedom.

253. It is one thing to recognize that the people of the world do not want war. It is quite another thing to attribute the same good motives to regimes or political systems that have consistently demonstrated precisely the opposite in their behavior. There are political philosophies with understandings of morality so radically different from ours that even negotiations proceed from different premises, although identical terminology may be used by both sides. This is no reason for not negotiating. It is a very good reason for not negotiating blindly or naively.

254. In this regard, Pope John Paul II offers some sober reminders concerning dialogue and peace:

> [O]ne must mention the tactical and deliberate lie, which misuses language, which has recourse to the most sophisticated techniques of propaganda, which deceives and distorts dialogue and incites to aggression . . . while certain parties are fostered by ideologies which, in spite of their declarations, are opposed to the dignity of the human person, ideologies which see in struggle the motive force of history, that see in force the source of rights, that see in the discernment of the enemy the ABC of politics, dialogue is fixed and sterile. Or, if it still exists, it is a superficial and falsified reality. It becomes very difficult, not to say impossible, therefore. There follows almost a complete lack of communication between countries and blocs. Even the international institutions are paralyzed. And the setback to dialogue then runs the risk of serving the arms race. However, even in what can be considered as an impasse to the extent that individuals support such ideologies, the attempt to have a lucid dialogue seems still necessary in order to unblock the situation and to work for the possible establishment of peace on particular points. This is to be done by counting upon common sense, on the possibilities of danger for everyone and on the just aspirations to which the peoples themselves largely adhere.[108]

255. The cold realism of this text, combined with the conviction that political dialogue and negotiations must be pursued, in spite of obstacles, provides solid guidance for U.S.-Soviet relations. Acknowledging all the differences between the two philosophies and political systems, the irreducible truth is that objective mutual interests do exist between the superpowers. Proof of this concrete if limited convergence of interest can be found in some vitally important agreements on nuclear weapons which have already been negotiated in the areas of nuclear testing and nuclear explosions in space as well as the SALT I agreements.

256. The fact that the Soviet Union now possesses a huge arsenal of strategic weapons as threatening to us as ours may appear to them does not exclude the possibility of success in such negotiations. The conviction of many European observers that a *modus vivendi* (often summarized as "détente") is a practical possibility in political, economic, and scientific areas should not be lightly dismissed in our country.

257. Sensible and successful diplomacy, however, will demand that we avoid the trap of a form of anti-Sovietism which fails to grasp the central danger of a superpower rivalry in which both the U.S. and the U.S.S.R. are the players, and fails to recognize the common interest both states have in never using nuclear weapons. Some of those dangers and common interests would exist in any world where two great powers, even relatively benign ones, competed for power, influence, and security. The diplomatic requirement for addressing the U.S.-Soviet relationship is not romantic idealism about Soviet intentions and capabilities but solid realism which recognizes that everyone will lose in a nuclear exchange.

258. As bishops we are concerned with issues which go beyond diplomatic requirements. It is of some value to keep raising in the realm of the political debate truths which ground our involvement in the affairs of nations and peoples. Diplomatic dialogue usually sees the other as a potential or real adversary. Soviet behavior in some cases merits the adjective reprehensible, but the Soviet people and their leaders are human beings created in the image and likeness of God. To believe we are condemned in the future only to what has been the past of U.S.-Soviet relations is to underestimate both our human potential for creative diplomacy and God's action in our midst which can open the way to changes we could barely imagine. We do not intend to foster illusory ideas that the road ahead in superpower relations will be devoid of tension or that peace will be easily achieved. But we do warn against that "hardness of heart" which can close us or others to the changes needed to make the future different from the past.

3. Interdependence: From Fact to Policy

259. While the nuclear arms race focuses attention on the U.S.-Soviet relationship, it is neither politically wise nor morally justifiable to ignore the broader international context in which that relationship exists. Public attention, riveted on the big powers, often misses the plight of scores of countries and millions of people simply trying to survive. The interdependence of the world means a set of interrelated human questions. Important as keeping the peace in the nuclear age is, it does not solve or dissolve the other major problems of the day. Among these problems the pre-eminent issue is the

continuing chasm in living standards between the industrialized world (East and West) and the developing world. To quote Pope John Paul II:

> So widespread is the phenomenon that it brings into question the financial, monetary, production and commercial mechanisms that, resting on various political pressures, support the world economy. These are proving incapable either of remedying the unjust social situations inherited from the past or of dealing with the urgent challenges and ethical demands of the present.[109]

260. The East-West competition, central as it is to world order and important as it is in the foreign policy debate, does not address this moral question which rivals the nuclear issue in its human significance. While the problem of the developing nations would itself require a pastoral letter, Catholic teaching has maintained an analysis of the problem which should be identified here. The analysis acknowledges internal causes of poverty, but also concentrates on the way the larger international economic structures affect the poor nations. These particularly involve trade, monetary, investment and aid policies.

261. Neither of the superpowers is conspicuous in these areas for initiatives designed to address "the absolute poverty" in which millions live today.[110]

262. From our perspective and experience as bishops, we believe there is a much greater potential for response to these questions in the minds and hearts of Americans than has been reflected in U.S. policy. As pastors who often appeal to our congregations for funds destined for international programs, we find good will and great generosity the prevailing characteristics. The spirit of generosity which shaped the Marshall Plan is still alive in the American public.

263. We must discover how to translate this personal sense of generosity and compassion into support for policies which would respond to papal teaching in international economic issues. It is precisely the need to expand our conception of international charity and relief to an understanding of the need for social justice in terms of trade, aid and monetary issues which was reflected in Pope John Paul II's call to American Catholics in Yankee Stadium:

> Within the framework of your national institutions and in cooperation with all your compatriots, you will also want to seek out the structural reasons which foster or cause the different forms of poverty in the world and in your own country, so that you can apply the proper remedies. You will not allow yourselves to be intimidated or discouraged by over-simplified explanations which are more ideological than scientific—explanations which try to account for a complex evil by some single cause. But neither will you recoil before the reforms—even profound ones—of attitudes and structures that may prove necessary in order to recreate over and over again the conditions needed by the disadvantaged if they

are to have a fresh chance in the hard struggle of life. The poor of the United States and of the world are your brothers and sisters in Christ.[111]

264. The Pope's words highlight an intellectual, moral, and political challenge for the United States. Intellectually, there is a need to rethink the meaning of national interest in an interdependent world. Morally, there is a need to build upon the spirit of generosity present in the U.S. public, directing it toward a more systematic response to the major issues affecting the poor of the world. Politically, there is a need for U.S. policies which promote the profound structural reforms called for by recent papal teaching.

265. Precisely in the name of international order papal teaching has, by word and deed, sought to promote multilateral forms of cooperation toward the developing world. The U.S. capacity for leadership in multilateral institutions is very great. We urge much more vigorous and creative response to the needs of the developing countries by the United States in these institutions.

266. The significant role the United States could play is evident in the daily agenda facing these institutions. Proposals addressing the relationship of the industrialized and developing countries on a broad spectrum of issues, all in need of "profound reforms," are regularly discussed in the United Nations and other international organizations. Without U.S. participation, significant reform and substantial change in the direction of addressing the needs of the poor will not occur. Meeting these needs is an essential element for a peaceful world.

267. Papal teaching of the last four decades has not only supported international institutions in principle, it has supported the United Nations specifically. Pope Paul VI said to the U.N. General Assembly:

> The edifice which you have constructed must never fail; it must be perfected and made equal to the needs which world history will present. You mark a stage in the development of mankind for which retreat must never be admitted, but from which it is necessary that advance be made.[112]

268. It is entirely necessary to examine the United Nations carefully, to recognize its limitations and propose changes where needed. Nevertheless, in light of the continuing endorsement found in papal teaching, we urge that the United States adopt a stronger supportive leadership role with respect to the United Nations. The growing interdependence of the nations and peoples of the world, coupled with the extra-governmental presence of multinational corporations, requires new structures of cooperation. As one of the founders of and major financial contributors to the United Nations, the United States can, and should, assume a more positive and creative role in its life today.

269. It is in the context of the United Nations that the impact of the arms race on the prospects for economic development is highlighted. The numerous

U.N. studies on the relationship of development and disarmament support the judgment of Vatican II cited earlier in this letter: "The arms race is one of the greatest curses on the human race and the harm it inflicts upon the poor is more than can be endured."[113]

270. We are aware that the precise relationship between disarmament and development is neither easily demonstrated nor easily reoriented. But the fact of a massive distortion of resources in the face of crying human need creates a moral question. In an interdependent world, the security of one nation is related to the security of all. When we consider how and what we pay for defense today, we need a broader view than the equation of arms with security.[114] The threats to the security and stability of an interdependent world are not all contained in missiles and bombers.

271. If the arms race in all its dimensions is not reversed, resources will not be available for the human needs so evident in many parts of the globe and in our own country as well. But we also know that making resources available is a first step; policies of wise use would also have to follow. Part of the process of thinking about the economics of disarmament includes the possibilities of conversion of defense industries to other purposes. Many say the possibilities are great if the political will is present. We say the political will to reorient resources to human needs and redirect industrial, scientific, and technological capacity to meet those needs is part of the challenge of the nuclear age. Those whose livelihood is dependent upon industries which can be reoriented should rightfully expect assistance in making the transition to new forms of employment. The economic dimension of the arms race is broader than we can assess here, but these issues we have raised are among the primary questions before the nation.[115]

272. An interdependent world requires an understanding that key policy questions today involve mutuality of interest. If the monetary and trading systems are not governed by sensitivity to mutual needs, they can be destroyed. If the protection of human rights and the promotion of human needs are left as orphans in the diplomatic arena, the stability we seek in increased armaments will eventually be threatened by rights denied and needs unmet in vast sectors of the globe. If future planning about conservation of and access to resources is relegated to a pure struggle of power, we shall simply guarantee conflict in the future.

273. The moral challenge of interdependence concerns shaping the relationships and rules of practice which will support our common need for security, welfare, and safety. The challenge tests our idea of human community, our policy analysis, and our political will. The need to prevent nuclear war is absolutely crucial, but even if this is achieved, there is much more to be done.

IV. The Pastoral Challenge and Response

A. The Church: A Community of Conscience, Prayer and Penance

274. Pope John Paul II, in his first encyclical, recalled with gratitude the teaching of Pius XII on the Church. He then went on to say:

> Membership in that body has for its source a particular call, united with the saving action of grace. Therefore, if we wish to keep in mind this community of the People of God, which is so vast and so extremely differentiated, we must see first and foremost Christ saying in a way to each member of the community: "Follow Me." It is the community of the disciples, each of whom in a different way—at times very consciously and consistently, at other times not very consciously and very consistently—is following Christ. This shows also the deeply "personal" aspect and dimension of this society.[116]

275. In the following pages we should like to spell out some of the implications of being a community of Jesus' disciples in a time when our nation is so heavily armed with nuclear weapons and is engaged in a continuing development of new weapons together with strategies for their use.

276. It is clear today, perhaps more than in previous generations, that convinced Christians are a minority in nearly every country of the world—including nominally Christian and Catholic nations. In our own country we are coming to a fuller awareness that a response to the call of Jesus is both personal and demanding. As believers we can identify rather easily with the early Church as a company of witnesses engaged in a difficult mission. To be disciples of Jesus requires that we continually go beyond where we now are. To obey the call of Jesus means separating ourselves from all attachments and affiliation that could prevent us from hearing and following our authentic vocation. To set out on the road to discipleship is to dispose oneself for a share in the cross (cf. Jn. 16:20). To be a Christian, according to the New Testament, is not simply to believe with one's mind, but also to become a doer of the word, a wayfarer with and a witness to Jesus. This means, of course, that we never expect complete success within history and that we must regard as normal even the path of persecution and the possibility of martyrdom.

277. We readily recognize that we live in a world that is becoming increasingly estranged from Christian values. In order to remain a Christian, one must take a resolute stand against many commonly accepted axioms of the world. To become true disciples, we must undergo a demanding course of induction into the adult Christian community. We must continually equip ourselves to profess the full faith of the Church in an increasingly secularized society. We must develop a sense of solidarity, cemented by relationships with mature and exemplary Christians who represent Christ and his way of life.

278. All of these comments about the meaning of being a disciple or a follower of Jesus today are especially relevant to the quest for genuine peace in our time.

B. Elements of a Pastoral Response

279. We recommend and endorse for the faithful some practical programs to meet the challenge to their faith in this area of grave concern.

1. Educational Programs and Formation of Conscience

280. Since war, especially the threat of nuclear war, is one of the central problems of our day, how we seek to solve it could determine the mode, and even the possibility, of life on earth. God made human beings stewards of the earth; we cannot escape this responsibility. Therefore we urge every diocese and parish to implement balanced and objective educational programs to help people at all age levels to understand better the issues of war and peace. Development and implementation of such programs must receive a high priority during the next several years. They must teach the full impact of our Christian faith. To accomplish this, this pastoral letter in its entirety, including its complexity, should be used as a guide and a framework for such programs, as they lead people to make moral decisions about the problems of war and peace, keeping in mind that the applications of principles in this pastoral letter do not carry the same moral authority as our statements of universal moral principles and formal Church teaching.

281. In developing educational programs, we must keep in mind that questions of war and peace have a profoundly moral dimension which responsible Christians cannot ignore. They are questions of life and death. True, they also have a political dimension because they are embedded in public policy. But the fact that they are also political is no excuse for denying the Church's obligation to provide its members with the help they need in forming their consciences. We must learn together how to make correct and responsible moral judgments. We reject, therefore, criticism of the Church's concern with these issues on the ground that it "should not become involved in politics." We are called to move from discussion to witness and action.

282. At the same time, we recognize that the Church's teaching authority does not carry the same force when it deals with technical solutions involving particular means as it does when it speaks of principles or ends. People may agree in abhorring an injustice, for instance, yet sincerely disagree as to what practical approach will achieve justice. Religious groups are as entitled as others to their opinion in such cases, but they should not claim that their opinions are the only ones that people of good will may hold.

283. The Church's educational programs must explain clearly those principles or teachings about which there is little question. Those teachings, which seek to make explicit the gospel call to peace and the tradition of the Church, should then be applied to concrete situations. They must indicate what the possible legitimate options are and what the consequences of those options may be. While this approach should be self-evident, it needs to be emphasized. Some people who have entered the public debate on nuclear warfare, at all points on the spectrum of opinion, appear not to understand or accept some of the clear teachings of the Church as contained in papal or conciliar documents. For example, some would place almost no limits on the use of nuclear weapons if they are needed for "self-defense." Some on the other side of the debate insist on conclusions which may be legitimate options but cannot be made obligatory on the basis of actual Church teaching.

2. True Peace Calls for "Reverence for Life"

284. All of the values we are promoting in this letter rest ultimately in the disarmament of the human heart and the conversion of the human spirit to God who alone can give authentic peace. Indeed, to have peace in our world, we must first have peace within ourselves. As Pope John Paul II reminded us in his 1982 World Day of Peace message, world peace will always elude us until peace becomes a reality for each of us personally. "It springs from the dynamism of free wills guided by reason towards the common good that is to be attained in truth, justice and love."[117] Interior peace becomes possible only when we have a conversion of spirit. We cannot have peace with hate in our hearts.

285. No society can live in peace with itself, or with the world, without a full awareness of the worth and dignity of every human person, and of the sacredness of all human life (Jas. 4:1–2). When we accept violence in any form as commonplace, our sensitivities become dulled. When we accept violence, war itself can be taken for granted. Violence has many faces: oppression of the poor, deprivation of basic human rights, economic exploitation, sexual exploitation and pornography, neglect or abuse of the aged and the helpless, and innumerable other acts of inhumanity. Abortion in particular blunts a sense of the sacredness of human life. In a society where the innocent unborn are killed wantonly, how can we expect people to feel righteous revulsion at the act or threat of killing non-combatants in war?

286. We are well aware of the differences involved in the taking of human life in warfare and the taking of human life through abortion. As we have

discussed throughout this document, even justifiable defense against aggression may result in the indirect or unintended loss of innocent human lives. This is tragic, but may conceivably be proportionate to the values defended. Nothing, however, can justify direct attack on innocent human life, in or out of warfare. Abortion is precisely such an attack.

287. We know that millions of men and women of good will, of all religious persuasions, join us in our commitment to try to reduce the horrors of war, and particularly to assure that nuclear weapons will never again be used, by any nation, anywhere, for any reason. Millions join us in our "no" to nuclear war, in the certainty that nuclear war would inevitably result in the killing of millions of innocent human beings, directly or indirectly. Yet many part ways with us in our efforts to reduce the horror of abortion and our "no" to war on innocent human life in the womb, killed not indirectly, but directly.

288. We must ask how long a nation willing to extend a constitutional guarantee to the "right" to kill defenseless human beings by abortion is likely to refrain from adopting strategic warfare policies deliberately designed to kill millions of defenseless human beings, if adopting them should come to seem "expedient." Since 1973, approximately 15 million abortions have been performed in the United States, symptoms of a kind of disease of the human spirit. And we now find ourselves seriously discussing the pros and cons of such questions as infanticide, euthanasia, and the involvement of physicians in carrying out the death penalty. Those who would celebrate such a national disaster can only have blinded themselves to its reality.

289. Pope Paul VI was resolutely clear: *If you wish peace, defend life.*[118] We plead with all who would work to end the scourge of war to begin by defending life at its most defenseless, the life of the unborn.

3. Prayer

290. A conversion of our hearts and minds will make it possible for us to enter into a closer communion with our Lord. We nourish that communion by personal and communal prayer, for it is in prayer that we encounter Jesus, who is our peace, and learn from him the way to peace.

291. In prayer we are renewed in faith and confirmed in our hope in God's promise.

292. The Lord's promise is that he is in our midst when we gather in prayer. Strengthened by this conviction, we beseech the risen Christ to fill the world with his peace. We call upon Mary, the first disciple and the Queen of Peace, to intercede for us and for the people of our time that we may walk in the way of peace. In this context, we encourage devotion to Our Lady of Peace.

293. As believers, we understand peace as a gift of God. This belief prompts us to pray constantly, personally and communally, particularly through the reading of scripture and devotion to the rosary, especially in the family. Through these means and others, we seek the wisdom to begin the search for peace and the courage to sustain us as instruments of Christ's peace in the world.

294. The practice of contemplative prayer is especially valuable for advancing harmony and peace in the world. For this prayer rises, by divine grace, where there is total disarmament of the heart and unfolds in an experience of love which is the moving force of peace. Contemplation fosters a vision of the human family as united and interdependent in the mystery of God's love for all people. This silent, interior prayer bridges temporarily the "already" and "not yet," this world and God's kingdom of peace.

295. The Mass in particular is a unique means of seeking God's help to create the conditions essential for true peace in ourselves and in the world. In the eucharist we encounter the risen Lord, who gave us his peace. He shares with us the grace of the redemption, which helps us to preserve and nourish this precious gift. Nowhere is the Church's urgent plea for peace more evident in the liturgy than in the Communion Rite. After beginning this rite of the Mass with the Lord's Prayer, praying for reconciliation now and in the kingdom to come, the community asks God to "grant us peace in our day," not just at some time in the distance future. Even before we are exhorted "to offer each other the sign of peace," the priest continues the Church's prayer for peace, recalling the Lord Jesus Christ's own legacy of peace:

Lord Jesus Christ, you said to your apostles: I leave you peace, my peace I give you. Look not on our sins, but on the faith of your Church, and grant us the peace and unity of your kingdom.

Therefore we encourage every Catholic to make the sign of peace at Mass an authentic sign of our reconciliation with God and with one another. This sign of peace is also a visible expression of our commitment to work for peace as a Christian community. We approach the table of the Lord only after having dedicated ourselves as a Christian community to peace and reconciliation. As an added sign of commitment, we suggest that there always be a petition for peace in the general intercessions at every eucharistic celebration.

296. We implore other Christians and everyone of good will to join us in this continuing prayer for peace, as we beseech God for peace within ourselves, in our families and community, in our nation, and in the world.

4. Penance

297. Prayer by itself is incomplete without penance. Penance directs us toward our goal of putting on the attitudes of Jesus himself. Because we are all capable of violence, we are never totally conformed to Christ and are always in need of conversion. The twentieth century alone provides adequate evi-

dence of our violence as individuals and as a nation. Thus, there is continual need for acts of penance and conversion. The worship of the Church, particularly through the sacrament of reconciliation and communal penance services, offers us multiple ways to make reparation for the violence in our own lives and in our world.

298. As a tangible sign of our need and desire to do penance we, for the cause of peace, commit ourselves to fast and abstinence on each Friday of the year. We call upon our people voluntarily to do penance on Friday by eating less food and by abstaining from meat. This return to a traditional practice of penance, once well observed in the U.S. Church, should be accompanied by works of charity and service toward our neighbors. Every Friday should be a day significantly devoted to prayer, penance, and almsgiving for peace.

299. It is to such forms of penance and conversion that the Scriptures summon us. In the words of the prophet Isaiah:

> Is not the sort of fast that pleases me, to break unjust fetters and undo the thongs of the yoke, to let the oppressed go free and break every yoke, to share your bread with the hungry, and shelter the homeless poor, to clothe the person you see to be naked and not turn from your own kin? Then will your light shine like the dawn and your wound be quickly healed over. If you do away with the yoke, the clenched fist, the wicked word, if you give your bread to the hungry and relief to the oppressed, your light will rise in the darkness, and your shadows become like noon (Is. 58:6–8; 10).

300. The present nuclear arms race has distracted us from the words of the prophets, has turned us from peace-making, and has focused our attention on a nuclear buildup leading to annihilation. We are called to turn back from this evil of total destruction and turn instead in prayer and penance toward God, toward our neighbor, and toward the building of a peaceful world:

> I set before you life or death, a blessing or a curse. Choose life then, so that you and your descendants may live in the love of Yahweh your God, obeying His voice, clinging to Him; for in this your life consists, and on this depends your long stay in the land which Yahweh swore to your fathers Abraham, Isaac and Jacob, He would give them (Dt. 30:19–20).

C. Challenge and Hope

301. The arms race presents questions of conscience we may not evade. As American Catholics, we are called to express our loyalty to the deepest values we cherish: peace, justice and security for the entire human family. National goals and policies must be measured against that standard.

302. We speak here in a specific way to the Catholic community. After the passage of nearly four decades and a concomitant growth in our understanding of the ever growing horror of nuclear war, we must shape the climate of opinion which will make it possible for our country to express profound sorrow over the atomic bombing in 1945. Without that sorrow, there is no possibility of finding a way to repudiate future use of nuclear weapons or of conventional weapons in such military actions as would not fulfill just-war criteria.

303. **To Priests, Deacons, Religious and Pastoral Ministers:** We recognize the unique role in the Church which belongs to priests and deacons by reason of the sacrament of holy orders and their unique responsibility in the community of believers. We also recognize the valued and indispensable role of men and women religious. To all of them and to all other pastoral ministers we stress that the cultivation of the gospel vision of peace as a way of life for believers and as a leaven in society should be a major objective. As bishops, we are aware each day of our dependence upon your efforts. We are aware, too, that this letter and the new obligations it could present to the faithful may create difficulties for you in dealing with those you serve. We have confidence in your capacity and ability to convert these difficulties into an opportunity to give a fuller witness to our Lord and his message. This letter will be known by the faithful only as well as you know it, preach and teach it, and use it creatively.

304. **To Educators:** We have outlined in this letter Catholic teaching on war and peace, but this framework will become a living message only through your work in the Catholic community. To teach the ways of peace is not "to weaken the nation's will" but to be concerned for the nation's soul. We address theologians in a particular way, because we know that we have only begun the journey toward a theology of peace; without your specific contributions this desperately needed dimension of our faith will not be realized. Through your help we may provide new vision and wisdom for church and state.

305. We are confident that all models of Catholic education which have served the Church and our country so well in so many ways will creatively rise to the challenge of peace.

306. **To Parents:** Your role, in our eyes, is unsurpassed by any other; the foundation of society is the family. We are conscious of the continuing sacrifices you make in the efforts to nurture the full human and spiritual growth of your children. Children hear the gospel message first from your lips. Parents who consciously discuss issues of justice in the home and who strive to help children solve conflicts through non-violent methods enable their children to grow up as peacemakers. We pledge our continuing pastoral support in the common objective we share of building a peaceful world for the future of children everywhere.

307. **To Youth:** Pope John Paul II singles you out in every country where he visits as the hope of the future; we agree with him. We call you to choose your future work and professions carefully. How you spend the rest of your lives will determine, in large part, whether there will any longer be a world as we know it. We ask you to study carefully the teachings of the Church and the demands of the gospel about war and peace. We encourage you to seek careful guidance as you reach conscientious decisions about your civic responsibilities in this age of nuclear military forces.

308. We speak to you, however, as people of faith. We share with you our deepest conviction that in the midst of the dangers and complexities of our time God is with us, working through us and sustaining us all in our efforts of building a world of peace with justice for each person.

309. **To Men and Women in Military Service:** Millions of you are Catholics serving in the armed forces. We recognize that you carry special responsibilities for the issues we have considered in this letter. Our perspective on your profession is that of Vatican II: "All those who enter the military service in loyalty to their country should look upon themselves as the custodians of the security and freedom of their fellow-countrymen; and where they carry out their duty properly, they are contributing to the maintenance of peace."[119]

310. It is surely not our intention in writing this letter to create problems for Catholics in the armed forces. Every profession, however, has its specific moral questions and it is clear that the teaching on war and peace developed in this letter poses a special challenge and opportunity to those in the military profession. Our pastoral contact with Catholics in military service, either through our direct experience or through our priests, impresses us with the demanding moral standards we already see observed and the commitment to Catholic faith we find. We are convinced that the challenges of this letter will be faced conscientiously. The purpose of defense policy is to defend the peace; military professionals should understand their vocation this way. We believe they do, and we support this view.

311. We remind all in authority and in the chain of command that their training and field manuals have long prohibited, and still do prohibit, certain actions in the conduct of war, especially those actions which inflict harm on innocent civilians. The question is not whether certain measures are unlawful or forbidden in warfare, but which measures: to refuse to take such actions is not an act of cowardice or treason but one of courage and patriotism.

312. We address particularly those involved in the exercise of authority over others. We are aware of your responsibilities and impressed by the standard of personal and professional duty you uphold. We feel, therefore, that we can urge you to do everything you can to assure that every peaceful alternative is exhausted before war is even remotely considered. In developing battle plans and weapons systems, we urge you to try to ensure that these are designed to reduce violence, destruction, suffering, and death to a minimum, keeping in mind especially non-combatants and other innocent persons.

313. Those who train individuals for military duties must remember that the citizen does not lose his or her basic human rights by entrance into military service. No one, for whatever reason, can justly treat a military person with less dignity and respect than that demanded for and deserved by every human person. One of the most difficult problems of war involves defending a free society without destroying the values that give it meaning and validity. Dehumanization of a nation's military personnel by dulling their sensibilities and generating hatred toward adversaries in an effort to increase their fighting effectiveness robs them of basic human rights and freedoms, degrading them as persons.

314. Attention must be given to the effects on military personnel themselves of the use of even legitimate means of conducting war. While attacking legitimate targets and wounding or killing opposed combat forces may be morally justified, what happens to military persons required to carry out these actions? Are they treated merely as instruments of war, insensitive as the weapons they use? With what moral or emotional experiences do they return from war and attempt to resume normal civilian lives? How does their experience affect society? How are they treated by society?

315. It is not only basic human rights of adversaries that must be respected, but those of our own forces as well. We re-emphasize, therefore, the obligation of responsible authorities to ensure appropriate training and education of combat forces and to provide appropriate support for those who have experienced combat. It is unconscionable to deprive those veterans of combat whose lives have been severely disrupted or traumatized by their combat experiences of proper psychological and other appropriate treatment and support.

316. Finally, we are grateful for the sacrifice so many in military service must make today and for the service offered in the past by veterans. We urge that those sacrifices be mitigated so far as possible by the provision of appropriate living and working conditions and adequate financial recompense. Military persons and their families must be provided continuing opportunity for full spiritual growth, the exercise of their religious faith, and a dignified mode of life.

317. We especially commend and encourage our priests in military service. In addition to the message already addressed to all priests and religious, we stress the special obligations and opportunities you face in direct pastoral service to the men and women of the armed forces. To complement a teaching document of this scope, we shall need the sensitive and wise pastoral guidance only you can provide. We promise our support in facing this challenge.

318. **To Men and Women in Defense Industries:** You also face specific questions, because the defense industry is directly involved in the development and production of the weapons of mass destruction which have concerned us in this letter. We do not presume or pretend that clear answers exist to many of the personal, professional and financial choices facing you in your varying responsibilities. In this letter we have ruled out certain uses of nuclear weapons, while also expressing conditional moral acceptance for deterrence. All Catholics, at every level of defense industries, can and should use the moral principles of this letter to form their consciences. We realize that different judgments of conscience will face different people, and we recognize the possibility of diverse concrete judgments being made in this complex area. We seek as moral teachers and pastors to be available to all who confront these questions of personal and vocational choice. Those who in conscience decide that they should no longer be associated with defense activities should find support in the Catholic community. Those who remain in these industries or earn a profit from the weapons industry should find in the Church guidance and support for the ongoing evaluation of their work.

319. **To Men and Women of Science:** At Hiroshima Pope John Paul said: "Criticism of science and technology is sometimes so severe that it comes close to condemning science itself. On the contrary, science and technology are a wonderful product of a God-given human creativity, since they have provided us with wonderful possibilities and we all gratefully benefit from them. But we know that this potential is not a neutral one: it can be used either for man's progress or for his degradation."[120] We appreciate the efforts of scientists, some of whom first unlocked the secret of atomic power and others of whom have developed it in diverse ways, to turn the enormous power of science to the cause of peace.

320. Modern history is not lacking scientists who have looked back with deep remorse on the development of weapons to which they contributed, sometimes with the highest motivation, even believing that they were creating weapons that would render all other weapons obsolete and convince the world of the unthinkableness of war. Such efforts have ever proved illusory. Surely, equivalent dedication of scientific minds to reverse current trends, and to pursue concepts as bold and adventuresome in favor of peace as those which in the past have magnified the risks of war, could result in dramatic benefits for all of humanity. We particularly note in this regard the extensive efforts of public education undertaken by physicians and scientists on the medical consequences of nuclear war.

321. We do not, however, wish to limit our remarks to the physical sciences alone. Nor do we limit our remarks to physical scientists. In his address at the United Nations University in Hiroshima, Pope John Paul II warned about misuse of "the social sciences and the human behavioral sciences when they are utilized to manipulate people, to crush their mind, souls, dignity and freedom . . ."[121] The positive role of social science in overcoming the dangers of the nuclear age is evident in this letter. We have been dependent upon the research and analysis of social scientists in our effort to apply the moral principles of the Catholic tradition to the concrete problems of our day. We encourage social scientists to continue this work of relating moral wisdom and political reality. We are in continuing need of your insights.

322. **To Men and Women of the Media:** We have directly felt our dependence upon you in writing this letter; all the problems we have confronted have been analyzed daily in the media. As we have grappled with these issues, we have experienced some of the responsibility you bear for interpreting them. On the quality of your efforts depends in great measure the opportunity the general public will have for understanding this letter.

323. **To Public Officials:** Vatican II spoke forcefully of "the difficult yet noble art of politics."[122] No public issue is more difficult than avoiding war; no public task more noble than building a secure peace. Public officials in a democracy must both lead and listen; they are ultimately dependent upon a popular consensus to sustain policy. We urge you to lead with courage and to listen to the public debate with sensitivity.

324. Leadership in a nuclear world means examining with great care and objectivity every potential initiative toward world peace, regardless of how unpromising it might at first appear. One specific initiative which might be taken now would be the establishment of a task force including the public sector, industry, labor, economists and scientists with the mandate to consider the problems and challenges posed by nuclear disarmament to our economic well-being and industrial output. Listening includes being particularly attentive to the consciences of those who sincerely believe that they may not morally support warfare in general, a given war, or the exercise of a particular role within the armed forces. Public officials might well serve all of our fellow citizens by proposing and supporting legislation designed to give maximum protection to this precious freedom, true freedom of conscience.

325. In response to public officials who both lead and listen, we urge citizens to respect the vocation of public service. It is a role easily maligned but not easily fulfilled. Neither justice nor peace can be achieved with stability in the absence of courageous and creative public servants.

326. **To Catholics as Citizens:** All papal teaching on peace has stressed the crucial role of public opinion. Pope John Paul II specified the tasks before us: "There is no justification for not raising the question of the responsibility of each nation and each individual in the face of possible wars and of the nuclear threat."[123] In a democracy, the responsibility of the nation and that of its citizens coincide. Nuclear weapons pose especially acute questions of conscience for American Catholics. As citizens we wish to affirm our loyalty to our country and its ideals, yet we are also citizens of the world who must be faithful to the universal principles proclaimed by the Church. While some other countries also possess nuclear weapons, we may not forget that the United States was the first to build and to use them. Like the Soviet Union, this country now possesses so many weapons as to imperil the continuation of civilization. Americans share responsibility for the current situation, and cannot evade responsibility for trying to resolve it.

327. The virtue of patriotism means that as citizens we respect and honor our country, but our very love and loyalty make us examine carefully and regularly its role in world affairs, asking that it live up to its full potential as an agent of peace with justice for all people.

> Citizens must cultivate a generous and loyal spirit of patriotism, but without being narrow-minded. This means that they will always direct their attention to the good of the whole human family, united by the different ties which bind together races, people, and nations.[124]

328. In a pluralistic democracy like the United States, the Church has a unique opportunity, precisely because of the strong constitutional protection of both religious freedom and freedom of speech and the press, to help call attention to the moral dimensions of public issues. In a previous pastoral letter, *Human Life In Our Day,* we said: "In our democratic system, the fundamental right of political dissent cannot be denied, nor is rational debate on public policy decisions of government in the light of moral and political principles to be discouraged. It is the duty of the governed to analyze responsibly the concrete issues of public policy."[125] In fulfilling this role, the Church helps to create a community of conscience in the wider civil community. It does this in the first instance by teaching clearly within the Church the moral principles which bind and shape the Catholic conscience. The Church also fulfills a teaching role, however, in striving to share the moral wisdom of the Catholic tradition with the larger society.

329. In the wider public discussion, we look forward in a special way to cooperating with all other Christians with whom we share common traditions. We also treasure cooperative efforts with Jewish and Islamic communities, which possess a long and abiding concern for peace as a religious and human value. Finally, we reaffirm our desire to participate in a common public effort with all men and women of good will who seek to reverse the arms race and secure the peace of the world.

Conclusion

330. As we close this lengthy letter, we try to answer two key questions as directly as we can.

331. Why do we address these matters fraught with such complexity, controversy and passion? We speak as pastors, not politicians. We are teachers, not technicians. We cannot avoid our responsibility to lift up the moral dimensions of the choices before our world and nation. The nuclear age is an era of moral as well as physical danger. We are the first generation since Genesis with the power to virtually destroy God's creation. We cannot remain silent in the face of such danger. Why do we address these issues? We are simply trying to live up to the call of Jesus to be peacemakers in our own time and situation.

332. What are we saying? Fundamentally, we are saying that the decisions about nuclear weapons are among the most pressing moral questions of our age. While these decisions have obvious military and political aspects, they involve fundamental moral choices. In simple terms, we are saying that good ends (defending one's country, protecting freedom, etc.) cannot justify immoral means (the use of weapons which kill indiscriminately and threaten whole societies). We fear that our world and nation are headed in the wrong direction. More weapons with greater destructive potential are produced every day. More and more nations are seeking to become nuclear powers. In our quest for more and more security, we fear we are actually becoming less and less secure.

333. In the words of our Holy Father, we need a "moral about-face." The whole world must summon the moral courage and technical means to say "no" to nuclear conflict; "no" to weapons of mass destruction; "no" to an arms race which robs the poor and the vulnerable; and "no" to the moral danger of a nuclear age which places before humankind indefensible choices of constant terror or surrender. Peacemaking is not an optional commitment. It is a requirement of our faith. We are called to be peacemakers, not by some movement of the moment, but by our Lord Jesus. The content and context of our peacemaking is set, not by some political agenda or ideological program, but by the teaching of his Church.

334. Thus far in this pastoral letter we have made suggestions we hope will be helpful in the present world crisis. Looking ahead to the long and productive future of humanity for which we all hope, we feel that a more all-inclusive and final solution is needed. We speak here of the truly effective international authority for which Pope John XXIII ardently longed in *Peace on Earth*,[126] and of which Pope Paul VI spoke to the United Nations on his visit there in 1965.[127] The hope for such a structure is not unrealistic, because the point has been reached where public opinion sees clearly that, with the massive weaponry of the present, war is no longer viable. There *is* a substitute for war. There is negotiation under the supervision of a global body realistically fashioned to do its job. It must be given the equipment to keep constant surveillance on the entire earth. Present technology makes this possible. It must have the authority, freely conferred upon it by all the nations, to investigate what seems to be preparations for war by any one of them. It must be empowered by all the nations to enforce its commands on every nation. It must be so constituted as to pose no threat to any nation's sovereignty. Obviously the creation of such a sophisticated instrumentality is a gigantic task, but is it hoping for too much to believe that the genius of humanity, aided by the grace and guidance of God, is able to accomplish it? To create it may take decades of unrelenting daily toll by the world's best minds and most devoted hearts, but it shall never come into existence unless we make a beginning now.

335. As we come to the end of our pastoral letter we boldly propose the beginning of this work. The evil of the proliferation of nuclear arms becomes more evident every day to all people. No one is exempt from their danger. If ridding the world of the weapons of war could be done easily, the whole human race would do it gladly tomorrow. Shall we shrink from the task because it is hard?

336. We turn to our own government and we beg it to propose to the United Nations that it begin this work immediately; that it create an international task force for peace; that this task force, with membership open to every nation, meet daily through the years ahead with one sole agenda: the creation of a world that will one day be safe from war. Freed from the bondage of war that holds it captive in its threat, the world will at last be able to address its problems and to make genuine human progress, so that every day there may be more freedom, more food, and more opportunity for every human being who walks the face of the earth.

337. Let us have the courage to believe in the bright future and in a God who wills it for us—not a perfect world, but a better one. The perfect world, we Christians believe, is beyond the horizon, in an endless eternity where God will be all in all. But a better world is here for human hands and hearts and minds to make.

338. For the community of faith the risen Christ is the beginning and end of all things. For all things were created through him and all things will return to the Father through him.

339. It is our belief in the risen Christ which sustains us in confronting the awesome challenge of the nuclear arms race. Present in the beginning as the word of the Father, present in history as the word incarnate, and with us today in his word, sacraments, and spirit, he is the reason for our hope and faith. Respecting our freedom, he does not solve our problems but sustains us as we take responsibility for his work of creation and try to shape it in the ways of the kingdom. We believe his grace will never fail us. We offer this letter to the Church and to all who can draw strength and wisdom from it in the conviction that we must not fail him. We must subordinate the power of the nuclear age to human control and direct it to human benefit. As we do this we are conscious of God's continuing work among us, which will one day issue forth in the beautiful final kingdom prophesied by the seer of the Book of Revelation:

> Then I saw a new heaven and a new earth; for the first heaven and the first earth had passed away and the sea was no more. And I saw the holy city, new Jerusalem, coming down out of heaven from God, prepared as a bride adorned for her husband; and I heard a great voice from the throne saying, "Behold, the dwelling of God is with men. He will dwell with them, and they shall be his people, and God himself will be with them, he will wipe away every tear from their eyes, and death shall be no more, neither shall there be mourning nor crying nor pain any more, for the former things have passed away." And he who sat upon the throne said, "Behold, I make all things new" (Rv. 21:1–5).

Notes

1. Vatican II, the *Pastoral Constitution on the Church in the Modern World* (hereafter cited: *Pastoral Constitution),* #77. Papal and conciliar texts will be referred to by title with paragraph number. Several collections of these texts exist although no single collection is comprehensive; see the following: *Peace and Disarmament: Documents of the World Council of Churches and the Roman Catholic Church* (Geneva and Rome: 1982) (hereafter cited: *Documents,* with page number); J. Gremillion, *The Gospel of Peace and Justice: Catholic Social Teaching Since Pope John* (Maryknoll, N.Y.: 1976); D. J. O'Brien and T. A. Shannon, eds., *Renewing the Earth: Catholic Documents on Peace, Justice and Liberation* (New York: 1977); A. Flannery, O.P., ed., *Vatican Council II: The Conciliar and Post Conciliar Documents* (Collegeville, Minn.: 1975); W. Abbot, ed., *The Documents of Vatican II* (New York: 1966). Both the Flannery and Abbot translations of the *Pastoral Constitution* are used in this letter.

2. John Paul II, "Message to the Second Special Session of the United Nations General Assembly Devoted to Disarmament" (June 1982) (hereafter cited: "Message U.N. Special Session 1982"), #7.

3. John Paul II, "Address to Scientists and Scholars," #4, *Origins* 10 (1981):621.

4. The *Pastoral Constitution* is made up of two parts; yet it constitutes an organic unity. By way of explanation: the constitution is called "pastoral" because, while resting on doctrinal principles, it seeks to express the relation of the Church to the world and modern mankind. The result is that, on the one hand, a pastoral slant is present in the first part and, on the other hand, a doctrinal slant is present in the second part. *Pastoral Constitution,* note 1 above.

5. Ibid.

6. Ibid., #43.

7. John Paul II, "Message U.N. Special Session 1982," #2.

8. *Pastoral Constitution,* #81.

9. Ibid., #80.

10. Ibid., #16.

11. Ibid., #80.

12. The exact opposite of this vision is presented in Joel 3:10 where the foreign nations are told that their weapons will do them no good in the face of God's coming wrath.

13. An omission in the New Testament is significant in this context. Scholars have made us aware of the presence of revolutionary groups in Israel during the time of Jesus. Barabbas, for example, was "among the rebels in prison who had committed murder in the insurrection" (Mk. 15:7). Although Jesus had come to proclaim and to bring about the true reign of God which often stood in opposition to the existing order, he makes no reference to nor does he join in any attempts such as those of the Zealots to overthrow authority by violent means. See M. Smith, "Zealots and Sicarii, Their Origins and Relations," *Harvard Theological Review* 64 (1971):1–19.

14. John Paul II, "World Day of Peace Message 1982," #12, *Origins* 11 (1982): 477.

15. Ibid., #11–12, pp. 477–78.

16. John Paul II, "Message U.N. Special Session 1982," #13; Pope Paul VI, "World Day of Peace Message 1973."

17. John Paul II, "World Day of Peace Message 1982," #12, cited, p. 478.

18. *Pastoral Constitution,* #79.

19. Ibid., #77.

20. Ibid., #80.

21. Ibid., #17.

22. Ibid., #78.

23. John Paul II, "World Day of Peace Message 1982," #9, cited. The *Pastoral Constitution* stresses that peace is not only the fruit of justice, but also love, which commits us to engage in "the studied practice of brotherhood" (#78).

24. *Pastoral Constitution,* #79.

25. Ibid., #82.

26. Ibid., #79.

27. Pius XII, "Christmas Message," 1948; The same theme is reiterated in Pius XII's "Christmas Message" of 1953: "The community of nations must reckon with unprincipled criminals who, in order to realize their ambitious plans, are not afraid to unleash total war. This is the reason why other countries if they wish to preserve their very existence and their most precious possessions, and unless they are prepared to accord free action to international criminals, have no alternative but to get ready for the day when they must defend themselves. *This right to be prepared for self-defense cannot be denied, even in these days, to any state.*"

28. *Pastoral Constitution,* #80.

29. Ibid.

30. John Paul II, "World Day of Peace Message 1982," #12, cited, p. 478.

31. Augustine called it a Manichaean heresy to assert that war is intrinsically evil and contrary to Christian charity, and stated: "War and conquest are a sad necessity in the eyes of men of principle, yet it would be still more unfortunate if wrongdoers should dominate just men." (*The City of God,* Book IV, C. 15)

Representative surveys of the history and theology of the just-war tradition include: F. H. Russell, *The Just War in the Middle Ages* (New York: 1975); P. Ramsey, *War and the Christian Conscience* (Durham, N.C.: 1961); James T. Johnson, *The Just War: Force and Political Responsibility* (New York: 1968), *Ideology, Reason and the Limitation of War* (Princeton: 1975), *Just War Tradition and the Restraint of War: A Moral and Historical Inquiry* (Princeton: 1981); L. B. Walters, *Five Classic Just-War Theories* (Ph.D. Dissertation, Yale University, 1971); W. O'Brien, *War and/or Survival* (New York: 1969), *The Conduct of Just and Limited War* (New York: 1981); J. C. Murray, "Remarks on the Moral Problem of War," *Theological Studies* 20 (1959):40–61.

32. Aquinas treats the question of war in the *Summa Theologica,* II-IIac, q. 40; also cf. II-IIac, q. 64.

33. *Pastoral Constitution,* #79.

34. Pius XII, "Christmas Message," 1948.

35. For an analysis of the content and relationship of these principles cf.: R. Potter, "The Moral Logic of War," *McCormick Quarterly* 23 (1970):203–33; J. Childress in Shannon, cited, pp. 40–58.

36. James T. Johnson, *The Just War: Force and Political Responsibility,* cited; *Ideology, Reason and the Limitation of War,* cited; W. O'Brien, *The Conduct of Just and Limited War,* cited, pp. 13–30; W. Vanderpol, *La doctrine scolastique du droit de guerre,* p. 387ff; J. C. Murray, "Theology and Modern Warfare," in W. J. Nagel, ed., *Morality and Modern Warfare,* p. 80ff.

37. John Paul II, "World Day of Peace Message 1983," #11.

38. United States Catholic Conference, *Resolution on Southeast Asia* (Washington, D.C.: 1971).

39. *Pastoral Constitution,* #80.

40. John Paul II, "World Day of Peace Message 1982," #12, cited.

41. "Declaration on Prevention of Nuclear War" (Sept. 24, 1982).

42. *Pastoral Constitution,* #80.

43. Ibid.

44. John Paul II, "World Day of Peace Message 1982," #12, cited.

45. Representative authors in the tradition of Christian pacifism and non-violence include: R. Bainton, *Christian Attitudes Toward War and Peace* (Abington: 1960), chs. 4, 5, 10; J. Yoder, *The Politics of Jesus* (Grand Rapids: 1972), *Nevertheless: Varieties of Religious Pacifism* (Scottsdale: 1971); T. Merton, *Faith and Violence: Christian Teaching and Christian Practice* (Notre Dame: 1968); G. Zahn, *War, Conscience and Dissent* (New York: 1967); E. Egan, "The Beatitudes: Works of Mercy and Pacifism," in T. Shannon, ed., *War or Peace: The Search for New Answers* (New York: 1980), pp. 169–187; J. Fahey, "The Catholic Church and the Arms Race," *Worldview* 22 (1979):38–41; J. Douglass, *The Nonviolent Cross: A Theology of Revolution and Peace* (New York: 1966).

46. Justin, *Dialogue with Trypho,* ch. 20; cf. also *The First Apology,* chs. 14, 39.

47. Cyprian, *Collected Letters;* Letters to Cornelius.

48. Suplicius Serverus, *The Life of Martin,* 4.3.

49. *Pastoral Constitution,* #79.

50. Ibid., #78.

51. United States Catholic Conference, *Human Life in Our Day* (Washington, D.C.: 1968), p. 44.

52. *Pastoral Constitution,* #80.

53. Ibid.

54. John Paul II, "Address to Scientists and Scholars," #4, cited, p. 621.

55. Cf. "Declaration on Prevention of Nuclear War."

56. Paul VI, "World Day of Peace Message 1967," in *Documents,* p. 198.

57. "Statement of the Holy See to the United Nations" (1976), in *The Church and the Arms Race;* Pax Christi-USA (New York: 1976), pp. 23–24.

58. R. Adams and S. Cullen, *The Final Epidemic: Physicians and Scientists on Nuclear War* (Chicago: 1981).

59. Pontifical Academy of Sciences, "Statement on the Consequences of the Use of Nuclear Weapons," in *Documents,* p. 241.

60. John Paul II, "World Day of Peace Message 1982," #6, cited, p. 476.

61. The following quotations are from public officials who have served at the highest policy levels in recent administrations of our government: "It is time to recognize that no one has ever succeeded in advancing any persuasive reason to believe that any use of nuclear weapons, even on the smallest scale, could reliably be expected to remain limited." M. Bundy, G. F. Kennan, R. S. McNamara and G. Smith, "Nuclear Weapons and the Atlantic Alliance," *Foreign Affairs* 60 (1982):757.

"From my experience in combat there is no way that [nuclear escalation] . . . can be controlled because of the lack of information, the pressure of time and the deadly results that are taking place on both sides of the battle line." Gen. A. S. Collins, Jr. (former deputy commander in chief of U. S. Army in Europe), "Theatre Nuclear Warfare: The Battlefield," in J. F. Reichart and S. R. Sturn, eds., *American Defense Policy,* 5th ed., (Baltimore: 1982), pp. 359–60.

"None of this potential flexibility changes my view that a full-scale thermonuclear exchange would be an unprecedented disaster for the Soviet Union as well as for the United States. Nor is it at all clear that an initial use of nuclear weapons—however selectively they might be targeted—could be kept from escalating to a full-scale thermo-nuclear exchange, especially if command-and-control centers were brought under attack. The odds are high, whether weapons were used against tactical or strategic targets, that control would be lost on both sides and the exchange would become unconstrained." Harold Brown, *Department of Defense Annual Report FY 1979* (Washington, D.C.: 1978).

Cf. also: *The Effects of Nuclear War* (Washington, D.C.: 1979, U. S. Government Printing Office).

62. For example, cf.: H. A. Kissinger, *Nuclear Weapons and Foreign Policy* (New York: 1957), *The Necessity for Choice* (New York: 1960); R. Osgood and R. Tucker, *Force, Order and Justice* (Baltimore: 1967); R. Aron, *The Great Debate: Theories of Nuclear Strategy* (New York: 1965); D. Ball, *Can Nuclear War Be Controlled?* Adelphi Paper #161 (London: 1981); M. Howard, "On Fighting a Nuclear War," *International Security* 5 (1981):3–17.

63. "Statement on the Consequences of the Use of Nuclear Weapons," cited, p. 243.

64. Pius XII, "Address to the VIII Congress of the World Medical Association," in *Documents*, p. 131.

65. *Pastoral Constitution*, #80.

66. Ibid.

67. M. Bundy, et al., "Nuclear Weapons," cited; K. Kaiser, G. Leber, A. Mertes, F. J. Schulze, "Nuclear Weapons and the Preservation of Peace," *Foreign Affairs* 60 (1982):1157–70; cf. other responses to Bundy article in the same issue of *Foreign Affairs*.

68. Testimony given to the National Conference of Catholic Bishops Committee during preparation of this pastoral letter. The testimony is reflected in the quotes found in note 61.

69. Our conclusions and judgments in this area although based on careful study and reflection of the application of moral principles do not have, of course, the same force as the principles themselves and therefore allow for different opinions, as the Summary makes clear.

70. Undoubtedly aware of the long and detailed technical debate on limited war, Pope John Paul II highlighted the unacceptable moral risk of crossing the threshold to nuclear war in his "Angelus Message" of December 13, 1981: "I have, in fact, the deep conviction that, in the light of a nuclear war's effects, which can be scientifically foreseen as certain, the only choice that is morally and humanly valid is represented by the reduction of nuclear armaments, while waiting for their future complete elimination, carried out simultaneously by all the parties, by means of explicit agreements and with the commitment of accepting effective controls." In *Documents*, p. 240.

71. W. H. Kincade and J. D. Porro, *Negotiating Security: An Arms Control Reader* (Washington, D.C.: 1979).

72. Several surveys are available, for example cf.: J. H. Kahin, *Security in the Nuclear Age: Developing U.S. Strategic Policy* (Washington, D.C.: 1975); M. Mandelbaum, *The Nuclear Question: The United States and Nuclear Weapons 1946–1976* (Cambridge, England: 1979); B. Brodie, "Development of Nuclear Strategy," *International Security* 2 (1978):65–83.

73. The relationship of these two levels of policy is the burden of an article by D. Ball, "U.S. Strategic Forces: How Would They Be Used?" *International Security* 7 (1982/83):31–60.

74. *Pastoral Constitution*, #81.

75. United States Catholic Conference, *To Live in Christ Jesus* (Washington, D.C.: 1976), p. 34.

76. John Cardinal Krol, "Testimony on Salt II," *Origins* (1979):197.

77. John Paul II, "Message U.N. Special Session 1982," #3.

78. Ibid., #8.

79. John Paul II, "Address to UNESCO, 1980," #21.

80. John Paul II, "Letter to International Seminar on the World Implications of a Nuclear Conflict," August 23, 1982, text in *NC News Documentary,* August 24, 1982.

81. Particularly helpful was the letter of January 15, 1983, of Mr. William Clark, national security adviser, to Cardinal Bernardin. Mr. Clark stated: "For moral, political and military reasons, the United States does not target the Soviet civilian population as such. There is no deliberately opaque meaning conveyed in the last two words. We do not threaten the existence of Soviet civilization by threatening Soviet cities. Rather, we hold at risk the war-making capability of the Soviet Union—its armed forces, and the industrial capacity to sustain war. It would be irresponsible for us to issue policy statements which might suggest to the Soviets that it would be to their advantage to establish privileged sanctuaries within heavily populated areas, thus inducing them to locate much of their war-fighting capability within those urban sanctuaries." A reaffirmation of the administration's policy is also found in Secretary Weinberger's *Annual Report to the Congress* (Caspar Weinberger, *Annual Report to the Congress,* February 1, 1983, p. 55): "The Reagan Administration's policy is that under no circumstances may such weapons be used deliberately for the purpose of destroying populations." Also the letter of Mr. Weinberger to Bishop O'Connor of February 9, 1983, has a similar statement.

82. S. Zuckerman, *Nuclear Illusion and Reality* (New York: 1982); D. Ball, cited, p. 36; T. Powers, "Choosing a Strategy for World War III," *The Atlantic Monthly,* November 1982, pp. 82–110.

83. Cf. the comments in Pontifical Academy of Sciences "Statement on the Consequences of the Use of Nuclear Weapons," cited.

84. Several experts in strategic theory would place both the MX missile and Pershing II missiles in this category.

85. In each of the successive drafts of this letter we have tried to state a central moral imperative: that the arms race should be stopped and disarmament begun. The implementation of this imperative is open to a wide variety of approaches. Hence we have chosen our own language in this paragraph, not wanting either to be identified with one specific political initiative or to have our words used against specific political measures.

86. Cf. President Reagan's "Speech to the National Press Club" (November 18, 1981) and "Address at Eureka College" (May 9, 1982), Department of State, *Current Policy* #346 and #387.

87. John Paul II, "Homily at Coventry Cathedral," #2, *Origins* 12 (1982):55.

88. The two treaties are the Threshold Test Ban Treaty signed July 3, 1974, and the Treaty on Nuclear Explosions for Peaceful Purposes (P.N.E.) signed May 13, 1976.

89. John Paul II, "Message to U.N. Special Session 1982," #8.

90. Mr. Weinberger's letter to Bishop O'Connor specifies actions taken on command and control facilities designed to reduce the chance of unauthorized firing of nuclear weapons.

91. Ibid. Cf. United States Catholic Conference, *At Issue #2: Arms Export Policies —Ethical Choices* (Washington, D.C.: 1978) for suggestions about controlling the conventional arms trade.

92. The International Security Act of 1976 provides for such human rights review.

93. John Paul II, "Address to the United Nations General Assembly," *Origins* 9 (1979):268.

94. John Paul II, "Homily at Coventry Cathedral," cited, p. 55.

95. *Pastoral Constitution,* #78.

96. G. Sharp, *The Politics of Nonviolent Action* (Boston: 1973); R. Fisher and W. Ury, *Getting to Yes: Negotiating Agreement Without Giving In* (Boston: 1981).

97. John Paul II, "World Day of Peace Message 1982," #7, cited, p. 476.

98. *To Establish the United States Academy of Peace: Report of the Commission on Proposals for the National Academy of Peace and Conflict Resolution* (Washington, D.C.: 1981), pp. 119–20.

99. United States Catholic Conference, *Statement on Registration and Conscription for Military Service* (Washington, D.C.: 1980). Cf. also *Human Life in Our Day*, cited, pp. 42–45.

100. Paul VI, *The Development of Peoples* (1966), #76.

101. Cf. V. Yzermans, ed., *Major Addresses of Pius XII*, 2 vols. (St. Paul: 1961) and J. Gremillion, *The Gospel of Peace and Justice*, cited.

102. Cf. John XXIII, *Peace on Earth* (1963), esp. #80–145.

103. A sampling of the policy problems and possibilities posed by interdependence can be found in: R. O. Keohane and J. S. Nye, Jr., *Power and Interdependence* (Boston: 1977); S. Hoffmann, *Primacy or World Order* (New York: 1978); The Overseas Development Council, *The U.S. and World Development* 1979; 1980; 1982 (Washington, D.C.).

104. John XXIII, *Peace on Earth* (1963), #137.

105. This has particularly been the case in the two U.N. Special Sessions on Disarmament, 1979, 1982.

106. United States Catholic Conference, *Marxist Communism* (Washington, D.C.: 1980), p. 19.

107. The debate on U.S.-Soviet relations is extensive; recent examples of it are found in: A. Ulam, "U.S.-Soviet Relations: Unhappy Coexistence," *America and the World, 1978; Foreign Affairs* 57 (1979):556–71; W. G. Hyland, "U.S.-Soviet Relations: The Long Road Back," *America and the World, 1981; Foreign Affairs* 60 (1982):525–50; R. Legvold, "Containment Without Confrontation," *Foreign Policy* 40 (1980):74–98; S. Hoffmann, "Muscle and Brains," *Foreign Policy* 37 (1979–80):3–27; P. Hassner, "Moscow and The Western Alliance," *Problems of Communism* 30 (1981):37–54; S. Bialer, "The Harsh Decade: Soviet Policies in the 1980s," *Foreign Affairs* 59 (1981):999–1020; G. Kennan, *The Nuclear Delusion: Soviet-American Relations in the Atomic Age* (New York: 1982); N. Podhoretz, *The Present Danger* (New York: 1980); P. Nitze, "Strategy in the 1980s," *Foreign Affairs* 59 (1980):82–101; R. Strode and C. Gray, "The Imperial Dimension of Soviet Military Power," *Problems of Communism* 30 (1981):1–15; International Institute for Strategic Studies, *Prospects of Soviet Power in the 1980s*, Parts I and II, Adelphi Papers #151 and 152 (London: 1979); S. S. Kaplan, ed., *Diplomacy of Power: Soviet Armed Forces as a Political Instrument* (Washington, D.C.: 1981); R. Barnet, *The Giants: Russia and America* (New York: 1977); M. McGwire, *Soviet Military Requirements*, The Brookings Institution (Washington, D.C.: 1982); R. Tucker, "The Purposes of American Power," *Foreign Affairs* 59 (1980/81):241–74; A. Geyer, *The Idea of Disarmament: Rethinking the Unthinkable* (Washington, D.C.: 1982). For a review of Soviet adherence to treaties cf.: "The SALT Syndrome Charges and Facts: Analysis of an 'Anti-SALT Documentary,'" report prepared by U.S. government agencies (State, Defense, CIA, ACDA and NSC), reprinted in *The Defense Monitor* 10, #8A, Center for Defense Information.

108. John Paul II, "World Day of Peace Message 1983," #7.

109. John Paul II, "The Redeemer of Man," #16, *Origins* 8 (1980):635.

110. The phrase and its description are found in R. S. McNamara, *Report to the Board of Governors of the World Bank* 1978; cf. also 1979; 1980 (Washington, D.C.).

111. John Paul II, "Homily at Yankee Stadium," #4, *Origins* 9 (1979):311.

112. Paul VI, "Address to the General Assembly of the United Nations" (1965), #2.

113. *Pastoral Constitution,* #81.

114. Cf. Hoffman, cited; Independent Commission on Disarmament and Security Issues, *Common Security* (New York: 1982).

115. For an analysis of the policy problems of reallocating resources, cf: Bruce M. Russett, *The Prisoners of Insecurity* (San Francisco: 1983). Cf.: *Common Security,* cited; Russett, cited; *U.N. Report on Disarmament and Development* (New York: 1982); United Nations, *The Relationship Between Disarmament and Development: A Summary,* Fact Sheet #21 (New York: 1982).

116. John Paul II, "The Redeemer of Man," #21, cited, p. 641. Much of the following reflects the content of A. Dulles, *A Church to Believe In: Discipleship and the Dynamics of Freedom* (New York: 1982), ch. 1.

117. John Paul II, "World Day of Peace Message 1982," #4, cited, p. 475.

118. Paul VI, "World Day of Peace Message 1976."

119. *Pastoral Constitution,* #79.

120. John Paul II, "Address to Scientists and Scholars," #3, cited, p. 621.

121. Ibid.

122. *Pastoral Constitution,* #75.

123. John Paul II, "Address at Hiroshima," #2, *Origins* 10 (1981):620.

124. *Pastoral Constitution,* #75.

125. *Human Life in Our Day,* cited, p. 41.

126. John XXIII, *Peace on Earth* (1963), #137.

127. Paul VI, "Address to the General Assembly of the United Nations," (1965), #2.